MORAVIAN ARCHITECTURE AND TOWN PLANNING

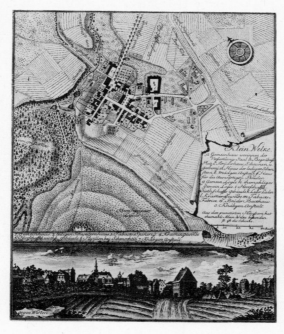

MORAVIAN ARCHITECTURE
AND TOWN PLANNING

BETHLEHEM, PENNSYLVANIA, AND OTHER EIGHTEENTH-CENTURY
AMERICAN SETTLEMENTS

by

WILLIAM J. MURTAGH

THE UNIVERSITY OF NORTH CAROLINA PRESS · CHAPEL HILL

To Maudie and Freddie

PREFACE

This volume had its genesis about ten years ago when I first became interested in the architecture of the Pennsylvania Germans through the request to do a research paper on the subject for a graduate seminar at the University of Pennsylvania. When I was subsequently appointed first executive director of the Annie S. Kemmerer Museum and executive secretary of Historic Bethlehem, Inc., both in Bethlehem, Pennsylvania, I was given ample opportunity for work in Moravian Archives, primarily in Bethlehem. Through this contact, an existing interest in the broader subject of Pennsylvania German architecture narrowed to a concentration on Moravian communities and their buildings.

A search of bibliographical sources reveals no study of major proportion on the architecture created by Germanic immigrants to this country in the eighteenth century despite the contributions that even a summary perusal of the subject indicates these people have made to our heritage. Of all the so-called Pennsylvania Dutch (that term so loosely applied to any non-English settler of the Pennsylvania colony in the eighteenth century), the most architecturally conscious structures reflective of a closely knit society of an inordinately high order were created by Moravians. It is to bring these achievements to light in architecture and community planning that this study has been undertaken.

I have chosen to deal primarily with Moravian buildings at Bethlehem for several reasons: first, on the basis of its accessibility and my familiarity with that community through two years residence there as director; secondly, and more important, because I consider the Bethlehem structures the purest expression of Moravian thought and their Germanic background to have been erected in this country as well as the largest group of such buildings. Nazareth has structures equally as foreign in architectural character, but these are limited in number and type. Salem, in North Carolina, has a group of buildings numbering as many or perhaps more than those in Bethlehem, but architecturally speaking they are later and therefore more removed from European prototypes in style and time than the Bethlehem structures.

I have chosen to end this study with the building of the eastern wing of the Single Sisters' House, since this was the last major structure to be erected in the eighteenth century in the Bethlehem community which had architectural affinities with the continental origins of the Moravians. Even this structure, which continues the use of materials and architectural details of the earlier buildings of the community, heralds change in its less intimate scale and straight gable roof. With the erection of the Central Moravian Church in a quasi-Federal style, the strength of the Germanic building tradition of the Moravians in Bethlehem and its continental architectural vocabulary was dissipated. This architectural change reflects the gradual change in the community which ultimately opened the village to non-Moravians and set the stage for the industrial flowering of the city of today. One might postulate that this change could have been a willful plan begun as a means to identify the Germanic community with the essentially English origins of the new republic, in addition to a recognition by Moravian church leaders that the closed communitarianism of the eighteenth-century village would destroy their effort if allowed to continue into the nineteenth century. But this is beyond the scope of this study. Whatever the cause, the revolution and the influx of outside pressures that it brought undoubtedly changed the community in many ways, not the least of which was the architectural expression of the group. Although Bethlehem and Salem have been emphasized in this study because of the quality of the architecture and the plethora of existing eighteenth-century fabric at these sites, one must not forget other Moravian communities treated perhaps less gently by time which are but mentioned in passing, especially those in Ohio, where the village of Schoenbrunn has been reconstructed and where the villages of Salem, Gnadenhuetten, New Schoenbrunn, and Goshen were important outposts in the Moravian world in the early years.

This study has progressed intermittently over such a length of time that a true list of acknowledgments of everyone who has helped, in some way, would almost produce a book of major proportions in itself. The reader will note some specific names recorded in the footnotes at the proper places. To Professor Smith, however, goes the credit for having first aroused in me the interest in the subject. I am also indebted to various organizations, notably The Archives of the Moravian Church in Bethlehem and the Moravian Archives in Salem, as well as Historic Bethlehem, Inc., and Old Salem, Inc., for making illustrative material and other source material available. To those who aided me in the translations and in preparing the manuscript, a note of special indebtedness is also expressed. Finally, financial assistance in the publication of this book is gratefully acknowledged to the Holden Trust, Old Salem, Inc., and Historic Bethlehem, Inc.

William J. Murtagh

ACKNOWLEDGMENTS FOR ILLUSTRATIONS

The following plates are reproduced by permission of the Provincial Archives Committee of the Moravian Church, Bethlehem, Pennsylvania; further reproduction of these plates may be done only with the written permission of the Committee.

Plates 1, 2, 3, 6, 7, 8, 9, 13, 14, 15, 18, 22, 23, 24, 31, 32, 33, 37, 40, 42, 44, 47, 48, 49, 50, 51, 52, 53, 54, 55, 56

The following plates are reproduced by permission of Historic Bethlehem, Inc., Bethlehem, Pennsylvania:

Plates 4, 12, 16, 17, 19, 20, 21, 27, 28, 29, 30, 34, 35, 36, 38, 39, 41, 43, 45, 46, 57, 58

The following plates are reproduced by permission of the Moravian Church Archives, Winston-Salem, North Carolina:

Plates 11, 60, 64, 65, 66

The following plates are reproduced by permission of Old Salem, Inc., Winston-Salem, North Carolina:

Plates 59, 61, 62, 63

Copy after an original in the Moravian Historical Society Collection, Nazareth, Pennsylvania, courtesy of Walter Peters:

Plate 10

The following plates originally appeared in Hellmuth Erbe, *Eine-Kommunistische Herrnhuter Kolonie des 18. Jahrhunderts* (Herrnhut, Germany, 1929), and are reproduced here by permission of the author:

Plates 5, 25, 26

CONTENTS

———◆———

ILLUSTRATIONS

MORAVIAN ARCHITECTURE AND TOWN PLANNING

I

INTRODUCTION

———◆·◆———

The stream of immigration of Germanic peoples to this country can be divided roughly into three periods: the late seventeenth-century migration centering near Philadelphia; the influx of Swiss Mennonites, as well as Lutheran and Calvinist Palatines, into the area known today as the Pennsylvania Dutch country, which began about 1710 and lasted in varying strength until just before the American Revolution; and the third wave in the nineteenth century, resulting from political upheavals in Germany, which chiefly washed the mid-west.

The late seventeenth century *Auswanderung* founded Germantown, now part of Philadelphia, in 1683, under the leadership of Daniel Pastorius of Krefeld, Germany. This settlement was a flourishing community when the eighteenth-century migration began gathering force. Architecturally speaking, the handsome use of cut field-stone masonry and the ample proportion of the so-called "Germantown hood" of many extant eighteenth-century structures in the area are the chief indications of the fusion of a non-English element in the essentially English conception of these buildings. In comparison with structures erected by Germanic settlers in the Pennsylvania Dutch counties of the state, the purity of the Germantown house, as a reflection of the culture of its builders, stands more in a transposed than a transported position. The proximity and plethora of

English-speaking settlers in the Philadelphia area were apparently sufficient to exert an early influence on builders of Germanic origins. While Germantown structures enjoy a distinctive architectural quality that easily differentiates them from buildings erected by the English, the purer Germanic architectural characteristics noted in structures of the Pennsylvania Dutch counties is lacking.

The eighteenth-century Germanic immigrants, today loosely termed Pennsylvania Dutch, were actually a polyglot group from varying levels of the socio-economic scale which originated in diverse sections of Europe. In popular parlance, the term includes Mennonites, Moravians, Amish, Dunkards, Schwenkfelders, Lutherans, Reformed, Huguenots, etc. Like their seventeenth-century Krefeld predecessors, the common denominator was the induced poverty generated by the Thirty Years' War and their protesting views against the state religions in the areas from whence they came.

Geographically, the majority of these people hailed from the Palatinate or the Pfalz area of the Rhine Valley. Mennonites were primarily Swiss in origin, earlier driven into the Schwarzwald area of Germany and thence to the Palatinate. As the eighteenth century wore on, the migration continued to be dominated by the Palatines, although an increase of *émigrés* from Schwabia can be noted. The preponderance of this migration was of peasant stock, preoccupied with the yield of the land, an obsession which is still reflected in the manicured farms of the descendents of these settlers. Ships' passenger lists, however, also note occasional tradesmen and persons of commerce.

Unlike the other groups, Moravians hailed chiefly from Bohemia and Moravia, later known as Czechoslovakia. Christianity is said to have first come to Moravia about 823 from Bulgaria through the interest of the sister of a Bulgarian king, who had been Christianized in Constantinople.[1] From there it was carried into Bohemia.[2] Both areas subsequently witnessed a succession of religious dissension through succeeding centuries.

It was into such an atmosphere that John Huss was born in Husinec, July 6, 1369, in southern Bohemia.[3] He took his name from the castle of Huss, one of an original group of twenty-four villages owned jointly by the Barons of Janowic and the Royal Exchequer. His family name is not known and little is known of his early years,[4] but it is to this courageous man that Moravians in Europe and America ascribe the foundation of their beliefs. In 1393 he took his first degree at the University of Prague, and in 1396 he received a Master of Arts Degree. Two years later he became a professor at the university; in 1401 he was elected dean of the Philosophical Faculty, and in 1402 rector of the university.[5]

Huss, whose first lectures were largely philosophical, became increasingly theological. On March 4, 1402, after his ordination into the priesthood, he became a preacher at the Bethlehem Chapel in Prague.[6] He was immediately successful and shortly became the greatest reformer of his time as well as a storm center of controversy. He finally spoke out so fervently against papal indulgences that he was excommunicated.[7] A church council was called to convene at Constance on November 5, 1414, and Huss was invited to plead his cause with promise of safe conduct, fair hearing, and safe return. Unfortunately, these were breached. He was imprisoned, accused of heresy, and burned at the stake.

The result of Huss's burning was a widespread dissension that raged for years throughout the area. Followers of Huss formed the Hussite League and became known as Hussites. They were assigned a district in Lititz near the border of Silesia and Moravia, where they were free to worship as they pleased and to enjoy liberty of conscience in the village of Kunwald, and they settled there about 1453.[8] This became the original organization known as the Ancient Church of the Brethren out of which grew the Fratres Legis Christi or Brethren of the Law of Christ. This was soon changed to Unitas Fratrum (The Unity of the Brethren) or Fratres Unitatis (The United Brethren).[9]

With the decrees of the Council of Trent in 1545, Protestants in the area were incited to revolt against accepting a new king, Ferdinand II (1619–37), and chose Frederic, the Elector of Palatine, in his stead.[10] This open revolt originated one of the bloodiest periods in history, the Thirty Years' War, which resulted in virtual extermination of protestantism in Bohemia and Moravia, climaxed by what present-day Moravians refer to as the Day of Blood, June 21, 1621, when twenty-seven leaders of Bohemia and Moravia, including fifteen leaders of the brethren's church, were executed.[11] Thousands of persons fled, and whole districts of the area were depopulated. The leader of the brethren during this period was John Amos Comenius, who hid in the moun-

1. John Heckewelder, *A Narrative of the Mission of the United Brethren Among the Delaware and Mohegan Indians*, edited by William Elsey Connelley (Cleveland, 1907), p. 3. Connelley took his information from Edward H. Reichel, *Historical Sketch of the Church and Mission of the United Brethren, Commonly called Moravians* (Bethlehem, 1848).

2. Edward Langston, *History of the Moravian Church* (London, 1956), p. 11.

3. There is some disagreement about this date. More recent writers hold to the date mentioned, but earlier historians mention 1373.

4. Edmund DeSchweinitz, *History of the Church Known as the Unitas Fratrum* (2nd ed.; Bethlehem, 1901), p. 28.

5. *Ibid.*, p. 29. The University of Prague was modeled after the University of Paris and was considered one of the most distinguished seats of learning in Europe at that time.

6. It stood next to the College of Lazarus and supposedly seated three thousand persons. The pulpit was square, with the stair near it leading to the room where Huss lived. Eventually given to the Bohemian Brethren, it later became the property of the Jesuits. It was finally closed in 1786 and later demolished. DeSchweinitz, *Unitas Fratrum*, p. 33, n. 2.

7. *Ibid.*, p. 43.

8. Langston, *Moravian Church*, p. 29.

9. They bore the name "Unitas Fratrum" until 1847, when the American church adopted the name "Moravian Brethren" as a distinguishing title from other groups calling themselves United Brethren.

10. The Council of Trent was opened in 1545 under Pope Paul III. It was called to unify the reaction of the Roman church to the Reformation and was largely guided by the Jesuit Order (founded in 1540). It effected internal reform in the Roman Catholic church and reaffirmed its dogmatic basis.

11. A gripping word picture of the day is recounted in DeSchweinitz, *Unitas Fratrum*, pp. 503–31. This account is apparently based on contemporary description of what occurred during the executions and exactly the form that each execution took, whether it was hanging, beheading, or having one's tongue ripped out.

tains of Bohemia and later led a group of exiles to Lizza, Poland, where he became a bishop of the church.[12]

The Peace of Westphalia, 1648, ending the Thirty Years' War, left no respite in its conditions for the brethren, and the dispersion that had started about 1624 continued. Many escaped to such places as Silesia, Poland, and Prussia. The greatest number went to Saxony and Upper Lusatia, gradually losing their identity among the local inhabitants. It has been suggested that eighty thousand Bohemians fled after 1624.[13]

This period of dispersion, following the execution of many of the nobles and ministers and the exile of most of the others, lasted for approximately a century (1627–1720) and is known among Moravian theologians as the Time of the Hidden Seed.[14] It is a singularly obscure time during which what is known today as the Moravian church was almost extinct, and the few members of the movement were found in the region of Fulneck, Kunwald, Zerawic, and Zanchtenthal, in Moravia, worshipping in secret and maintaining family worship.

A prophecy that the Hidden Seed would be saved came to pass in the person of Christian David.[15] In his capacity as traveling preacher, David met the Neissers of Schlen who asked him to find asylum for them in a Protestant country. In 1722 he reported

his contact with Nicholas Lewis, Count of Zinzendorf, who had recently acquired an estate in Upper Lusatia (part of Saxony) where it was his intention to set up a pastorate to work for the cause of protestantism. Soon after, the Neissers emigrated.[16] They were given land on which to settle near the Hutberg, on the road to Zittau, not far from Bertholdsdorf.[17] On June 17, 1722, the first trees were felled to found what was to become Herrnhut.[18]

The community grew steadily. Christian David made many return trips to Moravia, and upon one such trip to Zanchtenthal, he contacted Melchior Zeissberger through David Nitschmann and John Toeltschig. These were the connecting links between what present-day Moravians refer to as the Ancient and Renewed church, since they had continued to hold meetings after the church was legally suppressed.

There is no need to discuss the developments of Herrnhut as a settlement, but it must be mentioned that it was not solely a Moravian endeavor. Moravians, then, as now, were primarily a missionary group interested in "spreading the word." They existed at that time, in an era where church and state were one. The fact that they resorted to a Christian communism in which the individual was sublimated to the aims of the group was natural, taken in the context of existing church-state conditions. The ideology that they were not a separate sect but the servant of all Christian groups attests the age of pietistic idealism current after the religious wars of the seventeenth century. It is therefore not difficult to understand their prime motivation for emigration to the American colonies to Christianize the heathen, the Indian. Because of the Moravians' success in es-

12. According to Langston, *Moravian Church*, pp. 51–53, he was born in Komna. DeSchweinitz, *Unitas Fratrum*, p. 479, agrees with Langston on his birth date, i.e. March 21, 1592, but maintains that he was born in Niwnitz, in Moravia, a market town near Ungarish-Brod on the domain of Ostrau. He also states that Comenius is the Latin form of his true name, Komenskyl. His parents both died when he was young. He was schooled in the brethren's schools at Ungarish-Brod and Straznic. He entered the Theological Institute at Herborn, in Nassau, in 1611, and on June 19, 1613, the University of Heidelberg. Upon graduation he traveled in Holland and perhaps England. Returning to Moravia, he became rector of the school at Prerau. His treatise on grammar was published in 1616 as a result of his investigations into education. Soon after he became the pastor of the Fulneck Parish and rector of the school. With increased persecution, Comenius was the leading seeker for help from other sources. He died in Amsterdam, in 1670. His writings number many, including a catechism which was printed in Amsterdam.

13. David Cranz, *The Ancient and Modern History of the Brethren*, translated by Benjamin LaTrobe (London, 1780), p. 53.

14. Langston, *Moravian Church*, p. 55.

15. DeSchweinitz, *Unitas Fratrum*, p. 643. A prophecy had been made that there would soon be a deliverance. David was born at Senftlehen on December 31, 1690, and was schooled as a Roman Catholic. Influenced by Evangelical Christians after he became a carpenter, he decided to become a Lutheran, and went to Hungary for this purpose, then to Saxony, settling finally in Goerlitz, where he first plied his trade, but after marriage, became a preacher.

16. This was on Wednesday, after Whitsunday, in 1722. Beside Augustine and James Neisser and their families, there was their cousin Michael Joeschke and Martha Neisser, niece of Augustine. Langston, *Moravian Church*, p. 58.

17. The count was at the Court in Dresden at the time and negotiations were effected through his grandmother, the Countess of Gersdorf, of Great Hennersdorf. It was she who had educated Nicholas to the sympathies of Protestantism. *Ibid.*

18. *Ibid.*, p. 59. This name was not commonly used until 1724. It originated with the master of the count's household, a Mr. Heitz. He said in his report to the count, on July 8, "God has given Mr. Marche great courage to engage in this work. May He bless it, according to His loving kindness, and grant that Your Excellency may build a city on the hill, called the *Hutberg* (Watch Hill) which may not only stand under the guardianship and watch of the Lord, but where even all the inhabitants may stand upon the watch of the Lord (*Des Herrn Hut*) so that they may not hold their peace day nor night." Cranz, *History of the Brethren*, p. 101. Herrnhut is still the Moravian headquarters in eastern Germany.

tablishing Herrnhut, Nisky, and Klein Welke, one tends to forget the existence of other Protestants on the scene; but displaced folk of other persuasions settled there also, mainly from the Lutheran church, along with some individuals with Calvinist leanings. The honor and impetus of first settlement goes, however, to the Moravians. The first articles of agreement by which the inhabitants of Herrnhut were to live was the result of a meeting on May 12, 1727. These articles stated that Herrnhut was not to be considered a rising town or village so much as an establishment for the brethren and other protesting groups. With this stated purpose, the brethren gradually assumed responsibility for their own preaching.[19] Church affairs were the business of a conference of elders. More general questions were referred to the Council of the Church and cases of doubt were decided by lot.[20]

It was in Herrnhut that a service peculiar to the Moravian church came into usage. Known as the love feast, it is celebrated in addition to Holy Communion and apparently developed through social gatherings of friends. While together, they partook of soup, cake, and water, and joined in singing praises of the Lord.[21] A second institution begun at Herrnhut was the division of all brethren into "choirs," or living units, as follows: (1) The Married People; (2) the Widowers; (3) the Widows; (4) Single Brethren; (5) Single Sisters; (6) Youths; (7) Big Girls; (8) Little Boys; (9) Little Girls; and (10) Infants in Arms.[22]

At this time (1729) there were at least forty-seven families living in Herrnhut, and the population of the village numbered about two hundred. Approximately seventy letters of inquiry were received per day, and the fame of the settlement grew to such proportions that the Count of Saxony on two occasions (1732 and 1736) ordered an inquiry into the affairs of the colony.[23] As a result of the first inquiry, additional peoples from Bohemia, Moravia, and Silesia

were forbidden to move to Zinzendorf's estates in Upper Lusatia. The Herrnhut settlement turned its thoughts, therefore, to colonies elsewhere where it might continue in freedom to receive followers. A certain faction, mostly Lutherans, remained at Herrnhut. The remainder, i.e., the Moravian brethren, wishing to preserve their religion, prepared to establish themselves in other lands where they could form settled residences in order to receive others inclined to leave Moravia and also where they could do mission work among the heathen.

Missionaries were sent to the West Indies as early as 1732 and to Greenland in 1733.[24] Meanwhile, Zinzendorf was in correspondence with the managers of the Georgia colony, and upon completion of satisfactory arrangements, a company of missionaries under Augustus Gottlieb Spangenberg, left for England and from there sailed for Savannah.[25] This was in 1736. Embarking on the "Two Brothers" were ten brethren in the company of other colonists, mostly of Swiss origin; the group included Edward James Oglethorpe, governor of Georgia, as well as young John Wesley, who later founded Methodism. Thus was the first Moravian settlement established on the continent of North America. As early as 1737 these Moravians began to experience oppression from neighbors who insisted that they render military service in conjunction with the raging dispute of the area between the Spanish and the English. Spangenberg and David Nitschmann had traveled to Pennsylvania in the spring of 1736 in the interest of ministering to the Schwenkfelders.[26] With the continuance of military pressure, not to mention the hot

19. For some years such duties were the care of a Lutheran pastor at Bertholdsdorf.

20. Settlement of questions by lot was apparently much used in Herrnhut, even of marriage. It was never treated lightly, however, and only after prayer for guidance.

21. This service is still employed in the Moravian church a limited number of times per year. The "feast" today consists of coffee with cream and rolls.

22. Langston, *Moravian Church*, p. 77. See also Cranz, *History of the Brethren*, p. 124. It is important especially to mention the choir system, since this was adopted in Bethlehem during the general economy, i.e. that period of approximately the first twenty years of settlement.

23. See Langston, *Moravian Church*, p. 22 ff. for a full account of these.

24. See W. N. Schwarze and S. H. Gapp, *A History of the Beginnings of Moravian Work in America*, (Bethlehem, 1955), pp. 6–9, for the individuals involved in these missions.

25. Augustus Gottlieb Spangenberg was born in Clettenberg, Germany, on July 15, 1704, son of a minister. He matriculated at Jena University in 1722 and took a Master of Arts Degree in 1729. By 1732, he was assistant professor of theology at Jena. He became Zinzendorf's assistant in 1733 and thereafter served the Moravian Brethren's church in many places and in many capacities. He was ordained a bishop of the church at Marienborn on June 15, 1744. Among the other missions, he visited Bethlehem four times. Between the years 1763 and 1775 he wrote a *Life of Zinzendorf*. He died in Berthelsdorf on September 18, 1792. *Ibid.*, p. 68, 69.

26. These were followers of Kasper von Schwenkfeld, a nobleman born in Ossig, Silesia, in 1490. He was a contemporary of the zealous reformers of his day but refused to organize a demonstration. After his death at Ulm on December 10, 1561, his followers organized and experienced much the same religious persecution as the Moravians. Schwenkfelders were present at Berthelsdorf and it was Zinzendorf who helped them to Pennsylvania in 1734 after they had been ordered out of the country. See Schwarze and Gapp, *Moravian Work*, p. 95.

climate which some found detrimental to their health and their lack of notable success in converting the native Indians, the brethren decided to leave Georgia as soon as their debt was paid off.[27] Starting in 1737 and continuing until 1740, the Moravians abandoned Savannah. Some returned to Germany, some to England, and the remainder sailed north to Pennsylvania to undertake the erection of a school for Negroes at Nazareth for George Whitefield, the noted preacher.[28] As the result of a disagreement between Whitefield and John Hagen, a Moravian missionary, Whitefield ordered the brethren to quit his lands in the fall of 1740.[29]

About this time the Moravians had the opportunity to purchase their first land in Pennsylvania. This was a tract of five hundred acres, owned by William Allen and his wife, south of Nazareth and located at the confluence of the Monocacy Creek and the Lehigh River (called the West Fork of the Delaware in the eighteenth century). Henry Antes, representing the brethren, carried out the transaction through Nathaniel Irish, an agent of Allen's.[30] This completed, the Moravians began what proved to be their first permanent settlement in the American colonies—Bethlehem.

27. The trustees of Georgia had advanced the brethren a sum of money for their venture and had accommodated them in housing until they had their settlement established. See John Holmes, *History of the Protestant Church of the United Brethren* (London, 1825), I, p. 369.

28. The actual owner of the tract at Nazareth was a Mr. Seward, financial agent and traveling companion of Whitefield, founder of Calvinistic Methodism. An Englishman, Whitefield was born in Gloucester on December 16, 1714, and had gone to Georgia with Wesley. He spent most of his life traveling and preaching and died on September 30, 1770, at Boston. Schwarze and Gapp, *Moravian Work*, p. 103-4.

29. Upon the death of Seward, Whitefield was left in such poor financial position that he was forced to sell his land.

Thus, the entire tract of five thousand acres came into the possession of the Moravians on July 15, 1741, and Nazareth developed thenceforth into a settlement of Moravian Brethren. *Ibid.*, p. 105.

30. The Moravians' ownership of this land was the second in succession following the original proprietor of the Province of Pennsylvania. It was part of an original grant of five thousand acres to William Penn, which he passed on to John Lowther and his wife, of London, who, in turn, passed it to Joseph Turner, also of London. William Allen purchased it from Turner in 1731, located and surveyed it in 1736. Until that time, it had been merely an unlocated claim. See Joseph Mortimer Levering, *A History of Bethlehem, Pennsylvania, 1741–1892, With Some Account of Its Founders and Their Early Activity in America* (Bethlehem, 1903), p. 61.

1. Plans of Herrnhut (1722), Nisky (1742), and Klein Welke (1756)

II

EUROPEAN PRECEDENTS
AND COMMUNITY PLANNING

————— ❖ —————

Moravians are responsible for having created some of the most Germanic architecture in the American colonies. They warrant interest, not only for the buildings they erected, but also for their conscious concern for the total visual and functional environment of their communities, in the American colonies as well as in Europe. It must be borne in mind that the Moravians never acted as isolated individuals but always worked with the concept of group endeavor. This sense of group identity is the basis for their planned communities, the genesis of which can be seen in the original Moravian communities in Europe. With the dependence of the American Moravian colonists upon church headquarters at Herrnhut, Germany, it is little wonder that they carried on this practice and planned their settlements in the New World as assiduously as they had worked out the relationship of structures in their old-world villages.

As opposed to most immigrants who came to America for personal gain, it must be emphasized that Moravians came to these shores to find religious asylum and bring Christianity to the Indians of the American wilderness. From initial concept to actual settlement, Moravian communities were a unified effort pre-planned by Moravian leaders. Whether creating church householder villages or industrial centers such as Bethlehem, Moravians were conscious of the necessity to secure approval of plans from the church headquarters at Herrnhut. This accounts for the plethora of documentary material to be found in Moravian archives for proposed settlements which, before such schemes could progress, had to receive approval from Zinzendorf and Herrnhut. A copper engraving (Plate 1), published in 1782, shows the plans of Herrnhut, Nisky, and Klein Welke.[1] Al-

1. In translation, the title of this sheet reads as follows:
Ground Plans and Elevations of the Three Evangelical Brethren's Congregational Towns in the Margrave of Upper Leusitz
Herrnhut
Very first establishment of the Brethren's Church. Count Zinzendorf founded this town in the year 1722, on his manor at Bertelsdorf.
Nisky
Arose in the year 1742. Here is located the Grammar School and the Boys' Boarding School of the Evangelical Brethren's Unity.
Klein Welke
Erection was begun in the year 1756. The major part of the inhabitants are Wends.
Published on occasion of the Synod held in the year 1782 and dedicated to the illustrious Count Henry

though the plans of these settlements vary in details, one or two points are characteristic of all. First, each of the three settlements was planned around a central square. In the case of Nisky, this was an open plaza; at Herrnhut, it formed the setting for the *Gemeinhaus* and church, as it did at Klein Welke. Moreover, each town was visually dominated by the church building, a dominance that one would expect in such a communal church society as that of the *Bruder Gemeinde*. The small elevations that accompany the three plans give ample evidence of this with their towers terminating in onion domes of the type still commonly found in Austria, Czechoslovakia, and eastern Germany.

A building-by-building tour of the three villages indicates a self-sufficient settlement of the type that was continued in the American colonies. Thus, in Herrnhut one notes the *Gemeinhaus* with the chapel and the girls' boarding school in one large building dominating the central square of the village. Behind this structure, but still on the main square, was a fire station and guard house next to the butcher's stalls.

Starting at a point southeast of the church building and reading roughly clockwise around this central *Gemeinhaus* and church building, other structures in the village included the Sisters' House and garden; the Manor House and garden; the Count of Reuss's house and garden; a house or hostel for visiting brethren from out-of-town; the elector's post office and the elector's office for excise; the Brethren's House with its garden; the Widows' House; a leather store; a soap boiling shop; a retail store; a trading house; a tobacco factory; the widows' yard, garden, and orphanage; the boys' boarding school; and the Congregational Inn. The last was strategically placed at the northwest corner of the central square along the main road from Zittau to Laubau, which skirted this end of the square. The burying ground, called "God's Acre," was placed apart from the community at the foot of the Hutberg and had an access from the public road to Bertholdsdorf, which also intersected the short end of the central square at its northeastern side.

28th Reuss, the venerable and aged Spangenberg and the entire Evangelical Brethren's Unity of the Hemispheres.

Engraved on copper by M. Keil   By I. G. Krause, Saxon Drawing Master   Corporal of the Noble Knight and Elector's   Infantry Regiment of the Academy in Dresden   Electorate of Saxony

Nisky had a clearer and more symmetrical plan. As in Herrnhut, the central square was bisected by the main road from Goerlitz, leading to the royal dye works in Kattenburg. Perpendicular to this road, the other two sides of the rectangular square were bounded by a road from the lake and another from Budissin. These led beyond the town on its eastern side to a road noted simply as "the field road to new houses." The central square in Nisky was thus planned to be devoid of buildings save for the small firehouse that was situated in the lower right quadrant of the four-part garden into which the square was divided. (It is interesting to note that a small firehouse was also the only structure built on the central square at Salem in North Carolina.) The *Gemeinhaus*, with its church hall, was situated in this case on the northwestern side of the square. Reading once more roughly clockwise, the other buildings in the community consisted of the Single Sisters' House, with its garden; the Widows' House and an earlier Widows' House; a house for out-of-town brethren; a grammar school; a boys' boarding school; the apothecary; the store; the Congregational Inn or Hotel; the aforementioned firehouse on the square; the Single Brethren's House, with its various workshops and its attendant garden; and a tannery. As in the case of the inn at Herrnhut, the Congregational Hotel here was located on the main road from Budissin to Oedernitz. And, like the Hutberg at Herrnhut, the cemetery at Nisky was south of the community and placed on a slight rise.

There are two further items noteworthy on the plan and elevation of Nisky. One is the windmill immediately to the south and west of the cemetery (the works of which appear in the foreground of the elevation) and the other is the garden. Although some formal gardens are indicated at the Manor House and the Count Reuss House at Herrnhut, there is a singular emphasis on both the formal and informal garden here at Nisky. In the same general area as the cemetery, for example, this very interesting garden is noted as "Mon Plaisir." (At Nazareth a similar area laid out to the north of the "Residence" or hall was known for a hundred years as the "Pleasure Garden.") It was to be used as a promenading and recreation spot for the boys from the boarding school. This garden has a typical eighteenth-century scheme with a formal area and an asymmetrical section in the other portion of an informal, romantic character. Farther north and due east of the community, leading from the boys' boarding school, a second small, oval, formal garden can be seen. This is noted as the promenading spot for the little boys, which was generally called "Astrazen."[2]

A very interesting comparison can be made with the plan of Klein Welke, since an earlier settlement scheme is also known. This provides an excellent illustration of the difference between the planned, organized concept of the church village of the Moravians and the scattered, non-centralized arrangement that had evolved in Klein Welke before the advent of these people to the village. As in Herrnhut, the *Gemeinhaus* and its chapel dominated the central square in the community. Likewise, the cemetery was situated to the south and west of the town outside the central community. With less of the formal plan of the other two villages, the central square was still bounded on two sides by two streets, which ultimately joined together to form one thoroughfare in the older village of Klein Welke and led to the main highways leading to Lubach, Bautzen, and Hoyerswerde. At the edge of the town, between these two streets, the *Gemein Logis*, or Congregational Inn, was situated. A through-street to Nischwitz bordered the northwestern side of the square. Scattered around this were the Brethren's House and the barns; a tannery; the Single Sisters' House; the little girls' boarding school; a house for visiting brethren from out-of-town; the Congregational Inn; an earlier Congregational Inn; a manor house and farm buildings; a leather store; storage vaults for the store; a tobacco factory; the brethren's bakery; and the little boys' boarding school. There was also a brewery, which apparently was operated by the brethren at that time since it is noted, but which was situated in the earlier section of Klein Welke along the road from Hoyerswerde to Lubach and Bautzen.

In 1734 Zinzendorf inaugurated a colonization policy because of certain imminent problems of dispersion which faced the Moravians in Europe and in Saxony itself.[3] Moreover, such colonization furthered the evangelistic plan of Zinzendorf by establishing new centers from which work could be carried on. The first Moravian settlement occurred in 1734 on the island of St. Croix in the Virgin Islands. Later the same year, a second was founded in the

Duchy of Holstein, but this was quickly abandoned because of political and ecclesiastical difficulties. In 1737 it was transferred to the royal division of Holstein, and out of this grew Pilgerruh, which was abandoned in 1740 because of unsuitable individuals among the colonists. The fourth colony was the settlement of Heerendyk in the Barony of Ysselstein, in Holland, established in 1736, but apparently this was also soon abandoned.[4]

Preparations for the third settlement had been begun in 1735, for Savannah, Georgia,[5] in the New World. There, on March 10, the first Moravian settlement in America was organized as a regular congregation at Savannah, planned after that of Herrnhut. There is scant evidence in the Moravian Archives in Bethlehem of the efforts of the Moravians in Savannah. There does exist, however, a plan of the community, "copied July 1765" (Plate 2).[6] This manuscript is important since it locates the lots be-

2. It is also interesting to note that the garden of the Widows' Choir was somewhat removed from the Widows' House and was situated north and east of the village proper.

3. See Joseph Mortimer Levering, *A History of Bethlehem, Pennsylvania, 1741–1892, With Some Account of Its Founders and Their Early Activity in America* (Bethlehem, 1903), p. 105.

4. Colonists from these two abandoned settlements were eventually assigned to the Pennsylvania colony of Bethlehem, along with those from the Georgia colony.

5. Count Zinzendorf had given refuge to a colony of Schwenkfelders at Berthelsdorf in 1725. In 1732 they were required by royal edict to leave Saxony. In the meantime, the trustees of the Georgia colony in America had invited the Schwenkfelders to settle in Savannah, and when events turned their eyes to Pennsylvania instead of Georgia, the Georgia trustees invited the Moravians to colonize there. Thus, in the last week of July, 1735, Bishop David Nitschmann left Herrnhut for England with a colony of sixteen men and eight women. This colony sailed from Hamburg for England in September from whence they left for the new world. They arrived at the mouth of the Savannah River on February 16 and finally landed on the twentieth of that month in 1736. See Levering, *Bethlehem*, p. 35.

6. The accompanying explanation reads in translation as follows:

Savannah
Town in Georgia, one of the southern English Provinces in North America, 32 degree North Latitude and 76 degree Longitude west from London on the Savannah River and on a plain. Copied July 1765.
Explanation
1. The entire city site is 126½ rds. long and 102 rds. wide, a good 80½ acres.
2. In it are laid out 320 building sites, each 90 ft. long and 60 ft. wide, in 20 rds.
3. Therefore, the building sites total 40 acres and the streets and squares 40½ acres.
4. Each of the 4 squares, including the streets which run through them, are 440 ft. in length and 420 ft. wide and contain 4 acres, 10 rds.
5. Streets are three different widths, namely b. is 60 ft. wide, c. is 45 ft. and d. is 30 ft.
6. Special lots are: e. the Council House, f. Silk House, g. English Church, h. English Parsonage, i. are 2 lots.
7. Fort
8. The Trustees' Garden behind the Citadel.
9. Here lie 5 acre lots around Grovernor's Plantation.

Note is also made elsewhere on the sheet that there is a

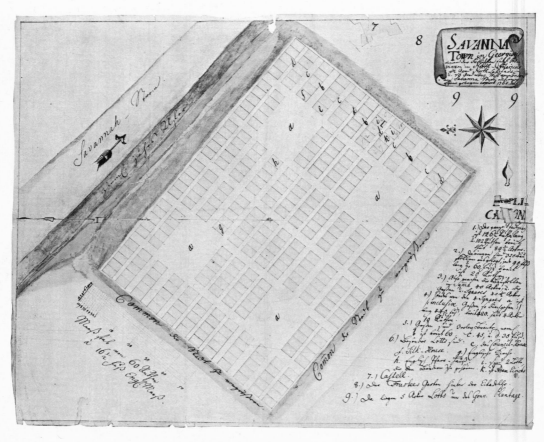

2. Plan of Savannah, Georgia, dated 1765

longing to the brethren in the settlement. There were two, in the southeast quadrant of the city, separated by an alley thirty feet wide. The sites were sixty feet wide and ninety feet long. These lots were on the more heavily populated side of the original plan for Savannah, since the Council House and the silk house were not too many blocks distant in a northeasterly direction from the Moravian plots. The English church and parsonage were, however, a little farther away. It is significant to note that much of this settlement was close to the fort outside the city proper, all lying on the banks of the Savannah River.

The plan that was developed for Bethlehem in Pennsylvania is shown most clearly on a map dated 1758 (Plate 3). By that year, a large percentage of the various "choir" buildings in the new community had been erected; only the last wing of the Single Sisters' House and the Widows' House of 1768 were to be added. The industrial community in the Monocacy Creek valley had likewise been developed.

"rather abrupt shore" along the river and that land "Common to Enlarge City" has been set aside on two sides of the settlement.

Following the town planning precedent established in Herrnhut, the plan of Bethlehem is organized around a central open square, known to eighteenth-century Bethlehemites as *Der Platz*. Unlike the European squares, which often had this open space developed into a series of garden plots, the Bethlehem *Platz* was an open green that was apparently always intended to remain so.

The main road from Philadelphia to the south of the settlement led up from the Lehigh River to this central square and continued from the northern extremity of this clearing toward Nazareth. Two main east-west streets were developed. That known today as Church Street was called in the eighteenth century "Sisters' Lane," and it was along this lane that the main "choir" buildings were erected between the years 1742 and 1773. *Ladengasse* farther to the north no doubt took its name from the fact that the first store of the community was established there.

Der Platz was bordered on the south by the Single Brothers' Choir building (Plate 4). On its eastern side were the doctor's house, the laboratory, and the *Kinderanstalt*. Its northern extremity was determined by the *Hof* barns, and other stable structures that were erected in this section of the community. Adjacent to these agricultural buildings, and running on a slight angle from the western extremity of the *Hof* southward and forming the western side of *Der Platz*, was the easternmost row of buildings defining the industrial Monocacy Creek area. Since Bethlehem was planned to be the industrial center into which the surrounding Moravian agricultural plantations poured their raw products and from which they took finished articles, the large industrial concentration, marveled at by so many eighteenth-century travelers, contained a variety of special-use structures. In 1758 the industrial community of the Monocacy Creek valley consisted of a blacksmith house and locksmith house, a potter's house, a cabinetmaker's and turner's shop, water works, oil mill, three buildings having to do with the tanning of leather and another simply known as "the leather-house," a spring house, a charcoal shed, a nailsmithy, a grist mill, and a slaughter house, while on the other side of the creek were situated the Indian Chapel, a kitchen, and Indian House which served as an inn for visiting Indians. A second concentration of industry grew up on Sand Island, bordering the Lehigh River. Here were located a flax house, a building for the breaking and drying of flax, a saw-mill, a house for boiling soap, and a wash house or community laundry used by the single sisters of the community. The agricultural *Hof* consisted of a horse stable, hay and straw barns, cow stables, pig

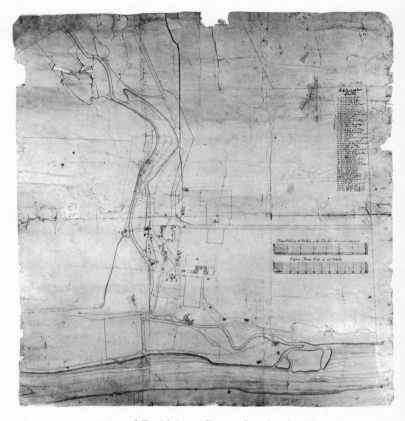

3. Plan of Bethlehem, Pennsylvania, dated 1758

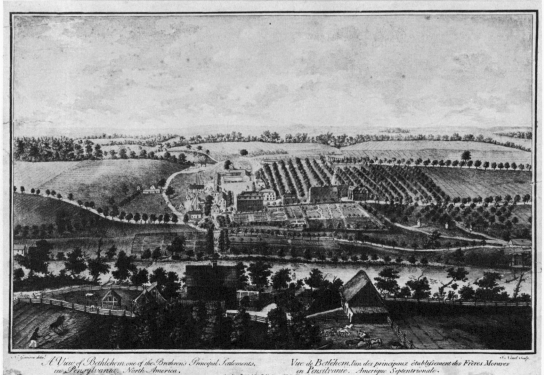

4. Nicholas Garrison View of Bethlehem, 1757

stable, and dwellings for stable hands, as well as other types of stables, some of stone masonry and some of half-timber construction. Clustered near the *Hof* was the original building of the village, then known as the "family house," as well as a wheelwright's shop, a hatter's shop, a currier's shop, and the cooper's house and shop.

To the north and somewhat removed from the center of the community was the Sun Tavern, erected by 1760, and its accompanying horse stable. As mentioned above, a community store was located on *Ladengasse*, as well as the residence of Timothy Horsefield, the storekeeper. The various "choir" buildings and attendant non-industrial structures were strung along the east side of *Der Platz* and Sisters' Lane (today called Church Street). These structures consisted of the Single Brothers' House; the Single Sisters' House, with its little log kitchen across the lane to the south; the girls' institute; the chapel; the *Gemeinhaus*; the Married Men's House; the boys' institute or *Kinderanstalt*; the doctor's house; and the laboratory. To the south, across the Lehigh River, was located the Crown Inn. Thus, in the short seventeen years between the founding of the community and the date of the map under discussion, the village had grown in a specified, orderly manner with the various functions of the community judiciously separated but related one to the other. A map of 1766 (Plate 5), now in the Unitas Archives in Herrnhut, further clarifies the orderly development of the community along the lines originally planned with the more detailed delineation of the gardens and the continuing development of the public way (now known as Broad Street) north of the community and the public tavern, known as the Sun Inn.

The fact that the Moravians were constantly alert to the values of the planned community, religiously, socially, and otherwise, is borne out by a manuscript in the Moravian Archives, signed by John Ettwein and dated February 16, 1791 (Plate 6). The enlightening memo reads in translation:

Memoranda

I do not say that Bethlehem will become like this! But I can still say, that it can become like this! Herrnhut has 100 building sites, this plan already contains 80! Why should one consider it foolish, if one says: in 20, 30, 40 years, all these lots will be resided on, when the plan, has provided for it.

The topography favors such a plan, and the location makes it natural. Some towns lie higher and still have water. Precautions should however be taken, that no

EXPLANATION
OF BUILDINGS

1. Inn
2. Farm or Plantation
3. Cuckler House
4. Cartwright's Shop
5. Store
6. Boemper House
7. Horsefield House
8. God's Acre
9. Ant. Schmich House
10. Cas. Fischer House
11. Hirt House
12. Okeley House
13. Schober House
14. Bakery
15. Ths. Fischer House
16. Langen House
17. Children's Boarding School
18. Drug Store
19. Family House
20. Water Tower
21. Family House
22. Church Building
23. Single Sisters' House
24. Girls' House
25. Single Brothers' House
26. Schaaf House
27. Cabinetmaker's Shop
28. Pottery
29. Locksmith Shop and Smithy
30. Nailsmith Shop
31. Family House
32. Small Market Houses
33. Water Works
34. Oil Mill
35. Tawer's Shop
36. Spring House
37. Tannery
38. Slaughter House
39. Soap Boiling House
40. Dye Shop
41. Grist and Fulling Mill
42. To the Tannery
43. To the Fulling Mill
44. Workshop and Building Yard
45. Flax House
46. Carding House
47. Sawmill
48. Dwelling House
49. Laundry
50. Bleaching House
51. Citizens' Gardens
52. Monocacy Creek
53. Lehigh
54. Orchards

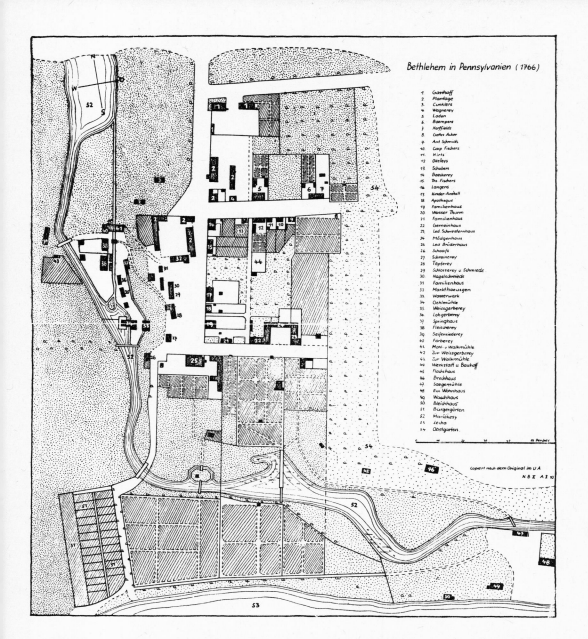

Bethlehem in Pennsylvanien (1766)

1. Gasthoff
2. Plantage
3. Cunklers
4. Wagnerey
5. Laden
6. Boempers
7. Horffields
8. Gottes Acker
9. Ant Schmids
10. Casp Fischers
11. Hirts
12. Okeleys
13. Schobern
14. Baeckerey
15. Ths. Fischers
16. Langens
17. Kinder-Anstalt
18. Apotheque
19. Familienhaus
20. Wasser Thurm
21. Familienhaus
22. Gemeinhaus
23. Led. Schwesternhaus
24. Mädgenhaus
25. Led. Brüderhaus
26. Schaafs
27. Schreinerey
28. Töpferey
29. Schlosserey u Schmiede
30. Nagelschmiede
31. Familienhaus
32. Markthaeusgen
33. Waserwerk
34. Oehlmühle
35. Weissgerberey
36. Lohgerberey
37. Springhaus
38. Fleischerey
39. Seifensiederey
40. Färberey
41. Mani. u. Walkmühle
42. Zur Weissgerberey
43. Zur Walkmühle
44. Werkstatt u Bauhoff
45. Flachshaus
46. Brechhaus
47. Saegemühle
48. Ein Wohnhaus
49. Waschhaus
50. Bleichhaus
51. Burgergärten
52. Manäkesy
53. Lecha
54. Obstgarten

Copiert nach dem Original im U A
N B X A I 10

5. Plan of Bethlehem,
   dated 1766

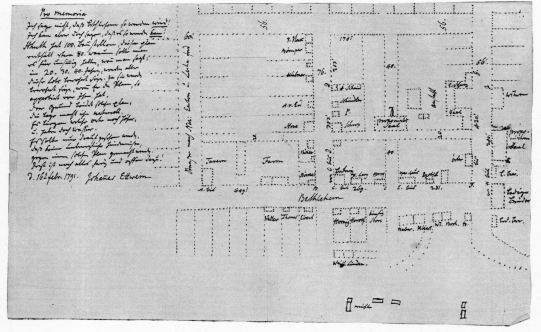

6. John Ettwein Plan of
   Bethlehem, dated 1791

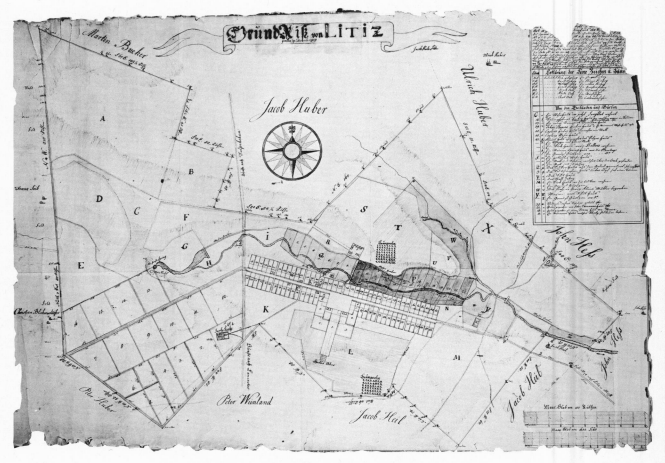

7. Plan of Lititz, Pennsylvania, dated 1759

immovable obstructions are made against such a plan. Now everything is still free and open for it!

February 16, 1791

John Ettwein

It is clear that even at this relatively late date, Ettwein was still interested in further consolidating and enhancing the plan of the community. The most significant change of this proposed plan of 1791 from that of 1758 is the elimination of the in-town agricultural *Hof*, which was now to be projected as a series of town lots for private homes, with the exception of the southernmost lot as the site of a "future store." Noteworthy also is the introduction of a narrow street from Sisters' Lane running north along the eastern side of the *Gemeinhaus* to *Ladengasse* and through to the future Broad Street, then the main road to Nazareth, Easton, and the Lehigh Ford. It is interesting to speculate as to whether the building shown on the south side of Sisters' Lane at the end of the aforementioned street and the structure that straddles a new street between Sisters' Lane

and *Ladengasse* and parallel to them, both noted as "proposed chapel," are actually proposals for two new chapels or whether Ettwein was suggesting alternate sites for a single new chapel. Documentary evidence does not indicate which was the probable intention. The latter site, however, would make a "vista building" of the proposed chapel by having it straddle the proposed street. Since the rising ground almost reaches its highest point at this particular spot, it is quite possible that the chapel was planned to dominate the community physically as church rule dominated it ideologically, following once more European precedent.[7]

7. When the present Central Moravian Church was erected between the years 1803 and 1806 at the corner of West Church Street and the present Main Street, its bulky scale dominated the village, a dominance that was accentuated by the steep approach to it by the main highway as it climbed from the Lehigh River. This sense of church dominance was destroyed when the present hill-to-hill bridge was erected in the early part of this century, bringing the visitor to the church at the level of the basement of the building instead of much below as it formerly was.

Lititz, Pennsylvania, (Plate 7) was planned as a long, narrow, "householders" village with a central axis that was bisected at the center by a large, open square with an additional perpendicular area leading to the burial ground or God's Acre, according to the plan dated December, 1759. Orchards were planned on both sides of the central portion of the community, and to the left of the northernmost two, a special yard or "liberty" for cattle was set aside near a watering ditch parallel to the main axis of the community. Eighty-one building lots for settlers' homesteads were laid out along both sides of the main street. A secondary street running perpendicular to the main thoroughfare divided every six lots on the two outer extremities on both ends, and a similar secondary street led directly into the center square in the middle of the plan. Although much of the explanation of the sheet has been lost, it is known that the church buildings were planned to cluster around the main square, where they are today.

Another diagram in the same archive, titled "Ground Plan of Emmaus in Salisbury and the land belonging to it, as this has been divided into lots in February 1760, copied from plans in Emmaus, December 29, 1767," shows a rather unusual plan for this Pennsylvania Moravian settlement (Plate 8).

A more modest "householders" village, this plan has no central square as has been the case in all other schemes considered thus far. A translation of the notes in the upper left section of the sheet reads:

The Plan of this Community is as follows:

1. Two rows of houses shall be erected in a distance of 7 rds. between which a street 3 rds. wide goes straight through, so that a width of 2 rds. remains in front of the houses for a front yard.

2. There is to be between every 3 lots a cross street 3 rds. wide, and between every 4 lots an alley 12 ft. in width.

3. Between the house and field lots as well as along the lines a road is to be left 1 rd. in width.

4. Each house lot is 18 rds. long and 4 rds. wide.

5. Each field lot wherever possible should consist of 3 acres.

6. The forest or bush shall remain standing for the present as also the square at the schoolhouse for its use.

Note that the schoolhouse was situated outside the regularly divided section of the village in a wooded area and had a planned garden. Possibly the school was so located before the village had been conceived. This school was to the northeast of the central section of the community, and the cemetery was situated to the southeast. A summary of the description

8. Plan of Emmaus, Pennsylvania, dated 1767

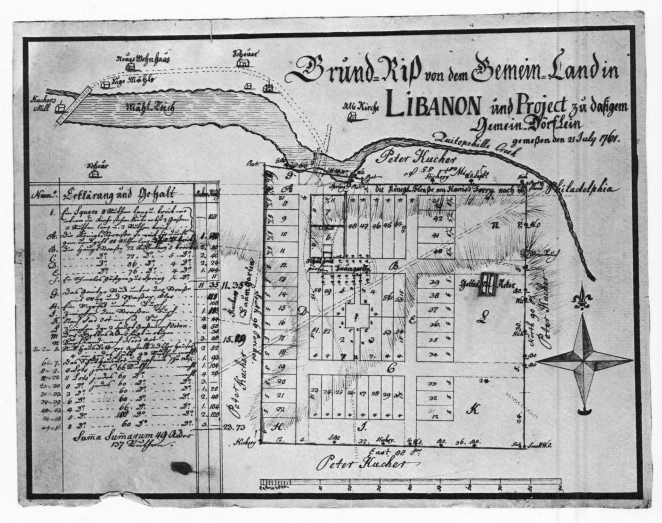

9. Plan of Lebanon, Pennsylvania, dated 1761

and contents of each of the sections of the planned community, shown to the lower right of the sheet, indicates that there were thirty-two house lots planned, each to contain one-fourth of an acre and thirty-two rods. There were also to be thirteen field lots, each three acres in size, two field lots of two acres, and two other field lots of three acres. The entire schoolhouse square (Number 18), with its yard area, meadows, roads, building lots, woodland, and what was cleared next to it, comprised nineteen acres, three rods, nine feet. The cemetery, various streets, and lanes used ten acres, one rod, thirteen feet, making the size of the village a grand total of one hundred two acres, two rods.

In the plan for Lebanon, Pennsylvania, a return to the more familiar town plan developed around a center square was followed (Plate 9). This sheet is titled: "The Ground Plan of the Church Land in Libanon and the Project for a little Church Village there. Surveyed July 21, 1761." The King's Highway from Harris' Ferry to Philadelphia bordered the northern extremity of the community. A site to the east of the planned center and slightly south and west of a stone quarry was set aside for the cemetery. The general plan of the village is reminiscent of the European Nisky in its symmetry. Like Klein Welke, however, it is obviously a new plan superimposed upon an older settlement. This is indicated by various references to a Peter Kucher around the newly planned village, the notation of a number of buildings—a new dwelling house, a barn, a saw mill, "Kucher's Mill" and millpond, another barn—in the upper left corner, and immediately to the left of the word "Libanon" in the title, a building marked "the old church." This is further shown by the manner in which the orchard area near the central square of the community straddles one of the main streets of the planned village. To the left of this orchard is the schoolhouse with a small garden in front, which is located in one of the newly proposed streets.[8] Again, the schoolhouse may have predated the planned town.

It should be borne in mind that each community held a specific purpose for these eighteenth-century Moravians. Bethlehem was to serve as the capital, the nerve center of the North American Moravian empire. It was the site of the planning for all other projects. It had direct liaison with European church headquarters at Herrnhut from which all direction of activity in North America was dispatched. Bethlehem was also the major industrial center that gathered raw material from other Moravian communities such as Lebanon or Hope, New Jersey, either con-

verting them into finished products or exchanging them for manufactured goods.

Nazareth, nine miles north, was primarily the central manor town equivalent to Bertholdsdorf in Germany. This ground had, after the original misunderstanding, been purchased from Whitefield. It was to be the seat of the ruler and contained Count Zinzendorf's retirement residence, which the Moravians had lovingly lavished upon him although death unfortunately denied him its use. References to the 5,000–acre Nazareth tract usually call it the "Barony of Nazareth."

Nain, located at some unknown spot on a prominence west of Monocacy Creek, was planned as a small village for Christianized Indians and as a more permanent establishment than the Indian tent village near Wunden Island behind the Bethlehem Brothers' House.

While Lititz, unlike the productive agricultural centers of Lebanon or Emmaus in Pennsylvania, or Hope, New Jersey, was conceived as an educational center, settlements like Gnadenhuetten were points of contact with the red men on the frontier, functioning as missionary and trade outposts. The fact that all of these communities, large and small, were thoughtfully planned, is the point to be noted. Their careful disposition not only gave them a niche in the socio-economic scheme of the church's network but gave them a pattern upon which to develop all of the visible, practical aspects of their communities.

Nazareth, nine miles north of Bethlehem, had been a Moravian settlement from 1741, when the five thousand acres of this tract were purchased from George Whitefield. (The heart of this old manor settlement was near the area of the present Walnut and New Streets.) By the end of the 1760's the old system of communal economy had been broken up and a system of controlled private enterprise took its place. As a result, by 1771, a new Nazareth town plan was laid out (Plate 10), streets were located, and the available plots were marked off. This is the plan of the present town, which centers around a *Platz* (A on plan) that originally contained a stone market house, a water works, and a fire house. Nearby was the Single Sisters' House, Single Brothers' House, the store, and Community Inn.

In 1766 the Bethlehem Moravians decided once more to attempt a settlement in the south and founded Salem, now Winston-Salem, in North Carolina. The earliest map to show the plan adapted for this community is dated April 2, 1766, and is attributed to Frederic William Marshall, then *Oeco-*

8. Translation of the explanation and contents of the sheet reads as follows:

No.	Explanation and Contents	A	Rds
1.	A square 8 rds. long and wide where church could stand with 8 alleys 11 rd. long and 2 rd. wide		108
A	The King's Highway as far as it goes through the Church land 88 rds. long and 2 rd. wide	1	148
B	The main street 72 rd. long, 5 rd. wide	2	40
C	The main street 72 rd. long, 5 rd. wide	2	40
D	The main street 86 rd. long, 4 rd. wide	2	24
E	The main street 76 rd. long, 4 rd. wide	1	144
F	A narrow alley to spring ½	–	11
		11	35
G	Entire section below street with road and water, clear	–	111
H	A rectangle below Bush	–	108
I	Between the Streets Bush	1	118
K	Towards Southeast in corner Bush	4	44
L	Between 2 main alleys tow. East	4	50
M	The God's Acre lies in the above	–	30
N	Bushland tow. Northeast	3	48
		15	29
From 2–5	Are house lots for Boarding School and Choirhouses 4, each contains 93 rd. makes	2	52
6–7	Schoolhouse lot and another one, 126½	1	93
8–11	4 lots, each 66 rd. makes	1	104
12–22	11 lots, each 60 rd. makes	4	20
23–30	8 lots, each 60 rd. makes	3	1
31–33	3 lots, each 60 rd. makes	1	20
34–39	6 lots, each 60 rd. makes	2	60
40–43	4 lots, each 66 rd. makes	1	104
44–48	5 lots, each 188 rd. makes	2	120
49–56	8 lots, each 60 rd. makes	3	1
	Entire total 49 A 137 Rds.	23	78

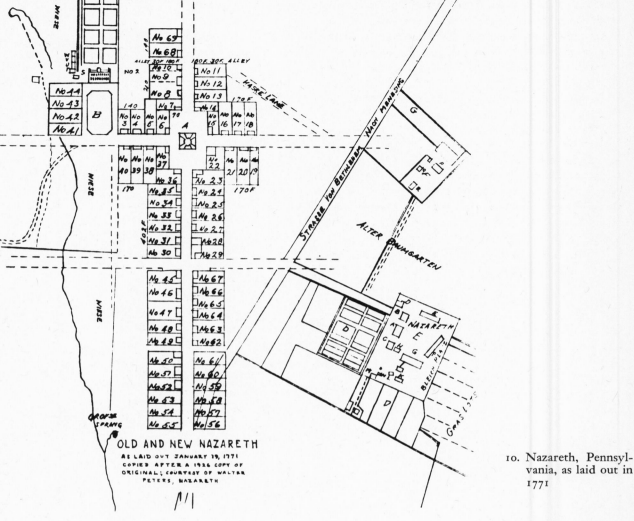

10. Nazareth, Pennsylvania, as laid out in 1771

nomus (administrator) of Wachovia (Plate 11). Ettwein mentions Nisky as a model for the plan in a letter dated August 6, 1765: "Br. Reuter's idea of a straight street through the town and your idea that one should not sacrifice convenience to appearance can be readily reconciled. Whether the long street, on leaving the town, continues or turns right or left, is of little moment; the way to the lower entrance of the town will probably be able to run straight for a long course, after Br. Reuter looks for and finds the right line."

In a letter of November 20, 1765, he gives further evidence of Moravian concern for the appearance of the city: "Regarding the plan of the town, we in the Conference are agreed how it should be. (Br. Reuter will give you his thoughts on your letter separately.) Regarding the Square, we all thought it too long; because none but two-story houses will be built on the Square; the place in the middle is made to appear so much larger than if three- or four-story houses were built around it. Besides, if it were shorter it would be more even and level."

These comments leave no doubt that the Moravian was conscious of the values of a planned community. It is also noteworthy that he had little or no compunction in laying a planned pattern upon an existing community. This has been noted at Klein Welke in Europe and as well as at Lebanon in

America. Whether good or bad, the ultimate conclusion that the Moravian never settled in a haphazard manner nor allowed his settlements to grow in a disorderly way is inescapable. Moravians have made a contribution to planning in the New World which is indeed noteworthy and may be compared favorably with the planning efforts of English settlers in New England and in the South.

After the several abortive attempts at permanent settlement in the New World, Bethlehem proved to be the first settlement to flourish and expand rapidly. If for no other reason, it is therefore worthy of close inspection. In creating this center from which all eighteenth-century activity of the Unitas Fratrum in the New World emanated, the church leaders and master builders of the community erected perhaps the largest and purest concentration of vernacular Germanic architecture in the United States. With a vocabulary of native materials, adapted to a European "language," the building-by-building growth of this pietistic settlement as outlined in the following sections attempts to not only illustrate in detail, scale, materials, and the unique architectural qualities of these structures but to give an insight into the social fabric of the community as well. Only the major structures of the town are discussed. It should be understood that these were supplemented by many other buildings, notably of log construction, all of which contributed to the fabric of a community that can be called one of the largest industrial concentrations of its place and age.

11. Frederic William Marshall Plan of Salem, North Carolina, dated 1766

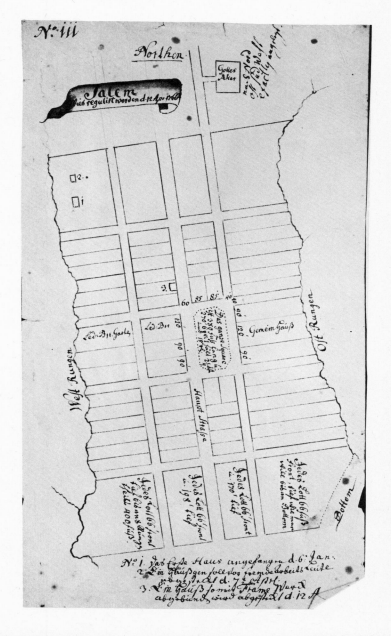

12. Watercolor of First House of Bethlehem (Extreme Left) by Rufus Grider, 1874

III

BETHLEHEM

—— ◆•◆ ——

FIRST HOUSE
(Erected, 1741; Demolished, 1823)

The felling of trees at the site on which the first structure of Bethlehem was to be erected occurred in the last days of 1740, when Father Nitschmann and several Moravian leaders came down from Nazareth to look over the Allen tract in anticipation of its purchase. The site they chose was, as Levering says, "some distance from the river" and beside an Indian path that led from the ford in the river to the north and west.[1] It was on a wooded slope at the top of a steep incline leading down to Monocacy Creek where there was a fresh spring. The spring was a primary reason for the purchase of William Allen's tract of land since the water never froze over in the winter and, therefore, offered the Moravians an unfailing source of fresh water.

Nothing more transpired for a little over a month, but on February 4 more timbers were felled in preparation for the eventual erection of a second and larger house. On this occasion, plans were made for

the erection of the small house at the spot that had been selected in December of the previous year. The logs of this first house of Bethlehem, which were square hewn, were completely framed by March 9, 1741 (Plate 12). It was a small building only twenty by forty feet in dimension and one story high, with a very steep sloping roof, containing an attic with adequate sleeping quarters for a number of persons. A unique feature of the building was a long partition dividing it into two sections, one of which was used for housing animals. Such buildings combining living and barn facilities under a single roof were rare in this country and almost unique in this section. Arrangements of this nature occurred in the Dutch settlements of New York State, but in the Pennsylvania colony this particular building is the only one of this type known to the writer. Precedent for the arrangement is found in continental Europe, especially in the Black Forest area of southern Germany and in the valley of the Emmenthal in Switzerland. The original house in which the brethren organized the Unitas Fratrum in 1457 in the valley of the Kunwald in Czechoslovakia shows a striking architectural similarity to the First House of Bethlehem. Photographs show it to have had the same long, low proportions, a similar wide overhanging roof on the entrance side, and a pent along the gable end separat-

1. Joseph Mortimer Levering, *A History of Bethlehem, Pennsylvania 1741–1892, With Some Account of Its Founders and Their Early Activity in America* (Bethlehem, 1903), p. 57.

ing the first from the second floor. The First House of Bethlehem was torn down in 1823 to make way for a stable that was needed when the third store of the community was converted into the second hotel known as *Der Gasthof zum Goldenen Adler*.[2]

There is some conjecture concerning the specific site of this first house. There are two drawings, one of which is illustrated by Plate 12, showing the building on the west side of what became Rubel Street.[3] According to a Bethlehem map of 1761, the First House was located in what would now be the northwest corner of the parking area of the present Hotel Bethlehem. However, the drawings lead one to conclude, by reason of its relationship to other buildings known to have been along the west side of Rubel Street, that the structure was situated in what would now be the southwest corner of the parking garage of the present hotel and on the north side of the street now known as Old York Road.

Numerous delineations of the house in its supposedly original form are extant. The Reverend C. F. Seidel reproduced an ink copy of one of them; Gustavus Grunewald, a Bethlehem oil painter of the mid-nineteenth century, reproduced the same view. J. A. Yerkes also painted the building, as have several anonymous artists. Since all of them are based, according to Levering, upon the two original pencil sketches made when the building was still standing, they invariably show it from the same angle and, even with minor variations in the structure in each of the pictures, it basically remains the same presentation.[4]

We know from Seifert and Levering's description of the house that the attic was used as the sleeping quarters of the building, that the entire south side was given over to human habitation, and that the smaller northern side housed the animals. This latter side was probably roofed with wooden shingles. It is usually shown as having a brick chimney, probably a later addition after the stabling occurred at the *Hof*. The roof covering the section used by the colonists is generally shown as red, indicating that it was probably tiled. Of interest also is the fact that most of the views show what can be interpreted as a clay and wood chimney on the tiled side of the structure.

This was an older and typical form. As a rule, the building is shown constructed completely of logs even to the tip of the gable, which is quite unusual. Two windows show in the upper floor of the gable end. Below this there is a small, pent roof running the width of the gable, and on the first floor are two fairly large-sized windows equally spaced across the façade. On what would be the eastern façade, the doors to both sections are side by side. These are flanked by a window to the left of the door lighting the area for human habitation and another window flanking the door entering the animal area.

The interior arrangement of the first floor is not known. Certainly the door to the area given over to human use must have opened into a *Küche* or kitchen and presumably there was a similar door in direct line on the other side of the building. The remainder of this floor may have been devoted to one large room or *Stube*. If privacy were required, this space could have had a board partition down the center of this room intersecting the fireplace wall of the *Küche* to create a *Kammer* or sleeping room. Since it is stated that the attic area was used for sleeping purposes, this partitioning is not very probable. However, the plan described above is the typical eighteenth-century house plan used by Germanic settlers throughout Pennsylvania.[5]

The fact that the building had at least a partial cellar is attested by the small gable-roofed appendage one notes on the forward or south side of the building in almost all of the representations. This probably was of stone and may have had a tile roof. It is always shown with a small window near the peak of the gable of the roof and slanting cellar doors that presumably led to a root or cooling cellar.

With the completion of the *Gemeinhaus* and the moving of the community into the latter building, the log structure that was the first building became the residence of the David Zeisbergers in the middle of August, 1742.[6] It was later occupied by Gotlieb Demuth and his wife until January 30, 1743, at which

2. See section on the Bethlehem Stores for further information on this building and site.

3. The gable windows shown on Plate XVI are presumably a later addition since none of the other views show them.

4. There are at least three more later versions of this view in the collections of the Annie S. Kemmerer Museum, Bethlehem.

5. The Miller's House at Muhlbach, the interiors of which are in the Philadelphia Museum of Art and "Fort Zeller," at Wolmelsdorf, near Reading, are but two of many examples which can be cited. Plans such as these and comparable interior arrangements may still be found in seventeenth- and eighteenth-century structures in outlying areas of southern Germany.

6. Levering, *Bethlehem*, p. 48. The dwelling part of the original building served as the place of worship for about a year. Tradition notes that it was in this building that the Moravians decided to adopt the name of Bethlehem for their settlement. The name is first used in the "Conference of Religions" in January, 1742.

13. Bethlehem *Gemeinhaus*, Watercolor by Rufus Grider, 1854

time Michael Miksch and his wife moved from Nazareth and occupied the building. The structure went through various unknown vicissitudes until its demolition in 1823.

It should be noted that the interval between the felling of trees for the First House and those for the *Gemeinhaus* is little more than a month. It is probable, therefore, that Bethlehem's first structure was never anything more than a temporary expedience in the minds of the settlers. The alacrity with which action was taken on the erection of the *Gemeinhaus* also leaves little doubt in one's mind that the brethren were thinking in terms of permanent settlement. The problems of clearing land, not only for the site, but for crops, and also the time consumed in the sowing and cultivating of crops undoubtedly contributed to the long interval between the beginning of preparation of log materials and the actual erection of the structure. The fact that the building was enlarged almost immediately is testimony to the sense of success of the settlement and the Moravian characteristic of planning ahead.

GEMEINHAUS[7]
(Erected, 1742–43; Extant)

The *Gemeinhaus*, the second structure erected in Bethlehem and one of the largest log structures ever erected in this country, was built of white oak logs (Plate 13). During the summer months of 1741, land was cleared south and east of the first log structure in accordance with the site plan. By June 22 the timbers cut the previous February were being squared for use and the excavation of the cellar was finished by September 22. The following day, Bishop David Nitschmann and Andrew Aschenbach laid the cornerstone at the southeast corner.[8] The field-stone

7. German *Gemein* = common, belonging in common to. The usual English translation of this name is Community House, or a house of many uses. Such multiple structures, used as headquarters of the parish or *Gemein*, were always the center of any eighteenth century Moravian settlement. It apparently grew out of the *Sbor* or *Dum* i.e., the Churchhouse of early Bohemia and Moravia.

8. Levering, *Bethlehem*, p. 69. He further states that a pewter box, containing the names of the fifteen persons present at the ceremony, was lowered in a cavity of the stone at this time.

used for these masonry foundations was taken from a nearby quarry which the Moravians had recently opened. Because of the growing needs of the community, an addition to the east was begun on August 12, 1742, and the cornerstone of this section was laid on September 10. By August 22 of the following year, work was finished and the interior was rearranged.[9]

According to Levering the original structure was thirty by forty-five feet when first erected.[10] The erection of the western end was begun first, a central block being constructed shortly thereafter, with the eastern addition of 1743 finishing the originally planned concept, which was thus actually achieved in three stages. This is suggested by the chain of events in the community at the time of Count Zinzendorf's arrival in Bethlehem in late 1741.

Ample evidence substantiates such a theory. Levering notes that when Count Zinzendorf arrived in Bethlehem on December 21, 1741, that: "In the unfinished Community House two rooms in the second story at the western end had been hurriedly prepared, as well as could be, for the use of the Count, and perhaps for his daughter. . . ."[11] These are presumably the two rooms to the west of the stair, since the chamber east of this stair was slated for use as the community chapel and was a single large room.

On December 24, the settlers gathered in the First House of Bethlehem for Christmas Eve vigil services, and Zinzendorf, struck by the similarity of the situation with that of the first Christmas, led those present into that half of the structure housing the cattle. By general consent, the name Bethlehem was thereupon adopted for the settlement. Certainly if the chapel in the *Gemeinhaus* had been in an even partially usable state at that time, it seems likely that Zinzendorf and the Moravian settlers would have used it on so momentous an occasion as the first Christmas in their new settlement.

That rooms for Zinzendorf had to be "hurriedly prepared" for him in the *Gemeinhaus*, plus the fact that the first special service was held in the First House instead of in the chapel of the *Gemeinhaus*, leads one to conclude that the central block of the structure either had not been started or, at most, was in such an early state of construction as to be unusable, despite the fact that the western end was clearly habitable for Zinzendorf, with only the addition of last minute touches.

It is also known that as late as June 15, 1742, Anton Seiffert and several carpenters went to Bethlehem after the close of the Pennsylvania Synod, specifically to help master builder Nitschmann and his assistants complete the *Gemeinhaus*.[12] These efforts must have then brought the structure to completion since it is recorded that Zinzendorf's secretary, John Jacob Mueller, who was also an artist, provided the first decorative art in Bethlehem when he set up a painting in the chapel.[13]

The structure undoubtedly looked much different in detail in 1743 than it does today. Howland has made a reconstruction drawing[14] based on his own researches and on a watercolor drawing of the "choir" house of the married couples, the building that was demolished in 1802 to make way for the Central Moravian Church (Plate 14).[15] This drawing, by "Old Mr. Oerter," appears to represent accurately the type of log construction that the Moravians employed at that time. There is no reason to suppose that the same system would not have been used in the *Gemeinhaus*, a structure erected only four years earlier than the Married Couples' House.

The roof of the *Gemeinhaus* was a steep gable,

9. *Ibid.*, p. 144. It is not clear whether the interior was actually physically rearranged, or whether the individuals living there were changed to different rooms for a more efficient use of the structure.

10. *Ibid.*, p. 68, n. 5.
Garth Howland, late chairman of the Fine Arts Department at Lehigh University, made a series of investigations of the *Gemeinhaus* during 1934–35 when the original logs were exposed for repair. His researches led him to the conclusion that the structure was originally an asymmetrical sixty-three foot-long edifice but that the 1743 addition was planned from the beginning. He notes that the central section of the building has cross walls with corner construction dovetailed into the logs of the front and rear façades and points out that the western end is made up of three outer walls with dovetailed corners, but mortised where it connects with the central block. It would seem that the central section was first constructed and the three-walled western end added later. Garth A. Howland, "Reconstructural Problems Associated with the Moravian Buildings in Bethlehem," *Transactions of the Moravian Historical Society*, Volume XIII, Parts III and IV (1944), 175.

11. *Ibid.*, p. 77.

12. *Ibid.*, p. 127. This was undoubtedly not only the eastern addition finally finished on August 22, 1743, but the original parts of the structure to which many things still needed to be done, such as the setting in of windows, the building of partitions, the laying of permanent floors, and the building of chimneys.

13. This was a picture of Christ bearing the cross, which was placed on the south wall of the Chapel, behind the table and chair of the minister. From it, right and left, and running around the room at the ceiling, he also placed a running border illustrating two hymns.

14. Original in the Moravian Archives, Bethlehem. See Howland, "Moravian Buildings in Bethlehem," p. 175.

15. Original in the Moravian Historical Society Collections, Whitefield Hall, Nazareth, Pennsylvania.

14. Married Brothers' Choir Building, Bethlehem, Undated Watercolor by "Old Mr. Oerter"

with a slight "kick" at the eave line, an architectural refinement characteristic of almost all German building efforts in America in the eighteenth century. In the upper attic, where one may still see the original five- to sixteen-inch-wide red pine boards, the original rafter structure remains intact, clearly showing that both extremities of the building had truncated ends at one time.[16] That of the west end was presumably changed when the Old Chapel building was put up, in order to make a smoother architectural transition in the joining of the two structures. The north and south sides of the roof originally had two rows of shed-roofed dormers, those in the upper attic being half as tall as those in the lower register and nearly square.[17] This is typical of medieval structures.

The lower attic was used as a dormitory, which was undoubtedly divided into more than one room. "Today we occupied our large house now that the rooms are ready. Each choir occupied its rooms, the dormitories also being exchanged since the Sisters moved into the new addition to the house."[18] The second floor center was completely given over for use as a chapel, thus making a square room approximately thirty by thirty feet. The walls of this room were plastered, and in February, 1750, four square walnut pillars were erected to support the ceiling. This is the floor that we also know contained the so-called Zinzendorf rooms at the west end.

The basement or ground floor is known to have housed the kitchens, which were entered through a door beneath the entrance stoop at the west end of the structure. This kitchen door (a "dutch door" divided horizontally in the middle) as opposed to the first floor door, which was the characteristic bi-leaf type, mortised, tenoned, and rabbited in a herringbone pattern, is still in place with its wooden hinges and latches well preserved. Vestiges of flagstone in this area give a clue to the probable original flooring.

We can only conjecture the original plan of the structure since the master builder's drawings for it are no longer extant. A 1752 inventory does, however, list twelve rooms in addition to the chapel and

dormitories. It is also known that a large, open hearth and oven provided cooking facilities in the basement kitchens. Heating was probably lacking in some of the rooms, notably the dormitories, but according to Howland, a tile stove heated the chapel as early as October, 1742.

There is an interesting master craftsman's drawing dated February 1, 1758, in the Bethlehem Moravian Archives titled, *Entwurf eines Gemein-Hauses in Bethlehem*, i.e., a plan for a community house (Plate 15). It indicates that the Moravians were probably outgrowing their log *Gemeinhaus* even at this early date and were thinking in terms of a new and architecturally more sophisticated building. Though never erected, it is important because of its baroque qualities and architectural affinity to some of the buildings in Nazareth and Lititz.

In plan, the structure was to be a rectangle, one hundred and seventy-four feet long by forty-eight feet wide. This was bisected in the middle by a large hall or chapel ninety feet long and fifty-four feet wide, placed perpendicular to the long side of the building. A note in the upper left corner of the sheet indicates that there was to be a kitchen, a kitchen room (presumably a preparation room), and a kitchen cellar or larder at the west end of the basement level, with a further note that "the dining hall" could be very well arranged along the south side. There are no other notations to tell what the remainder of this ground level was to be used for or whether the rest of it was even to be excavated.

At the northwest corner of the first floor, a twenty by forty-foot dining hall was planned with a sixteen by twenty-foot room to the east of it. On the opposite side of the hall, which divides the building longitudinally on both floors, two more twenty-by-twenty-foot rooms were planned with the entrance area containing the stairs to the second floor to the east. The large fifty-four by ninety-foot chapel or hall, with four windows on both north and south sides, was planned for the center of the structure. The east wing was exactly like that of the west, save for the fact that the forty-foot long dining hall area in the west wing was here divided into two twenty-foot rooms.

The second floor had a "small hall" directly over the first floor dining hall and its adjacent twenty-foot wide room. The remainder of this wing and the entire east wing was divided into twenty-by-twenty-foot or twenty-by-sixteen-foot rooms. Of special note is the balcony off the east wing which projected into the upper space of the first floor chapel.

16. This is borne out by inspection of the many eighteenth century drawings and prints that show the building in this manner.

17. The upper row of dormers has completely disappeared on the south side, as have the small lights in those remaining. For a fuller exposition of the fenestration problems and patterns, see Howland, "Moravian Buildings in Bethlehem."

18. Congregational Diary of Bethlehem, August 22, 1743, Moravian Archives, Bethlehem, Pennsylvania.

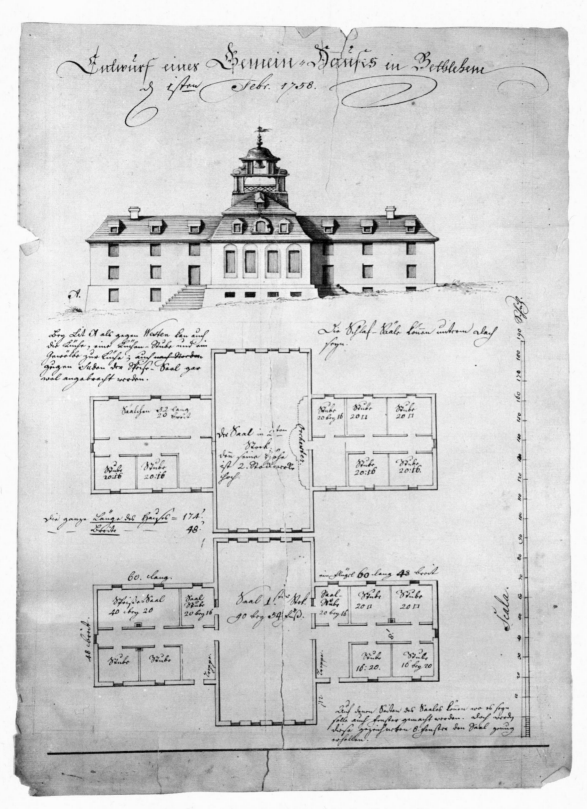

15. Proposal for a New *Gemeinhaus* for Bethlehem, dated 1758

This is marked *Orchester* on the plan and is presumably the area that seated the singing choir or musicians during special events and religious services.

A note at the upper right corner of the sheet consigns the attic area to dormitory use. The lack of open fireplaces on the plan gives rise to the conclusion that tile stoves were probably planned to heat the rooms.

The elevation holds perhaps even more interest for the architect and architectural historian than do the plans. The most striking element of the design is the elaborate bell tower crowning the building. Definitely baroque in concept, with scrolled supports flanking a graceful dome that is topped by an elaborate finial, it seems conceivable that this design was probably inspired by drawings from books on architecture in the libraries of such master builders as David Nitschmann and Henry Antes.[19] The symmetry of the plan and façade is characteristic of the Moravian architectural conception. Somewhat surprising is the lack of an upper attic, save in the gambrel-roofed chapel section of the building. One will note that both shed and gable-roofed dormers were projected. Of particular interest is the round-headed central dormer in the lower register of the chapel section. The baroque conception here is quite similar to the central dormer shown on the original plans for the Sun Inn at Bethlehem. These are dated the same year, i.e., 1758.

One cannot help but lament that this projected

19. There are at least one seventeenth-century and nine eighteenth-century architectural treatises in the Bethlehem Moravian Archives today. Most of them are profusely illustrated with many baroque designs, any one of which could have inspired the Bethlehem builders. These books are:

Grundliches Unterricht von Heng-Oder Sprengenwercken, Leonhard Christoph Sturms, Stockholm und Leipzig, 1726.
Synopsis Architecturae Civilis Eclecticae, Johann Jacob Schubler, Nurnberg, 1732.
Die Architectura Civilis, M. Albert Daniel Merckleins, Frankfurth und Leipzig, 1737.
Theatri Machinarum Hydraulicarum, Jacob Leupold, Leipzig, 1724.
Hutte-Werken, Christoph Andreas Schluter, Braunschweig, 1738.
Vulcanus Famulans, M. Johann Georg Leutmann, Wittenberg, 1720.
Scheuplazz des Mechanischen Mühlen Baues, Johann Georg Scopp, Frankfurth und Leipzig, n.d.
Neu eroffnete Vorraths-Kammer, (no author), Frankfurth und Leipzig, 1760.
Ars Vitraria Experimentalis, Johannis Kunckelii, Frankfurth und Leipzig, 1689.
Slang-Brand-Spuiten en Haarewyze van Brand-Blussen, Jan van der Heiden en Jan van der Heiden de Jonge, Amsterdam, 1735.

building was never actually erected. Certainly, the belfry of the structure would have been a fine addition to the growing skyline of this unusual settlement, not to mention the contribution it would have made to the architectural heritage of our country in general.

TANNERY
(First Building Erected, 1743;
Damaged by Fire, 1745)
(Second Building Erected, 1761; Extant)

The significance of Bethlehem as an eighteenth-century industrial community of note is attested by the fact that the first building of one of its major industries, i.e., tanning, was erected the same year that the third section of the *Gemeinhaus* was being erected. This structure was placed in the low-lying area of Monocacy Creek, along whose banks Bethlehem's industrial community was to be developed. By placing this first of many structures devoted to industry and crafts near the source of water power, the builders isolated it from the residential community on the hill above and set the pattern for a useful division of their community.

A traveler approaching Bethlehem from the south in 1743 saw a monumental log structure capping the hill over the Lehigh when he crested South Mountain. To the left on the hill and further back stood the first house, and in the valley to the left, the first tannery structure and grist mill. Undoubtedly the scene was also furnished with limited cleared plots of land under cultivation and a sprinkling of smaller outbuildings, but history does not bother to record the latter.

A small frame building was erected in 1743 on the east side of a mill race just south of the new grist mill as the first housing for the tanning, tawing, and currying industry which was to develop into such prominence in eighteenth-century Bethlehem. During the night of January 18, 1745, this building caught fire, but the blaze was soon extinguished.[20] The expansion of the industry rather than damage from fire was probably the cause for the erection of the larger stone structure which still stands (Plate 16). Erected on the west side of the mill race in May, 1761, this thirty-six by sixty-six-foot building was constructed of native limestone in the same architectural style as the large "choir" houses on Church

20. Congregational Diary of Bethlehem, 1745, Moravian Archives, p. 2.

16. Undated Nineteenth-Century Photograph of the Bethlehem Tannery

Street, with red brick arches over each of the nine-over-six-light windows evenly spaced across the front and end façades of the structure. The center window over the hooded door, slightly larger with twelve-over-nine lights, gave subtle accent to the center of the building. This emphasis may also be observed on such structures as the Bell House.[21]

According to a diaconal report,[22] the first floor was divided for use as a dyeing room in one half while the other half was devoted to "a leather room" and a small room for dressing the leather. The second floor was divided into a preparing room but the use of two other rooms is not noted. The entire third floor apparently was used as a drying area. The report also makes note of "a new scraping house" behind the building. Whether this was attached or not is unknown.

Two early photographs made in the latter part of the nineteenth century show the building already divided into two parts, with the northern end serving as a residence. Despite recent commercial use, much of the woodwork of this later residence portion of the structure remains within the building. Many of the window reveals give evidence of panelling, and a very graceful balustraded stairway can still be found within the structure.

GRIST AND FULLING MILLS
(First Grist Mill, Erected, 1743;
Damaged by Flood, 1747)
(Second Grist Mill, Erected and
Fulling Mill Added, 1751;
Fulling Mill Damaged by Fire, 1752)
(Fulling Mill Rebuilt, 1759;
Grist and Fulling Mills Destroyed by Fire, 1869)

Although the first grist mill, of which little is known, shared the Bethlehem scene with its neighbor, the log tannery, as well as the first house and the *Gemeinhaus* farther up the hill, the stone grist mill that replaced its predecessor in 1751 was erected in a community that was much more developed than the village of 1743. In addition to those structures already mentioned, the visitor in this later year must

indeed have been impressed by the size, number, and concentration of structures in this wilderness. Approaching from the south toward the ford of the Lehigh River, he would now have first encountered the Crown Inn and its outbuildings. Glancing across the river, the complex of "choir" buildings would undoubtedly have caught his eye first, beginning with the second stone structure of the single brothers and the two log family houses across Sisters' Lane; to the north and east of them, the log *Gemeinhaus*; the stone Bell House and the first Single Brothers' House, the latter then serving the Single Sisters' "choir." Behind these latter structures lay "God's Acre"—the cemetery—and before them the fenced doctor's garden and *Gemeinhaus* garden. Sisters' Lane was pleasantly bordered with black cherry trees eastward to a watch house with its cap roof and finial. Dotting the hill south of the Sisters' House, he would have noticed the laundry house, the flax drying house, the bleach house, and the saw mill. Beyond "God's Acre" he may have noted the beginnings of *Ladengasse* lined with cross-log fencing and graced with one small structure on the north side which led from the latter to *Der Platz* and the stable compound near the First House. Cascading down the slope and clustering around the power source of Monocacy Creek were a group of sixteen to twenty smaller structures to judge from the extant 1750 view of the community in the Bethlehem Moravian Archives. Thus, the village had grown swiftly in the decade since its founding from a single structure to a community of approximately ten to twelve major buildings with a supporting array of minor structures of unknown number. The industrial community was already sufficiently developed to a point of distinction. It was the new grist mill, with its attendant fulling mill, and soon to be established dye works and clothier's shop—all in one structure—which gave unmistakable impetus to this growth.

Although the first grist mill in this section of the country belonged to Nathaniel Irish, land agent from whom the Moravians had bought their five hundred acres to found Bethlehem, Moravians were concerned with the erection of their own building as early as 1743.[23] The master builder of Bethlehem, Henry Antes of Falckner's Swamp, was in the community to select the site as early as January 25 of

21. Of special note is the triple nine-over-six-light sash at the third level. Inspection of this sash and frame indicates possible original fabric. If this is correct, such an architectural feature is unusual and possibly unique in eighteenth-century Moravian architectural practice.

22. *Unity Directors Board X*, 145, Appendix VI (Archives of the Unitas Fratrum, Herrnhut, Germany), as cited in Hellmuth Erbe, *Kommunistische Herrnhuter Kolonie des 18. Jahrhunderts* (Stuttgart, 1929) p. 69, n. 38.

23. A. W. Schmich (compiler), *The Grist Mill: More about the Old Mill; W. C. Reichel's Tribute to the Old Mill; Petition for Stone Bridge at Luckenbach's Mill* (Bethlehem, 1925).

17. Undated Nineteenth-Century Photograph of the Second Bethlehem Grist Mill (Right Section), Erected in 1751 and Dye Works and Rebuilt Fulling Mill, 1759 (Left Section) Both Destroyed by Fire in 1869

that year.[24] The site was near the large spring that supplied the village with fresh water and near the creek the Indians called the Menaggassi (now Monocacy). Antes is known to have gone back to Bethlehem on the same project on April 21 and 28. It is also known that Gotthard Demuth, an original member of the Moravian colony in Georgia assisted him in building the mill. By June 20, Demuth had returned to Germantown where he was then living, and four days later Antes came up from his farm to superintend the fitting in of the mill works.

On June 28 the first flour was ground at the new mill. By 1744 four hundred and thirteen bushels of various types of grain were being ground at the mill annually.

Although the building material of which this first grist mill was made is not known, it is very probable that it was log set on a stone foundation. This

assumption is based upon documentary evidence that most of the first craft and industry buildings in Bethlehem were housed in log structures. Moreover, it is known that the stone substructure of the mill was damaged in the flood of 1747. Although the mill had been repaired, a decision was made in 1751 to erect a second mill (Plate 17). At the same time it was decided to enlarge the structure to the west and to incorporate the fulling mill under the same roof.[25] During the winter of 1751 preparations were made for the erection of this new structure, to be of stone quarried in what is now the Nisky Hill cemetery area. Timber was felled and hewn in January for the new water wheel and the masons began the foundation in June of that year.

By September 2, 1751, the first flour was ground in the second mill, and on November 18 the fulling

24. Congregational Diary of Bethlehem, 1743, Moravian Archives. See also Levering, *Bethlehem*, p. 161.

25. Antes had conferred with those in charge about the building of such a fulling mill as early as 1751. See Levering, *Bethlehem*, p. 153.

mill was started with the same power. It was not long before a second run of grinding stones was added to the mill to satisfy the ever-increasing demand of the residents of the community and that of the surrounding countryside; these began turning by May of 1753.

Unfortunately there are no plans known to the author which show the interior layout. It is known, however, that the building was entirely of stone; that it had a red tile roof made by Burnside, the Bethlehem potter, at his tile works on Monocacy Creek farther north of the settlement; that the upper floors and a gable area were precisely pointed with mortar, as proof against vermin; and that the inner walls of the gables were smooth-finished in lime stucco. Levering also says that the interior was plastered upon laths made at the sawmill at Christiansbrunn. There was a large, open fireplace in the east wall on the ground floor which gave warmth to the large room that served as a gathering place for the farmers. It is further known that in January, 1752, a meal room, presumably for storage, was built directly over the existing undershot water wheel. Earlier, the dam and the raceway had both been renovated to eventually provide sufficient power for the double run of stone mill wheels. A hoist and sundial were added at an early but unknown date.

Hans Christian Christiansen from Holstein in Europe is the person to whom the design of the works for the fulling mill has been attributed. This is the same man who built the oil and buckwheat mills and the famous first water works of Bethlehem. In February, 1752, the fulling mill caught fire. It was repaired, but by 1759 it was decided to rebuild.[26] By October 19 of that year the new fulling mill was started and as documents indicate it was "capable of running through three hundred yards of stuff at once."

DYE WORKS AND CLOTHIERS
(Erected, 1759; Destroyed by Fire, 1869)

About the same time, an addition that functioned as a dye house was erected to the west of the fulling mill, and to the north an adjoining room was added for the clothiers. With the addition of this dye house, the length of the front of the building was

26. The first mill probably only had a stone foundation with log walls. The second structure was completely of stone.

now approximately one hundred and eight feet from the eastern end of the grist mill. With the growing trade of the clothiers, Richard Popplewell and James Hall, both from Moravian headquarters in Yorkshire, England, were brought over to tend this part of the industry along with William Dixson. They supplemented John Bernhard Millar, a Württemburger, who had come to Bethlehem in the spring of 1753 as the first clothier.

A stone house, which was erected in 1784 next to the mill for the miller and his family, completed the complex of buildings concerned with the grist, fulling, dye, and clothiers industries. According to Levering, it is possible that the dye house and clothiers' addition were erected with the fulling mill in 1751. However, if this earlier building were of wood and the second rebuilt in stone in 1759, the latter two buildings—dye house and clothier—stem from this later date since they were also of stone.

A group of undated drawings in the Bethlehem Moravian Archives shows the plan and elevation for a small cloth weaver's shop to the north of the fulling mill. Judging from the thickness of the walls, this addition was a two-room structure of stone, situated immediately to the west of the mill race. Entry was from a door facing west into a ten by twenty-foot vestibule, which in turn gave entry into a drying room thirty by twenty feet. The building was heated by a tile stove that stood in the middle of the northern wall of the drying room. From notes on the sheet, it is also evident that part of the function of cloth weaving took place within the body of the main building as well. This small, one-story, gable-roofed structure was proposed to be connected with the fulling mill by a door on its southern extremity.

It is evident from other manuscript material that serious consideration was given at one point to creating a new fulling mill adjacent to the Indian Hotel, which was situated on the west bank of the Monocacy, incorporating the latter building into the functioning of the fulling mill (Plate 18). The cloth workers submitted this idea themselves, and the following resolution, apparently submitted to the proper authorities in 1758, petitioned them to consider the Indian House as a new site for the fulling mill, bolting mill, and the addition of the tawing mill. The petition reads as follows in translation:

Because the old Fulling Mill is in such poor condition that it can't possibly keep going through this winter, we therefore request that the Brethren who work in it be assisted as soon as possible.

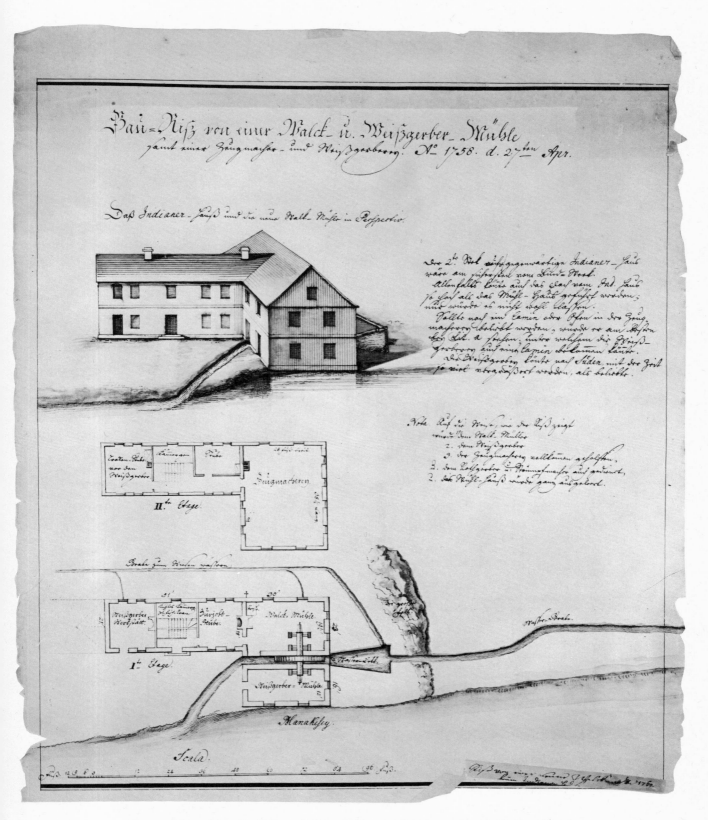

18. Proposal for a New Bethlehem Fulling Mill, 1758, Incorporating the Indian Hotel

[35]

The location of the Fulling Mill is good enough, but since it has to be rebuilt and the miller realizes that a bolting mill would be very useful and profitable, all the Brethren who have placed their signatures herein are of the mind and opinion that it should be attached to the Indian House with a tawer's mill added.

The Brethren are concerned, because they can see the prospect of customers going elsewhere if the fuller's mill cannot last through this winter and the Congregation would surely suffer a loss of £200, especially since the country people were getting accustomed to coming here.

Therefore, the undersigned Brethren, being of unanimous mind and opinion, request a decision soon.

Abr. Andrew   Casper Fisher   Richard Popplewell
            Johann Stoll

As soon as a decision is made, Brother Popplewell, and his colleagues offer, in his leisure hours (1) to break all the stones for it, (2) to dig the ground for the mill and the water ditch and the sooner he could start, the better he would like it.

At least four alternate schemes for this proposal are known to have been submitted.[27] It is obvious that

27. They first proposed a small, one-story wing to be built at right angles to the Indian House which would house the fuller and tawer's mill. This was proposed to be 24 by 29 feet and it was suggested as an alternate that what was then the fulling mill could best be utilized as the site of a bran mill.

A wheel 16.5 feet high was proposed, with a door giving entrance to both sides of the wheel; a small window in the larger of the two rooms was intended to be devoted to the work of the fuller.

A second proposal advocated building an extension north of the Indian House, which was to be 50 feet long and to contain a preparing room 20 feet long, a fuller's mill 15 feet long, a tawing mill 10 feet long, and space for the water wheel with wall thicknesses of 12.5 feet, making a total length of 108.5 feet by approximately 20 feet in width, which was the width of the Indian House.

A third plan called for building a two-story addition north of the Indian House but at right angles to it, which would be 30 by 50 feet, roughly the dimensions of the existing Indian House. This proposed a tawing and tanning room on the east side of the new addition, separated by the water wheel from the fulling mill which was to be on the west side. Upstairs, which was gained by a stair in the southwest corner of the fulling mill, there was to be a 6-foot-wide hall with a room 22 by 27 feet not designated for any use but heated by a tile stove, and a room over the tawing and tanning room on the first floor for the use of the tawer. One room of the existing Indian House was to serve as a preparing room for Brother Popplewell.

A fourth plan, the most elaborate and the only one dated, i.e. April 27, 1758, is titled in translation, "Building Plan for a Fulling, and Tawing Mill with Cloth Making and Tawing Works." This plan involved not only a new two-story structure at right angles to the existing Indian House but also raising the Indian House by a full floor height. On the first

this petition was not successful any more than were any of the schemes for conversion of the Indian Hotel, since the mill continued operating in its original location until destroyed by fire in 1869 when the existing structure was erected on the foundations of the third eighteenth-century building.

FIRST SINGLE BROTHERS' HOUSE AND ADDITIONS
(Erected, 1744; Extant)

In the residential part of town, the first Single Brothers' House must of necessity take importance over all other structures then built in Bethlehem. Not only was it the first of the individual "choir" houses to be erected in the village but it was the first to be built of stone and consequently set the architectural style of structures in the community throughout almost the remainder of the century and certainly until the immediate post-revolutionary years. Thus, a cognizance of its salient features and architectural characteristics is paramount to the understanding of the architectural contribution of Moravians to American culture. The exterior vocabulary of native lime-

floor, beginning at the southern end of the Indian House, was to be the tawer's work shop, then a cool chamber for storage behind the stair area, the latter of which was in a room off the main entrance, and then a preparing room. In the new section was to be the fuller's mill separated by the water wheel from the tawer's mill that was to be adjacent to the Monocacy Creek. Upstairs, the drying room for the tawer was to be situated in the southern end of the new floor of the Indian House, followed by two small chambers of undesignated use. The entire second floor of the new addition was to be given over to the clothmakers. This was to be approximately 28 by 38.5 feet long. The second floor was to be heated by tile stoves, no doubt getting their heat from the flues of the open fireplaces below.

It should be noted that in each of these proposals a new millrace was necessary with a reservoir of water as the race enters the building. In the later proposal, a secondary race was proposed to irrigate the meadow farther to the south. In translation, the notes to the right of this sheet read as follows:

The second floor of the present Indian House would be safest for open work. However, indeed the roof of the Indian House could be raised as high as that of the mill house; but it would not work well. If another fireplace or stove were desired in the cloth making shop, it had best stand at letter A, under which the Tawing Shop could also get a fireplace. With time, the Tawing Shop could be enlarged as much as desired toward the South.
Note: In the manner as shown by the ground plan,
1. the (fulling miller) fuller
2. the tawer
3. the clothmaker would be aided completely, and the red tanner and stocking knitter would also be served, and the mill would be emptied entirely.

19. Undated Nineteenth-Century Photograph of Church Street (Sisters' Lane), Bethlehem, Looking East, Showing the *Gemeinhaus*, Bell House Court, the First Single Brothers' House (Later Single Sisters' House), and the 1773 Additions to the East

stone, herringbone patterned wood doors, palm latches, red brick window arches, double-tiered roof dormers, small windows, and strict adherence to symmetry, coupled with square red floor tiles, whitewashed walls, deep window reveals, cock-head or strap hinges, tile stoves, walk-in fireplaces, and stairs of monumental proportions, even today speak the language of a non-English building tradition to the architectural observer. The continental European tradition was translated to America by this building.

The structure was erected to house the single men of the community after Count Zinzendorf had selected the site on July 7, 1742.[28] On July 13, 1744, the site was finally staked off and on August 8 of that year the cornerstone was laid. It was not until De-

cember 6 of the same year, however, that the building was occupied[29] (Plate 19). The single men occupied the house until November, 1748, when they moved to new and larger quarters farther west on the south side of Church Street.[30] The earlier building was then taken over by the single sisters in whose hands it remained until the "choir" system was dissolved and the buildings were finally changed into apartments. This, then, was the first unit of the series of stone structures ultimately to comprise what is known today as the Bell House group.

When erected, it was thirty feet deep and forty-

28. Kenneth G. Hamilton, *Church Street in Old Bethlehem* (Bethlehem, 1942), p. 13. See also Levering, *Bethlehem*, p. 144.

29. *Ibid.* Fifty men and several boys comprised the first occupants of the building.

30. This move was triggered by the rapid growth of the Single Brethren's Choir and the increasing space that it needed for its many crafts, for it was from this choir that the industrial Bethlehem of today had its genesis.

eight feet across the front.[31] As noted above, this structure set the architectural character for the later stone buildings in Bethlehem. Its style was obviously inspired by European precedents, modified by ideas from architectural books in the possession of Bethlehem's master builders.[32] The original building plan called for a simple central hall flanked on either side by single rooms. On the exterior, this was reflected in a façade with doorway on center, flanked by two windows on either side on the first floor, with five windows spaced evenly across the front on the second level.

The roof is a gambrel with three dormers in both lower and upper sections. This upper section is hipped at the western end, making the building appear today architecturally closer to German prototypes than the present gable roof of the earlier *Gemeinhaus*. The fenestration in the upper section of the roof is comprised of a series of small, square, shed-roofed dormers, while those in the lower register have gable roofs. It should be noted that the dormer in the center of this lower section, on a direct vertical line over the first floor entrance, is much larger than the two flanking it. This might indicate a later replacement of an earlier smaller dormer, but it seems more likely that it was probably made larger originally for the emphasis that such an architectural refinement would bring to the façade.

The end walls have three windows per floor and rise without interruption to the upper attic level. It is probable that the windows on all floors of these early buildings in Bethlehem had shutters for the double purpose of protection and heat conservation. One would expect casement windows to have been used in this relatively isolated eighteenth-century village, but it is known that double-hung windows were advertised at relatively inexpensive prices as early as the 1720's in Philadelphia, a scant forty-five miles south of Bethlehem, thus making them easy to attain.

One assumes that the even pattern of fenestration voids in relation to the solid expanse of wall certainly is an inspiration from northern Renaissance European architectural practices rather than from any essentially medieval predilection for asymmetry. Yet, despite the double-hung windows and the symmetrical placing of windows and doors, the buildings in Moravian Bethlehem still retain their continental Germanic flavor, reflecting an inspiration well outside the English Georgian Renaissance tradition that elsewhere dominated the heritage of colonial America.

Since this building was devoted chiefly to sleeping and work rooms, there was no provision for a kitchen. Consequently there is no basement, save for a small storage cellar under a portion of the building.

In addition to the use of native limestone, appearing in Bethlehem for the first time in this structure, the use of a concave cornice forming a simple transition from the wall to the overhang of the roof was also introduced in this structure. Noteworthy also are the red brick arches over each window as well as in the lintel between the square-headed sash and the flat arch.[33]

Flanking the center hall of the building were two fireplaces open to each room, which may have been fed from the hall as they were at the Oley Valley Moravian schoolhouse.[34] In the latter building, it is known that tile stoves or five-plate iron stoves, attached to a hole in the back of the fireplace, heated the flanking rooms. Such may have been the case in this structure also.

The original stairway to the second floor was probably in the center hall with the second floor plan essentially a repetition of that of the first floor. This hall stair was in all probability removed when the extension to the east was added in 1773, since, at that time, part of the first floor of the original building needed to be given over to a circulation area for access to the wing. Moreover, it would have no longer served a necessary function, since the new stair in this addition was placed in such a manner that it served both the old house and the new building.

To judge from existing stairways in other eigh-

31. This 48-foot measurement is taken from scale drawings now in the Congregational offices of the Central Moravian Church in Bethlehem. These are dated 1897. Levering states that the building was 30 by 50 feet while Hamilton says it was 30 by 40 feet.

32. For a list of the eighteenth-century architectural and engineering treatises in the Bethlehem Moravian archives, see n. 19, p. 30.

33. Some authorities have felt that these arches were only decorative because the actual structural arch behind the brick is an integral part of the stone wall and bricks are set in front of it, flush with the face of the exterior masonry surface. One may perhaps better account for them, however, by the fact that brick of uniform size is an easier building material to handle in creating a relieving arch immediately above a wooden window frame and that the flat stone arch behind the window frame acts as a reveal in the fabric of the thick stone wall. Against this hypothesis, however, is the fact that such brick arches are sometimes omitted over ground-floor entrances with a stone arch substituted. This can be noted on the Old Chapel as well as the north wing of the Sisters' House.

34. This important half-timbered structure, erected in the 1740's by Moravians in the Oley Valley, near Reading, Pennsylvania, has disappeared completely within the last decade.

teenth-century buildings of the Bell House group, one must presume that here too were stairs with a riser-tread ratio of an almost monumental proportion. This is another detail characteristic of these buildings. Such runs are excessively wide, the risers extremely low, and the treads very deep. The narrow flight that one finds on the second floor of the first Brothers' House is probably a later addition and not a continuation of the original stairway. Certainly the risers are too high and the flight too narrow to be comparable with other extant Moravian stairs of the earlier construction date.

In contrast to the plain whitewashed interior walls and the dark red, square floor tiles, the doors are of more than passing interest. On the third floor an original door remains which is a single full-length panel, with a quarter circle cut from each corner of the panel and a rectangular return at the center of each side. As opposed to the long strap hinges that one finds on the exterior herringbone patterned doors of the front and rear of the building, as well as on some interior doors, one finds hinges in a double "S" shape on this door, strongly suggesting once again the close ties this architecture has with the anonymous buildings of continental Germanic Europe.

It is noteworthy that many of these eighteenth-century doors also have wooden latches, worked by a leather thong; that some of them are "dutch doors" having upper and lower panels working independently; and that a few are constructed of a single board width.

NORTHERN EXTENSION (*Erected, 1752; Extant*)

As the initial dinner in the new dining room for married couples was taking place in the basement of what was then the new Old Chapel, the last gap in the quadrangle of the so-called Bell House group was being closed. At this time the northern end of the original Single Brothers' House, which had been taken over by the single sisters in 1748, was being extended northward to meet the eastern extension of the Bell House (Plate 20). Antes had conferred with those in charge of the work as early as 1750 and plans had rapidly progressed as a result of this conference. Thus, the third side of the court was completed in 1752 in order to provide additional space for the growing numbers within the Single Sisters' Choir. Required were a larger dining room, a new dormitory, and, later, a chapel. Architec-

turally, the building followed the pattern of the first Single Brothers' House from which this wing was then being extended. Likewise, the building was made of native limestone with red brick arches over each of the windows and a double-level attic with a double register of shed-roofed dormer windows in the gambrel roof on the east side of the building only, since the west façade rose uninterrupted to the level of the upper attic.

There were certain architectural adjustments necessary in effecting the connection of this wing with the two existing structures on either side of it. Since only the upper half of the gambrel roof of the original Brothers' House was hipped, this hip was continued northward, as the roof of the new extension. Thus, the new addition on the court side of the complex is a full three stories high instead of the usual two-story height, with two levels—the upper and lower attics—both under a gambrel roof on the east side only. This created a long narrow, relatively flat roof that was then covered with red clay tiles. Like its sister wing at the west side of the court (the Old Chapel), these tiles were removed in 1755 and were replaced by wooden shingles to lighten the roof load when certain indications of a failure in the limestone base and subsoil were discovered. It was presumably at this time also that the two ribbon buttresses were placed against the wall. Close inspection indicates that these buttresses were never an integral part of the wall but were built up against it, proving that they are later additions.[35]

On the opposite side of the new addition the roof was less of a problem than on the west. Only twenty-six feet wide, the new wing formed an "L" with the original building of 1744, and here the double level of the gambrel of the 1744 building was continued to meet a similar roof on the eastward extension of the Bell House. However, there was a certain awkwardness created by a disparity of floor heights between the two structures, and at the northwest juncture, we find at least a foot difference between the lower level of the gambrel of the Bell House roof and that of the extension of the single sisters' buildings. Moreover, following the lower roof line of

35. See Howland, "Moravian Buildings in Bethlehem," pp. 175–280. See also Hamilton, *Church Street*. Both of these writers feel the buttresses were in existence before the roof tiles were removed. Howland even states that they were erected during construction. This is a logical assumption if one looks at the removal of the heavy roof tiles as a further effort to lighten the load on a possibly poor foundational subsoil. Neither researcher quotes a source for this assumption.

20. Undated Nineteenth-Century Photograph of the 1752 (Northern) Extension of the Single Sisters' House, Bethlehem

the new extension, the windows of this new structure are slightly lower than those of the Bell House. Such details as these indicate to the discriminating observer that the entire complex actually grew piecemeal over a quarter of a century, although it appears to the casual eye to have been built at one time. Also, according to Hamilton, at the time the roof tiles were removed, "the dormitory was reinforced by additional pillars and beams."

On the interior, the building is almost as interesting today as when first built, since much of its original character remains. Thus, we find an access door on the west side opening into the court from a cross-hall. Originally there was a second door in line with the other opening on the other side of the building.[36] Later still, a second door was made from the window immediately north of the closed door, which has since been made again into a window. Large eighteenth-century square brick tiles floor the hall on the first floor, which leads to a large room at the north end of the structure. Probably this room was used originally as the dining hall, since the outline of an access door to the kitchen area of the Bell House is still visible from the room.[37]

On the second floor immediately above this dining area was the single sisters' chapel. This is now a series of exhibition spaces, partitions having cut the once large room into a series of small compartments. One can see the original supports for the room, however, imbedded in these partition walls.

As might be expected, the access stair to the second floor is monumental, the treads typically broad and the risers low. The heavy beam stringers exposed along the exterior stone wall and the entire character of this stair epitomize the character of the community—an unpretentious but distinctly Germanic culture and architectural expression.

36. This has since been closed and is now a window. See Howland, "Moravian Buildings in Bethlehem," p. 249, Figure 48, for a photograph of this original door entrance.

37. *Ibid.*, p. 248. This room corresponds in location to the ground floor dining hall in the Old Chapel. Thus, the kitchen, which was in the Bell House basement, could easily service either building. There is documentary evidence to prove, however, that the single sisters had a log kitchen and cow stable across Sisters' Lane (Church Street) from their buildings. It is perhaps correct to postulate that they only did their heavy cooking and preserving in this latter kitchen. A drawing in the Bethlehem Moravian Archives, titled in translation "Plan of the Single Sisters' Garden in Bethlehem marked off the 16th April, 1762," shows this log kitchen and cow stable and the six plots (each 2 by 2) of fenced vegetable garden of the single sisters to the south and east of it. A second but smaller garden immediately north of this new extension and the original building of 1744 were also presumably used by them.

EASTERN ADDITION (*Erected, 1773; Extant*)

This was the last of the buildings to be added to the Bell House group. Although the members of the Single Sisters' Choir had begun to agitate for an addition to their "choir" house as early as 1768, the date of the erection of the Widows' House across the street, it was not until October 19, 1773, that they were in possession of their building (Plate 21). Permission to erect the structure was finally forthcoming from the various boards involved in 1771, but work was not started until the following year, the cornerstone being laid and dedication taking place on May 4, 1772.

Although the structure conforms in general style with the stone buildings surrounding it, it lacks the character of a wing and gives the appearance more of a separate building. Stylistically, it is closer to the Widows' House across the street, which had been built only a few years before, than to any of the other structures to which it is attached.[38] Like the Widows' House, the intimacy of scale of the earlier structures is somewhat lessened. Moreover, a gable roof has taken the place of the earlier type of gambrel roof current in the community. In contrast to its neighbor, the 1744 Brothers' House, the building is much taller, mainly by virtue of its full basement. All floor levels are consequently higher than in the earlier building and a series of steps was therefore mandatory between the two structures on each floor level. A distinguishing characteristic of this particular building is the very simple water table above the basement level. This is an architectural adjunct absent in earlier structures of the community, including the Widows' House.

If one compares the original drawings with the building as it now stands, very little difference can be noted between the finished building and the structure proposed in 1771 (Plate 22). The large façade is broken by a central door, double-leaved and herringbone-patterned, with a frame and five over-lights above, topped by an arch of brick. This is flanked on either side by four windows, evenly spaced, and an equal number on the second floor. In contrast to other buildings in the Bell House group, the central window above the door is only three lights wide instead of the four-light window one finds

38. Upon comparison, there is little doubt that the plan of the Widows' House, dated July 23, 1760, inspired the plans for this structure of 1771. This conclusion is strengthened by the realization that the 1760 plan was intended for the site later used in 1771 for the other building.

over doors in the earlier buildings. In the lower attic register are a series of four gable-roofed dormers. Interspersing them on the second attic level are three shed-roofed dormers, slightly rearranged from the original scheme. The archive drawing shows three shed dormers, not interspersed between the lower dormers, but in line with them. Changed also are the entrance steps. The drawing indicates a straight run which has been changed to a double run east and west, presumably because of the narrow sidewalk. Moreover, a proposed hood over the entrance door no longer exists, if it once did.

An indication of the lessening Germanic character of these buildings and of this structure in particular might be noted in the greater number and closer spacing of windows with a larger relationship of voids to solids than had been the case when the earlier Bell House and its extensions were built.

The east end of the structure preserves more of the solid character of earlier Bethlehem architecture. On this end are only three voids in the large expanse of the stone wall. On the second floor a central door opens onto a balcony such as originally existed on the south side of the Bell House. This is probably a nineteenth-century replacement if one is to judge from the style of the railing and balcony supports. There is no doubt, however, that the door itself is original. In this case, the central window above is four lights wide in the manner of the earlier buildings of the settlement while the two windows flanking it are the usual three lights wide. Directly above the central window, in the upper attic, is a very small window directly beneath the chimney. This might seem to be an architectural anomaly until one visits the interior of the attic to learn that two separate flues rise in the structure flanking the central hallway, forming a pointed arch inside the attic, although expressed on the exterior as a single chimney.

On the rear or north façade, the general fenestration and door rhythm of the street or south façade is repeated, save that the door is thrown farther east by virtue of interior arrangements.[39]

Three manuscripts to be found in the Moravian Archives are undoubtedly the drawings of the unknown master craftsman responsible for the building (Plates 22, 23, 24). Comparing these plans with a plan of the original Brothers' House and its two extant wings drawn for Howland by Theresa H. Shute, one notes that the building's plan is essentially as originally intended with the exception of the interpolation of four later walls to create smaller rooms and a different flight direction of the stair run. In the case of the stair, it is not known whether the one indicated on the plans was never executed as projected or whether the existing stair resulted from a later change of mind. The point is clear, however, that there is an obvious difference between the original plans and the run of the stairs as they now exist.

Entering from the Church Street side, the circulation corridors form a "T".[40] The building was originally planned to be divided into four relatively large rooms, each over twenty feet in length. The stair area apparently was always planned for the northwest corner of the structure where it connected with the original "choir" building of 1744. It is presumable that the northeast corner of the latter building originally contained the stair and that this was removed when the eastern addition was erected. It is by reason of these stairs that the western chimney is not in a position commensurate with that of the eastern end, i.e., against the outside wall. The western chimney rises instead from basement through upper attic, about fifteen feet east of the west wall of the structure, in order to afford accessible flues for the free-standing tile stoves that the original plans indicate heated each of these rooms. Hamilton mentions that when the single sisters were agitating for this wing they complained of water standing near their premises. Hence, we find provision for the drainage of this water on the plans.

One of the three sheets (Plate 22) is titled in translation, "Plan for an addition to the Choir House for the Single Sisters in Bethlehem, 69' by 44' with approval of the Congregational Director's Board, Drawn December 19, 1771." The *Erklaerung* or table of explanation to the right of the sheet gives detailed information concerning the intended use of the structure.[41] In the lower left corner of the same

39. The large, flat-headed window to the left of the door as one faces the rear of the building is a late nineteenth-century addition.

40. As opposed to the usual cross plan for corridor circulation in Moravian buildings in Bethlehem.

41. This reads in translation as follows:
 A Basement in which are B, the kitchen and C, the kitchen room. D is the canal to lead water into the kitchen. F, the canal to draw water out of the kitchen. G, section of kitchen, cutting through kitchen at a. with the wall of the old house. H, portion of the foundation wall to be seen from the outside from the

21. Twentieth-Century Photograph (*circa* 1957) of the 1773 Addition to the Single Sisters' House

22. Plans, Elevations, and Section of the Eastern Addition to the Single Sisters' House, Bethlehem, 1771

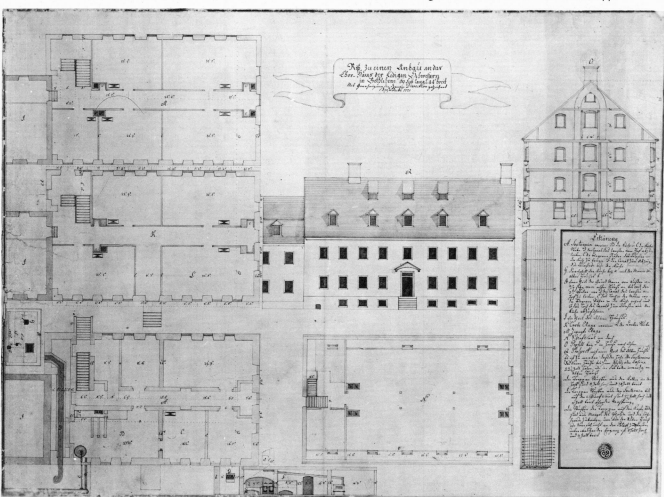

sheet, one notes the basement plan in which the kitchen and its adjoining larder were to be situated in the southwest corner of the building. At the extreme western end, an eighteen-inch canal or swale was planned, presumably to lead the water on the single sisters' premises away from the yard and into Church Street. Near this was to be a lead pipe that brought usable water into the kitchen and into a cistern, and near it was another small pared channel, presumably of brick, that allowed used water to be disposed of through the bottom of the kitchen wall to the outside.

At the bottom of the sheet, one may note a descriptive elevation of this kitchen and larder area showing the exact relationship of the drainage water trough to the large baking oven and the small stove, situated in the larder, with a small pipe leading into the flue in the next room over the oven. This stove is lower than would normally be expected and it was planned to stand on feet about twelve inches off the floor. The open fireplace is very wide with an arched top. There is also an indication of two large bake-ovens.

Another partial elevation of a portion of the foundation wall shows the general relationship of the canal taking the water from the yard, the lead pipe for clean water, and the trough that takes the water from the kitchen. Above this, at "K," is the first floor, where a room called the *Buba Zimmer* or "boys' room" is found in the southeast corner. A separate room for small boys was set aside in the Single Sisters' House so that they could be cared for by these young women while their parents worked or were away on extended missions on the Indian frontier or elsewhere. The plan also shows at this point a minimum of three steps to reach the level of the adjoining 1744 "choir" house.

The floor above, i.e., "M," in the upper left corner of the sheet, shows the second floor in which there were three rooms planned along the south side of the building and two along the north. Above this was the dormitory in the lower attic. This *Schlafsaal* or sleeping room impressed many eighteenth-century visitors who had the privilege of going through these buildings. Thus, a Lieutenant Anburey, in 1781, noted, among other things: "The superintendent of these young women conducted us to the apartment where they slept, which is a large vaulted room, the whole dimension of the buildings, in which were beds for every woman."[42] Another visitor, the Marquis de Chastellux, also wrote of the Sisters' House upon the occasion of his visit in 1782: "The superintendent . . . conducted us to the first [sic] floor, where she made us enter a large vaulted room, kept perfectly clean, in which all the women slept, each having a bed apart, in which are plenty of feathers. There is never any fire in this room and though it be very high and airy, a ventilator is fixed on the roof like those in our play houses."[43]

This *Schlafsaal* has remained essentially as Anburey and Chastellux saw it. It is not a truly vaulted room, but the wood and plaster framing beneath the lower part of the roof and along the underside of the upper attic floor creates the impression of a vault. In the center, one can still see the opening with its fancy grill, like a wheel window, which served as the ventilator. This room is not shown on the floor plan as having been heated in any way, thus bearing out the observation of the Marquis de Chastellux.

According to the explanation, "It is to be observed that the height of the new basement in the new house, to the landing or casing, is 22½″ higher than the floor inside the old house. The stair steps from the basement up to the yard are 8″ high and 10″ wide. The stair steps from the basement up to the dormitory are 7½″ high and 11″ wide without the ledge."

The two other drawings of this building are basically framing plans (Plates 23, 24), one showing the

old house and including the third pillar where d, the canal, brings water from the yard. E, the hole in the wall where the lead pipes are laid into the kitchen and F, the hole where the canal lets water run out of the kitchen.
I   A portion of the old house.
K   First floor, L. in which is the Boy's Room.
M   Second Floor.
N   Dormitory under the roof.
O   Profile at P. in the house toward the east.
Q   Perspective with a portion of the old house.
    It is to be observed that the height of the basement in the new house to the landing or casing is 22½ in. higher than the floor inside the old house. The steps from the basement to the dormitory in the yard are 8 in. high and 10 in. wide. The steps from the basement to the dormitory are 7½ in. high and 11 in. wide without the ledge.
    The steps of the stairway to the trunk attic and its height are to be made turning outward, in order not to knock oneself against the door lintel, from the old house into the new one, under which entrance is a step 8 in. high and 9 in. wide, on account of the space and to manage with the height of the addition.

42. Howland, "Moravian Buildings in Bethlehem," p. 276, n. 54.
43. Marquis de Chastellux, *Travels in North America in the Years 1780–81–82* (New York, 1827), pp. 350–51.

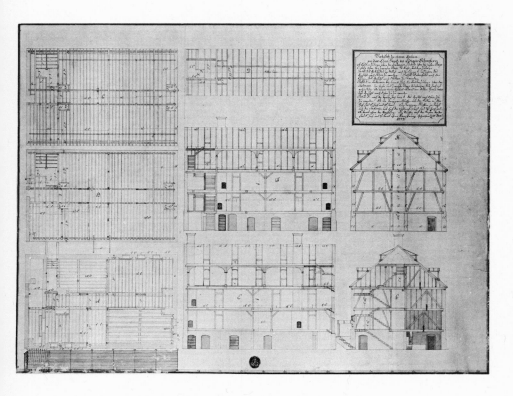

23. Framing Sections and Plans of the Eastern Addition to the Single Sisters' House, Bethlehem, dated 1772

construction of three floors plus a section without any notation whatsoever. The other is titled, in translation, "Legend for an Addition to the Choir House of the Single Sisters."[44]

The framing alternates, running north and south in the northeastern and southwestern sections of the building and east and west in the two opposite ends of the structure. The plans also clearly show the special head framing needed for the stair areas and around the chimneys.

The longitudinal and transverse sections are extremely enlightening, showing as they do in the basement level of all sections various door openings

44. Translation of the legend reads as follows:
A Framing addition above the basement. B The same above the first floor. C The same over the second floor. D Keystone beams added. Profile of building in middle according to the length, the view towards the north, Profile G, in the basement at line "a" notice the beam framing above the basement. The first and second floor also. The roof is to be viewed as if there were no gable wall at the old house, the view will be towards the east. Profile H according to width by line "b". The view turned towards the East. M The steps from the cellar into the yard are 8 in. high and 10 in. wide. The steps in the house in the basement to the dormitory are 7½ in. high and 12 in. wide without the projection. The steps to the trunk floor are 8 in. high and 9 in. wide without projection. Drawn Jan. 28th, 1772.

24. Undated Chimney Flue Section and Plans of the Eastern Addition to the Single Sisters' House, Bethlehem

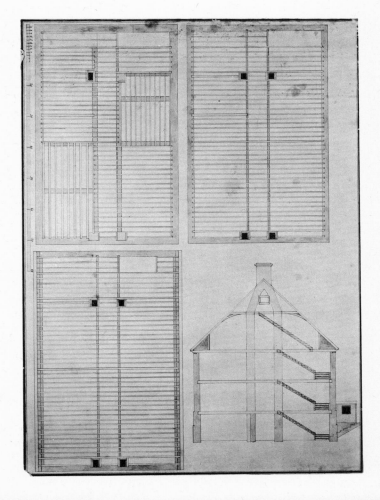

and built-in closets with shelves. One notes from the transverse sections that the walls were planned to be two feet four inches thick at the foundation level, reduced to two feet two inches in the upper basement, one foot ten inches on the first floor, and one foot eight inches on the second floor.

Also in the transverse sections, translated as profile "G," the master craftsman asks the observer to particularly notice the framing above the basement level. A number of upright studs can be noted which are braced by heavy diagonal members, presumably mortised and tenoned into a heavy central upright brace. Section "G" also shows quite clearly the means of vertical circulation originally intended, which has either disappeared, been replaced, or was never so built. The present stairs ascend from the north side of the building toward the south, while the original plan had the stairs approachable from the central hall and ascending toward the north, to a landing where they returned upon themselves in a southerly direction.

Despite the unusual quality of this structure, one feels that the simple gable roof, the larger scale, the gable-roofed dormers in the lower register of the roof, and the greater number and larger window openings in relation to the solid wall are all indications of a lessening of the earlier purity of the Germanic architectural design. This perhaps indicates the beginning of the transition that the community made from its pure continental Germanic background to an eventual absorption into the overwhelmingly English tradition of our American heritage. This trend was to culminate in Bethlehem with the erection of the Central Moravian Church, finished in 1806 in the American Federal style, and now completely non-Germanic in architectural character.

CROWN INN
(Erected, 1745; Demolished, 1858)

Notwithstanding the pace-setting first Brother's House, tradition dies slowly. The ease with which log structures could be erected was not forgotten when the necessity for a hostelry for visitors to the Bethlehem community was contemplated. Thus, the Crown Inn of 1745 south of the river ford reverted to this method of construction, undoubtedly because of its low cost and ease of construction. Before the erection of this structure, strangers had been lodged in various buildings in the community, until the number of travelers became so great that *Die Krone* had to be erected. For over a decade it stood as the single hostelry of the area until the necessity was felt for the construction of an inn within the town proper, at which time the more famous Sun Inn was erected in 1758. *Die Krone* stood for one hundred and thirteen years and was then razed, in the name of progress, to make way for a railroad, but vestiges of the structure, such as its key and other small artifacts, are preserved in the collections of the Moravian Historical Society at Nazareth, Pennsylvania.

The Crown Inn was built on what the Moravians termed "the Simpson tract." By February, 1743, the Moravians were negotiating with William Allen for the purchase of Simpson's two hundred and seventy-four acres. Finally, on June 3, 1746, the Moravians succeeded in acquiring it in the name of Jasper Payne, a winecooper of Bethlehem, for the sum of two hundred pounds, Pennsylvania money.[45] Meanwhile previous to this, on March 11, 1743, the Moravians had launched a ferry to link this tract on the south side of the Lehigh River with the five-hundred-acre tract on which Bethlehem was being built. Once this south side tract had been acquired, they began to cultivate it. This, then, was the beginning of the four Moravian farms that gradually developed on that side of the river, known at the time of their destruction to give way to development as the "Luckenbach Farm," the "Jacobi Farm," the "Fuehrer Farm," and the "Hoffert Farm."[46]

During these years expanding settlement northward made the Moravians increasingly aware that there should be some means of accommodating travelers. Arrangements in the large houses in Bethlehem precluded lodging of strangers in the village itself. It was thus eventually proposed to erect an inn on the south side of the river on the newly purchased Simpson tract. By spring of 1745 a site had

45. If one equates a single pound of this early Pennsylvania currency to $2.66, the purchase price was equivalent to approximately $533.33.

46. As early as January 25, 1743, a landing site for the ferry across the Lehigh had been selected, and in February, 1745, a Charles Schaus, a non-Moravian formerly of Falkner's Swamp, became the first ferryman. He ferried only for a year and then became a miller at the Bethlehem Mill. It is also known that in the spring of 1743 both he and his son had assisted Mr. Antes in erecting the grist mill for the community. Levering dates the beginning of construction in December, 1744, work resuming in March, 1745, with completion in October of that year.

been selected a little east of the terminus of the ferry, and work was soon commenced. The building was approximately forty by twenty-eight feet, constructed of white oak logs, and two stories high with a steep gable roof when finished in September, 1745. According to Reichel, there were four rooms on each floor and all were floored by one-and-a-half-inch white oak planks. The studding of the partition walls was of the same material. These members were grooved to receive cross pieces (or hand-split lath) and the interstices were completely filled with a mixture of cut straw and clay. The casings of all doors and windows were solid timber and, according to Reichel, had decorations of beading and fluting. There were also wooden latches and bolts. Apparently all nails used in the structure had been made by the local nailsmith at Bethlehem. Thus erected, the building stood for a hundred and thirteen years, until its demolition in 1858.

Perhaps the most reliable view of the structure is in Nicholas Garrison's "A View of Bethlehem, One of the Brethren's Principal Settlements, in Pennsylvania, North America," printed in London on November 24, 1757 (See Plate 4). The Crown Inn appears in the foreground of the print, and is indeed of log as Reichel describes it. The roof was a gable seemingly covered with red tiles from the local tile factory on Monocacy Creek. The evenly spaced fenestration on the long side of the structure consisted of four windows on the second floor and three on the first. Typical of Germanic structures in Pennsylvania, the chimney is near the center of the building, giving exterior evidence of the centrally located fireplaces.

A number of interesting subsidiary inn structures also appear in the print. To the left of the inn are three smaller buildings a story-and-a-half high with steep gable roofs, presumably tiled. These buildings appear to have been half timber constructions. To the right of the inn, another very small tile-roofed structure with chimney at the center can be noted. To the extreme right of the complex is a very interesting barn of vertical battens with a thatched roof which was erected in 1747 near the inn because it was inconvenient to ferry hay and fodder over the river to the farmyard in Bethlehem. The structure also housed the animals pastured on the south side of the Lehigh River. Immediately in front of the inn, from the viewer's side, a small structure can be seen with what also looks like a tiled roof. This could

have been a shed for stabling the horses of patrons. In the 1760's, it is known that one of the inn managers also erected an elaborate "apiary or beehouse."

It will be noted that the front of the inn faced south. This can possibly be attributed to routes of travel, for the hostelry had been built at a reasonably strategic spot to draw upon as many travelers as possible along the lines of travel north, south, east, and west.[47]

When first opened, the inn was called "The Tavern over ye Water" by the Bethlehem Moravians, "The Tavern near Bethlehem" by other people, or simply "The Bethlehem Tavern."[48] There were fifteen landlords during the lifetime of the inn, from its establishment in 1745 until October, 1794, when it no longer functioned as an inn.[49] Inventories and other sources of information provide a fairly complete picture of the contents of the inn, its growth, and its income. Thus, during Manager Hartmann's residency, we learn that the inn contained the following:

19th May 1746. Tavern over ye water Dr., for sundries, to wit: 2 cows 7 £., one churn 3s., one quart wine measure., one pint ditto, one half pint ditto, one gill ditto, one half gill ditto, all of pewter, and three gill and two dram glasses 1 £., two hogshead of cider 3 £., four casks ditto 2 £., 5s., one cask of metheglin 17s. 6p., a

47. The earliest known view of Bethlehem, dated 1750, can be found in the Bethlehem Moravian Archives. This is also taken from the south looking north, placing the Crown Inn and its attendant buildings in the foreground. Unlike the Garrison view, this shows but one building to the left of the Inn, the others presumably not having been built yet. What is more important, the inn building itself shows only two widely separated doors on the first floor with but two small windows on the second floor on a direct vertical line over the doors. The relative smallness of the windows and the lack of the two middle ones on the second and first floors, as shown in the Garrison view, thus creates a large blank wall area in relation to the small voids of the windows, giving a much more Germanic and medieval aspect to the structure. Moreover, in Reichel's view of the inn in its 1854 role as the Fuehrer House, which shows the north front, a similar arrangement of two windows on the second floor and a door and window on the first floor can be noted. William C. Reichel, *The Crown Inn, near Bethlehem, Pa., 1745* (Philadelphia, 1872), p. 117.

48. *Ibid.*, p. 31. It is first referred to as "Das Gasthaus Zur Krone" in records dated October 18, 1756.

49. After it ceased to be a public inn, it became a farmhouse, a function that it filled until its demolition. The landlords of the Inn, in the order of their succession, were as follows: Samuel Powell, Frederic Hartmann, Jobst Vollart, Hartman Verdriess, John Leighton, John Godfrey Grabs, John Nicholas Schaeffer, Ephreim Colver, Andreas Horne, John Lischer, Ephraim Culver, Augustus H. Franke, Valentine Fuehrer, John G. Stoll, and George Schindler.

small cupboard with an iron lock 8s., one walnut table 16s., a tin funnel, an iron strainer, a beef fork and a ladle 4s 6p., two iron candlesticks 1s 6p., six pewter plates 10s., twelve pewter spoons 5s 6p., and two soup dishes 12s.

During this same period, the chambers had green rugs, blankets, and "network window curtains." In the sitting room were two brass candlesticks. To the kitchen were added "six black handled knives and forks, one copper coffee pot, one grid iron for broils, one pewter tea pot, and the three brown cups and three saucers of china."

During the managership of Hartmann Verdriess, a "Neisser clock" with the legend "Ab hoc momento pendet aeternitas" was placed in the hall of the inn, and when Grabs was landlord, an hour glass was added to the furnishings. Shortly thereafter, during Lischer's residency (June, 1762), napkins were added to the table service. Under Ephraim Culver, an inventory of April 19, 1765, listed the following:

There is on hand at the Crown this day—

Kitchen furniture valued at 17 £ 17s 11p
Drinking vessels valued at 61 £ 18s 9p
Tea and coffee vessels valued at 6 £ 2s 10p
Earthern ware valued at 1 £ 11s 1p
Bedding valued at 32 £ 10s
Linen valued at 3 £ 2s 4p
Sundry utensils valued at 11 £ 13s 6p
Casks etc. valued at 5 £ 11s 6p
Tools at ye barn and stable 2 £ 4s 10p
Garden tools valued at 2 £ 11s 2p

Total 89 £ 15s 11p

Supplies at the Crown Inn in the 1760's included: Antigua rum, Barbados rum, New England rum; Lisbon and Madeira wine; coffee, sugar, limes; roll tobacco. In 1762, 233 gallons of liquor were in store. Christiansbrunn supplied the Crown with "small beer"; Christian Diemer, baker, supplied bread from the bakery in Bethlehem. Beef costing three pence per pound came from the Bethlehem butcher, Henry G. Krause.

The rates at the Crown Inn during the incumbency of Hartmann (1760) cast some light on the cost of the Inn's accomodations and the business that flourished there.

4p for breakfast of tea or coffee
6p for dinner
8p for dinner with a pint of beer
4p for supper cold
6p for supper hot
2p for a night's lodging
12p for a night's hay and oats for a horse

OIL MILL
(Erected, 1745; Rebuilt, 1763; Demolished, 1930's)

At approximately the same time that the Crown Inn was being erected, another wooden structure was being added to the industrial community along Monocacy Creek. This housed not only some of the processes for tanning leather but also that of crushing flax seed, a crop that the Moravians early recognized as an essential one to their Bethlehem economy. Like so many of the first log structures of this community, detailed knowledge of its appearance is almost non-existent and, as was the case with other buildings in the area, it was early replaced by a larger structure of native stone. Thus, with the grist mill and tannery, the oil mill helped to carry the architectural continuity of the village and visually increase the architectural importance of this section of the community.

The small wooden building that had been erected in 1745 as first housing for the tanning, tawing, and currying mills, on the east side of the mill race and south of the grist mill, also housed the oil mill where linseed oil was extracted from the native flax seed, while the fiber of the plant furnished linen thread and cloth to Bethlehem and its subsidiary communities.[50]

Although it is unknown whether this was a one or two-story building, it is recorded that the structure was forty-six feet by thirty-four feet wide and that it was valued at two hundred thirty pounds.[51] The ground plan and section that Erbe illustrates (Plates 25, 26) must be the plan and section of the second mill, if this first mill was the size already mentioned. Since this plan is more than twice as

50. Hellmuth Erbe, *Eine Kommunistische Herrnhuter Kolonie des 18. Jahrhunderts* (Stuttgart, 1929), p. 67. There is a discrepancy between the 1743 that Erbe gives for the building of this structure and two entries to be noted on page 3 of the Congregational Diary of Bethlehem, Moravian Archives, one for February 4, 1745, and another for February 12, 1745. The February 4 entry reads in translation: "Carpenters almost finished with main work on Oil Mill," while the February 12 entry reads in translation: "Oil Mill so far completed, members could make first linseed oil." Levering states that ". . . the mill was commenced in January, was finished in early February 1745." Therefore, it would seem that on the basis of the Congregational Diary and Levering, *Bethlehem*, that Erbe's dating is probably incorrect by two years.
51. Erbe, *Herrnhuter Kolonie*, p. 67, information from the Unity Directors Board, Volume X, p. 145.

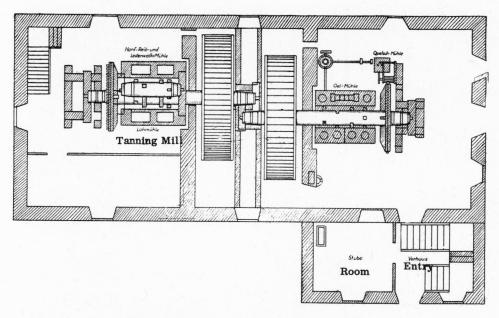

25. Undated First Floor Plan of the Bethlehem Oil Mill

long as it is wide, the proportions as given for the first mill do not hold true. However, it is known that a new tanning mill went up on the other side of the mill race in 1761 and that a second grist mill (Plate 27) farther up the race to the north had been erected earlier than that.

On the evening of November 18, 1763, this first timber structure oil mill in Bethlehem burned. The limestone building that went up on the site as a result of the destruction of the first wooden building was finished by October, 1765. Records state that it was referred to with some pride as "one of the most solid and durable structures in the country" (Plate 27).

The new building was sixty-six-and-one-half feet long by thirty feet wide. According to original plans in the Unitas Archives in Herrnhut, the building had two water wheels at the center. One propelled the tanning mill and leather fulling mill at the left of the first floor. At the same time a hemp mill was mechanically connected with the latter. On the second floor, space was left for installing further machinery. The other wheel set in motion the oil mill located on the right side of the first mill, as well as "the mill with a clapper," located on the second floor above it.

A wing (twenty-five and three-quarters by eleven and one-half) was added at some unknown date at the southeastern corner of the building, later serving the function of a tanbark grinding mill. Architecturally, this building followed the models of the "choir" houses up on the hill and was constructed of native Pennsylvania limestone with an even arrangement of windows on the north and south sides, three to a side, with the two original entrances on the east side. Windows were shuttered with solid shutters and over each was the characteristic red brick flat arch

26. Undated Section of the Bethlehem Oil Mill, from the North

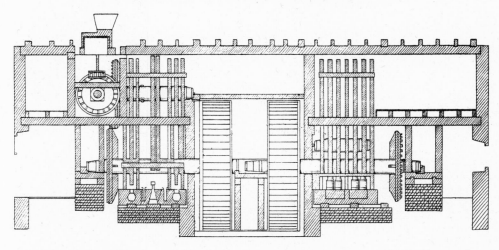

27. Undated Nineteenth-Century Photograph of the Bethlehem Oil Mill, from the North, Water Works to the Left

one finds on eighteenth-century Moravian structures. A single shed dormer gave light and ventilation to the attic area and the roof terminated at the eave line with a graceful kick, another characteristic Germanic architectural trait found on eighteenth-century Moravian buildings.

The oil industry continued with vigor through the post-revolutionary period in Bethlehem. The products, especially of the oil mill but also those of the oat and barley hulling mills, were used to procure provisions from Philadelphia at a cheaper rate than they could be furnished through the local Bethlehem store when a financial pinch resulting from heavy taxes and the postwar inflation forced the warden of the Brothers' House to embark on such a barter system. With the dissolution of the economy and the eventual opening up of Bethlehem to non-Moravians in the middle of the nineteenth century, the building passed into private hands. Later, it was used by the city to house the enlarged water supply system which the growing community demanded. Finally, in the 1930's, this eighteenth-century structure, then empty and neglected, was demolished as part of a WPA beautification project along Monocacy Creek.

Within months after the erection of the first wooden oil mill and a matter of almost a decade-and-a-half before that structure was burned and replaced by its stone successor, the growing needs of the community gave rise to the creation of the third building in the complex of structures now known as Bell House Square. Architecturally very similar to the first Brothers' House, it was also compatible with it in scale, its major distinctions being the cupola holding its bell and the long since demolished central balcony that originally graced the second floor of its façade.

The placing of the structure is of prime importance, as the building that defined the northern side of the complex later to develop into an urban square of more than little grace.

With additions east and west made several years after the erection of the central section, the square was further defined and almost visually completed if one were to view the structures head on. It remained, however, for the connecting links of the Old Chapel of 1751 and the eastern addition to the first Single Brothers' House of 1752 to enclose the space in actuality. The Widows' House visually closed the south side of the square in 1768, a composition that the widening of Sisters' Lane, now Church Street, and the routing of twentieth-century traffic has tended to destroy.

BELL HOUSE AND ITS EXTENSIONS[52]
(*Erected, 1746; Enlarged, 1748, 1749; Extant*)

According to Levering, Count Zinzendorf was "planning the location of the different classes of building" before the eastern addition to the *Gemeinhaus* had been begun.[53] Although he makes no mention of the Count's total plan, it is quite possible that Bell House Square reflects the Count's thinking in planning the community since such integral building relationships are characteristic of Moravian settlements in Europe. One need only look at the plans of the settlements of Nisky, Herrnhut, and Klein Welke (see Plate 1) to realize the careful deliberation that went into the placing and relationship of buildings in these Moravian communities. Such was true in Nazareth, in Lititz, as well as in Bethlehem. Bell House Square is obviously the result of a careful plan of development despite the fact that it was created over a period of a quarter of a century.

On October 24, 1745, the site was staked off for the third building of this group, which was to be erected, again in this instance, to provide for the growing needs of the community.[54] The site was selected at a point about seventy-two feet north of the *Gemeinhaus* and the first Brothers' House and midway between these two structures. This portion of the present building, i.e., the center, was not ready for occupancy until October, 1746. It thus became the focal point at the farther end of the square and assumed a relationship to the *Gemeinhaus* and the first Brothers' House commensurate with the relationship of the main structure to the advance wings of a Palladian plan.

Like the first Brothers' House, this new building was of native limestone, twenty-seven feet deep and thirty-five feet along the front. It had the same characteristic brick arches over the windows, the

52. Because of the bells that hung in its cupola, which were cast by Samuel Powell, this structure seems to have had this name from the very beginning of its existence.

53. Levering, *Bethlehem*, p. 144, in reference to the selection of the site of the first Brother's House.

54. It was intended that the structure contain a refectory for the single men and living quarters for married couples. This aimed to alleviate two conditions: congested quarters in the *Gemeinhaus* and the freeing of certain minor log structures, then serving as quarters for married couples, for other uses. *Ibid.*, p. 191.

same exposed native stone, and a similar gambrel roof, with the notable exception that the dormers were all shed-roofed rather than having gable roofs as those on the lower section of the first Brothers' House.

The large fireplace in the basement gives rise to the theory that here was the kitchen that supplied the two dining halls on the first floor.[55] Like the first Brothers' House, the Bell House had a center-hall plan. There was a fireplace in each of the flanking rooms, placed unlike those on the inside walls of the Brothers' House which were on what were originally the outside walls.[56] The rhythm of fenestration and door openings, however, is the same even pattern as that of the first Brothers' House façade.

The belfry was finished by June 9, 1746.[57] It shows quite clearly on a drawing of 1750.[58] On February 15, 1747, a brass clock by Augustine Neisser of Germantown was installed in the base of the belfry where it served for years as the town clock.[59] Architecturally speaking, the belfry is at great odds with the Germanic feeling of the rest of the structure

and of the other buildings of the Bell House complex. Howland accepts the English Chippendale character of the belfry in his writings, observing that the master builders may have seen such things during their stay in England. He also notes that the cupola is almost identical in design to one in the clock gate at Hampton Palace in England. To back up this theory, he makes further note of a book in the Moravian Archives, printed in Amsterdam in 1735, in which a cupola of this type is illustrated.[60]

It is quite possible that the un-Germanic architectural character of the cupola could have had its inspiration in the source Howland indicates, but the fallacy of the entire theory lies in the railing that uses a Chinese Chippendale motif and is identical to the railing around the tower of the Central Moravian Church. The latter was not erected until 1806, at a period when the pure Germanic architectural character of new Bethlehem buildings was long past its peak. Stylistically, the Central Moravian Church is in the Anglo-American tradition and specifically in the Federal style. There is a strong possibility, therefore, that at least the turret railing of the Bell House cupola could date from the early nineteenth-century period of the church. The aforementioned drawing of 1750, incidentally, shows no railing around the cupola. This high point became the traditional location for festal trombone players before the Central Church was constructed—hence possible justification for a later railing, perhaps after the balcony on the south façade was removed. The cupola itself is hexagonal in form, with six arches of an unadorned character except for a small molding at the point of springing. The bell-shaped dome has an extremely graceful reverse curve. Surmounting the whole is the weather vane designed by Moravian Bishop Cammerhoff. This illustrates the emblem of the Moravian church—a pascal lamb with a banner, which in turn is pierced with the German word *Heyl*, meaning "salvation." This is etymologically rooted in "to heal," "to be hale," and "to be whole."

Two extensions of the structure, each twenty-one feet long, were later added, one to the east in 1748 and another to the west in 1749 (Plate 28). The eastern extension brought the new wall in line with the west side of the first Brothers' House. The western extension, however, was about ten inches short of alignment with the east side of the *Gemeinhaus*

55. This theory of room use, which is Howlands' ("Moravian Buildings in Bethlehem"), is most likely correct since all kitchens in other eighteenth-century buildings in Bethlehem are in the basement. Moreover, the choir system would not admit to married couples and single men eating together, hence one room as men's dining chamber on the first floor and the other for the use of the married couples.

56. Such placing of chimneys is very un-Germanic in character. A touchstone of any structure erected by a German-speaking colonist in the Pennsylvania area, Moravian or not, is the interior fireplace that places the chimney in the center of the roof on the exterior. Thus, what would have been originally fireplaces on exterior walls leads one to several conclusions concerning the structure: first, the gambrel roof was probably never hipped before the east and west extensions were built. Second, remembering Levering's statement that Zinzendorf was "planning the different locations of buildings" even when the earlier structure the first Brother's House was being erected, the building was probably meant to have additions from the beginning. Third, the fireplaces could hardly have been placed on the interior walls since this would have made the chimneys appear on the roof immediately adjacent to either side of the cupola base. Fourth, such exterior placing of chimneys could possibly illustrate architectural inspiration from a non-Germanic source, a fact which the style of the cupola certainly bears out. Fifth, such exterior chimneys would have been considered ultimately interior chimneys if one accepts this pre-planned community theory that extensions were to be made on either side of the structure before they were erected.

57. See *Bethlehemisches Diarium*, Moravian Archives, Bethlehem, for this date.

58. This drawing, in the Bethlehem Moravian Archives, is clearly dated 1750.

59. Levering, *Bethlehem*, p. 191. This clock still exists and still strikes the hour from the tower of the Central Moravian Church in Bethlehem.

60. This is titled *Beschryving der Nieuwlyks Uitgevonden en Geostrojeertes Slang-Brand-Spuiten en Haarewyze van Brand-Brussen.*

28. Twentieth-Century Photograph of the Bell House, Bethlehem, with Additions, Old Chapel to the Left, 1752 Extension of the Single Sisters' House to the Right

and consequently the later addition of the so-called Old Chapel extends the differential of ten inches into the Bell House court.[61]

The dividing line between the two additions and the central portion of the present structure is evident in the masonry on both the front and rear of the building, but the extensions were architecturally conceived, nonetheless, to continue the symmetry of the façade of the first section of the Bell House. Each extension originally had a door and window on the first floor and two windows placed directly above them on the second floor, dormers being aligned only on the first level of the roof. The seemingly casual arrangement of shed dormers on the second roof

level, or the upper attic, breaks the general symmetry of the façade, but this may be the result of the subsequent disappearance of one of the dormers. As one faces the south façade today, there are two dormers to the left of center and one to the right.

The door of the eastern extension is now a window and must have been converted at an early date. It appears as a door in the drawing of 1750 but not in any later drawings or engravings. Simple observation of the masonry well indicates the change that has taken place in the building at this point. Moreover, this window is four lights wide instead of the usual three-light width of the other windows in the building.

The present central doorway on the south façade is post-1875 to judge from a photograph that Howland published from a negative in the Moravian

61. Such well-thought-out extensions seem to indicate clearly that the entire complex was planned to develop as it did from the start.

[53]

Archives. This photograph shows a door lower than the present one, the head of which is on line with the head of the window flanking it. This is not true today. It also shows a fragment of an arch above, which is no longer extant.

The enlarged doorway is not the only change that has taken place on the south façade of the original center portion of the Bell House. Although this court façade was originally symmetrically designed, horizontally and vertically, slight variations in this symmetry can now be noted. The most obvious change is the left shed dormer on the lower roof which is vertically out of line with the windows on the façade below it. As the building was originally conceived, the windows were placed slightly closer to the doorway than to the exterior wall. This emphasis on the center was reinforced by a balcony that extended above the doorway to the outer sides of the flanking windows. Ample proof for the former existence of this balcony can be established from the drawing of 1750 and from examination of the physical evidence of the building itself. A careful inspection of this wall, above the present doorway, shows a regular series of upright stones two to six inches apart which are presumably masonry fillers where timbers once projected to support the balcony.[62] Moreover, the central window on the second floor now has a plaster panel below it instead of the usual stonework, indicating that this window was obviously once a door opening onto a balcony.

The balcony evidently was removed in 1766, just twenty years after its construction.[63] The 1757 view of Bethlehem, which appears dependable judging by the correct proportion and general silhouette of the structures, does not show a balcony on the Bell House at that time, so it may have been removed as early as this date if we do not wish to ascribe its absence in this view to inadequacy on the part of the delineator. There are many later views of the city, but none show the balcony save for the view by Levin T. Reichel who worked during the 1850's and shows the balcony very clearly in his view of Bethlehem in 1755.

Thus, in the year 1749, three buildings stood in the area, the *Gemeinhaus* to the west, the first Brothers' House to the east, and the Bell House with its east and west extensions midway between them and to the north. These three buildings were not to be joined for two or three more years. Before this was undertaken, a new house for the single Brothers was erected further west and on the south side of Church Street.

SECOND SINGLE BROTHERS' HOUSE
(*Erected, 1748; Extant*)

Of the main structures thus far considered, the first house and *Gemeinhaus*, the first tannery and grist mill, first Single Brothers' House, Crown Inn, first oil mill, and the Bell House, without its additions, were all standing when construction of the second Single Brothers' House was begun. The eastern addition to the Bell House was under construction at the same time, the western addition to follow a year later. Of these buildings, only two—the first Single Brothers' House and the Bell House—were of stone. Other than these structures, Bethlehem was essentially a wooden log community with some half-timber construction.

It should also be noted that the second Single Brothers' House was the most ambitious structure begun up to that date by Bethlehem Moravians. Situated on a hill, it was six stories high, including the basement (which was at grade level on the lower side of the hill) with upper and lower attics. It served not only as residence for the single men and older boys of the community but also as a center for the various crafts under the jurisdiction of their "choir." Moreover, it more than once served as a hospital during the Revolutionary War, thus earning the structure the distinction of perhaps the most historic building in the community, with the possible exception of the Sun Inn. The fact that Moravian records contain so much detail of the progress of its construction is ample evidence of the importance attached to it in the mind of the eighteenth-century Bethlehemite.

Plans for the erection of this new building were contemplated as early as October 18, 1747, at which time the *Chor-Diarium der Ledigen Brüder* records that the two Spangenbergs were at love feast and discussed the fact that the first house of the single brethren was becoming so inadequate that it would soon be necessary to build a larger one. Moreover, there were some pounds, shillings, and pence avail-

62. Levering says it was the custom for musicians to play from this balcony during harvest festivals, in the morning and the evening on holy days, and for other gatherings in the court. See Levering, *Bethlehem*, p. 192.

63. Both Levering and Howland quote this date without giving the source. As with almost all of Levering's material, it is presumably from the *Bethlehemisches Diarium*, although a search of the appropriate volume of this diary has yielded no reference to this.

able since Mother Spangenberg, as she was referred to, had signified her willingness to give a hundred pounds toward the project.[64] The plan for a new building foresaw an early need for considerable space in the light of the expected influx of more single men from Europe and the growing multiplicity of crafts and trades in which this "choir" was engaged. When the structure was finally erected, the single men turned over their first "choir" house, which had been constructed in 1744, to the single sisters. Mother Spangenberg's gift was the first of many which were to follow.[65] Although most gifts were monetary, some were in goods and services.[66]

By October 27, the single brothers' diary records the following (translation): "In Workers' Conference, the new house was discussed, that the new foundation would soon be dug. It was decided where it is to stand. This is namely a new row or alley, begun towards the Lehigh, where it is to be the corner house not far from the Monocacy, which will be fine and convenient for the entire Choir."[67]

By the third week in November we learn that bricks are being made,[68] and on December 8, the floor plans and elevations were shown for the first time (translation): "In Helpers' Conference, at noon, the floor plan and elevation of our new house was shown and described to members. The larger boys' house is separate, but all under one roof. There is a door, from the workers' (single men) house into the boys' house. It was decided to keep a special book for recording all extraordinary things that might occur."[69] A week later, ground was broken and the felling of trees on the site was started.[70] The entry in the *Chor-Diarium* for January 9, 1748, has the following interesting account (translation):

Today the site for our new Single Brethren's House was pegged [staked out]. It will be 83 feet long and 30 feet wide. The single Brethren gathered in chapel after supper, and then marched in pairs with lovely music to the new single Brethren's site, formed a circle around it, and Br. Nathaniel began to sing: "Now Lamb I do beseech you, come enter into our midst, and bless people and house, etc. . ." Then he prayed earnestly to the Lamb for his new care and grace, that it also would in this building work, which was to be erected entirely alone for Him, and in which many a disciple's heart should be prepared for Him to remain with us from the start to finish and be present in all our labor, and after another hymn had been sung, all the Brethren immediately began to dig the ground and take it away, and in future on every moonlit evening is to be continued. It was quite a charming sight, so many Brethren working with spades, grubbers, and all kinds of other tools, as if all of them wanted to dig the earth out of the cellar at once.

The continuation of this cellar excavation is mentioned at least twice more in the "choir" diary. By March 18, we learn that the brethren were also busy cutting boards for the structure since the diary notes at this juncture (translation): "Br. Frey who on account of cutting boards for our new house had gotten behind in his language study, was given Philip Transou to go along as his assistant to the Sawmill."[71]

Visitors began to arrive for the cornerstone laying on April 6, and the following day this service took place.[72] Not long after, two unnamed masons arrived from Lancaster to help with the new building. Construction proceeded rapidly, so quickly that by August 1 the framework of the roof was com-

64. See *Chor-Diarium der Ledigen Brüder* for October 18, 1747, Bethlehem Moravian Archives.

65. *Ibid.*, entries for January 8, 12, 22, and March 13, 1748.

66. One of the Brethren, Johann Bonn, even offered to buy shingles for the new house. *Ibid.*, October 24, 1747. According to Levering, *Bethlehem*, p. 198, these came from Frederick Township.

67. This "row or alley" today is that portion of Main Street west of Church Street.

68. "Ludwig Huber starts ditch for making bricks for our new House, also preparations for further work," *Chor-Diarium*, November 19, 1747.

69. *Ibid.*, December 8, 1747. The author has never located any "special book for recording all extraordinary things that might occur."

70. "Our Single Br. Weise began breaking ground for new house; also tree felling started." *Ibid.*, December 15, 1747.

71. The logs were cut in Gnadenhuetten, a Moravian settlement up the Lehigh River where a sawmill was located, and were floated down river to Bethlehem. *Ibid.*, March 26, 1748. It is probably safe to assume that most logs were cut there into boards while others were cut at the Bethlehem sawmill. The diary records many entries of boards or logs arriving in Bethlehem. At one point (July 1, 1748), it mentions six thousand feet of board, at another (September 17, 1748), four hundred pieces, and as late as November 10 of the same year, three hundred pieces.

72. A translation of the description in the *Chor-Diarium* of this service on April 7, 1748, follows:
Today the cornerstone for our New Single Brethren's House was laid. All the single Brethren and large boys were individually interviewed by the Workers, and the purpose of the cornerstone laying discussed with them, because each one had to state whether he wished to have his name included in it, and it was considered a favor to all of them to be included and so therefore all preparations were made for it. And after dinner, instead of our quarters hour, the entire Single Brethren's and large boys' Choir met in our chapel, where first there was a talk on the reason and purpose of the entire project. Then we all walked in pairs with music to the site, and surrounded the same. The small Brethren from the boarding school we had in our middle, many of the married and other members around us on the outside. Br. Cammerhoff first made an address on today's Lamb's text.

pleted.[73] In celebration, a love feast—the first in the new building—was held in the structure the following day.[74]

By October, the single men were already using the dormitory of the building for services, although the actual move into the new structure did not take place until November 7.[75] Finally, on November 16, the consecration of the new house took place.[76] Less than a week later it is recorded that this social unit of the Bethlehem community became further self-sufficient when (translation): "Our kitchen was separated from the Congregation kitchen and finished separately because the number of members in Bethlehem is too large for one kitchen."

This second Brothers' House was the largest that the residents of the community had yet erected. Standing alone, as it did in the years immediately after its erection on the south side of what is now Church Street, the structure was invariably the first building to impress visitors. In the early prints of

eighteenth-century Bethlehem, it is always the most prominent structure. The earliest known print of Bethlehem (Plate 29), dated 1754, exaggerates the building to such proportions that it is only logical to conclude that the artist was more impressed by the size of the structure than any other building in the community.

Levering indicates that it was the fourth set of plans for the building which was finally adopted[77] (Plate 30). This is an India ink wash drawing on parchment titled "Single Brethrens' House in Bethlehem," with a scale at the top of the sheet. The first, second, and third floors are shown side by side across the drawing, but no elevations or roof plans are included. The first floor clearly shows the double entrance with a heavy wall-bearing partition separating the left side of the building, with one entrance door, from the right side and the other door. On the interior, however, the building was connected by a door in this separating partition. Two flights of steps

He indeed had to become like His Brethren, so that His External Godly power might save us through this flesh and very beautifully showed how the Savior truly had assumed our flesh and blood, and with it had endured everything that occurs in a human being, and from the time He was a boy and a young man to the time of the Cross, so that He knows very well how our boys and single Brethren feel, and they can be particularly grateful to Him, that He gathers such people for Himself in these days, in whom He can see His image; for that this house is being built, in order that the Elder of Disciples might encourage such emulators, whose mind is like His and whose bodies are His; for this we want to lay the first cornerstone, in the name of the Lamb and in the name of His Father and Holy Ghost as our Mother. Thereupon several hymns were sung, and so the cornerstone was laid in the first corner, under the Boys' House by the Brn. Joseph Spangenberg, Cammerhoff, Nathaniel Seidel, Gottlieb Bezold, Westmann and Heinr. Antes. Afterwards Br. Nathaniel stepped on the cornerstone and prayed to Father, Mother, and Man, for a blessing to this entire building, because They knew the purpose and intention, i.e., that it is to be a House Lodging, in which many people shall be raised for the Lamb, whom He could use, and where also many a poor heart might have a place, where it could stay and be brought to safety. Then we went into our chapel where a love feast had been set up, which we held during which time so many important and blessed conversations occurred, it was, above all, a day of blessing for our entire Choir. . . .
73. Translation from *ibid.*, August 1, 1748:
Today one Brethren completed the framework of our New House and everything went off happily without any damage. We immediately sang some stanzas of gratitude and praise for the Lamb. In the evening our musicians played for the first time in the New House.
74. Translation from *ibid.*, August 2, 1748.
This noon we had the first general love feast in our newly built House, and because there was nobody in

Bethlehem who had not had some share in its building (and the Harvest Festival also was included) so all of the congregation who were at all able came to it. The love feast was held under the hiproof, where all the members sat in circles. The little boarding school children sat in the center, everything made a charming appearance, and twice as many members would have had plenty of room to sit at the love feast because the space is as big as the entire house is long and broad. . . .
75. Translation from *ibid*, October 25 and November 7, 1748:
. . . All the Congregational Services and Synodic sessions were held in the now arranged disciples dormitory, under the hiproof in our new Single Brethren's House.
Today we started moving out of our old Single Brethren's House and first arranged for sleeping in the New House.
76. Translation from *ibid.*, November 16, 1748:
In the evening was the actual consecration of this our New House with a very charming love feast. The chapel was decorated with many lights and the Choir sat 110 strong around in the chapel. First from his heart, Br. Johannes sang some stanzas for us, and then there was a discussion on various matters, concerning the erection of this House as well as the entire cause of the Single Brethren in this country. . . . After all the services our dear Johannes also consecrated the dormitories. First he held an earnest quarter hour before we went to blessed rest in the wounded side. Then the Brethren as well as the larger boys each went to their dormitory where he again sang some charming stanzas for us and wished for the Brethren, each of whom stood by his bed, "Now lie deep into the (wounded) side."
77. Levering, *Bethlehem*, p. 198. He gives December 19, 1747, as the date of adoption of these plans but as usual does not quote his source or the source of the fact that four plans were considered. To the author's knowledge, such information does not appear in the Single Brother's Choir Diary. None of the earlier plans have survived in the Bethlehem Moravian Archives.

29. View of Bethlehem, 1754

show on the plan without indicating whether they are for access to the basement, the upper floors, or both. A regular pattern of windows is shown, and various masonry blocks would indicate interior chimneys (to which tile stoves would have been attached) and/or perhaps open fireplaces, although the latter is not probable.

The circulation area forms a "T" shape on the first floor. The left side of the building contained four rooms of equal size, two to either side of the longitudinal hall that ran the length of the building. On the right side, four rooms were arranged in a manner similar to those on the left, with the addition of an extra room the width of the entrance hall area. An area of similar size on the left side of the structure was presumably not a room, but might have been intended as a long closet.

The entrance on the right side shows two stairs, including one straight run that turns. The straight run presumably gave access to the basement, while the other stair, as shown on the second floor, appears to have led to that level. Upstairs, no division separated the east and west portions of the building, but a dividing hall ran lengthwise through the structure on this and the third floors. The most notable room on the second floor was the long chapel in the center of the south side of the building. This was flanked by two smaller rooms of equal size. The north side was equally divided into four rooms—two to a side—flanking the circulation areas of the stairs. On the third floor, the long *Bettsaal* or dormitory occupied the entire south side of the building. To the north and on the west side were three separate rooms, and to the east, two smaller rooms. Between these two, and dividing them, was an access stair that presumably gave entrance to the attic and ultimately to the roof belvedere from which the trombone choir sometimes played. Because of the large size of the new building, the stone quarry was undoubtedly very busy in 1748.[78] The site of the new building slopes west and south at this point permitting vaulted storage rooms below ground level at the east end, and the kitchens at the west end of the structure appear above grade.

Although the building rose three full stories in height, instead of the two stories of the previous structure, it retained the characteristic double attic under the gambrel roof. The roof top belvedere was surrounded by a protecting balustrade with a chimney at each of the four corners. There were also the characteristic upper and lower dormers in both levels of the gambrel roof. It is not exactly clear whether these were all shed-roofed dormers or not. Some of the early prints show shed dormers only on the lower roof slope on the front of the building. On the rear or south side of the structure, however, the present gable-roofed dormers appear to be original.

Architecturally, the façade of this stone building continued the character set by the Bell House and the first Single Brothers' House in the use of local fieldstone, with flat brick arches over each of the windows and a concave cornice at the eave line of the roof. On the short ends of the building, the upper part of the gambrel roof was hipped on the ends of the building. The fenestration along the front and back façades was evenly spaced, and the two central doorways on the north side were repeated on the south façade. These were flanked by four windows to a side on both façades. The placing of the doors and windows on the first floor regimented the rhythm of fenestration on the second and third floors of the structure, creating an even rhythm from the ends of the building toward the center, with a slight enlargement of the spacing between the next-to-the-innermost windows and those over the central doorways. This refinement, i.e., the wider central spacing on the upper floors over the two central doors, creates a certain architectural pause that brings attention to the center of the structure. This is further accentuated by the fact that the two central windows are four panes wide instead of the usual three panes used elsewhere on the building. This apparently was originally so on both the front and rear of the building, although, in reality, there was no front or back and both façades appear to be equally important. The building stood alone, and both north and south sides were as nearly identical as possible. Attention upon the center of the building was further emphasized by the insertion of two plaques into the walls of the building, one on the south and the other on the north.

According to the *Chor-Diarium*, these stones came from the same quarry across the river which had been the source of the other building stone for the

---

78. The stone most likely came from the quarry across the Lehigh River. According to the *Chor-Diarium*, May 27, 1748: (translation)
  Br. Gottlieb with Lorch and Scheburch went across the Ferry to fetch some stones for our New House.

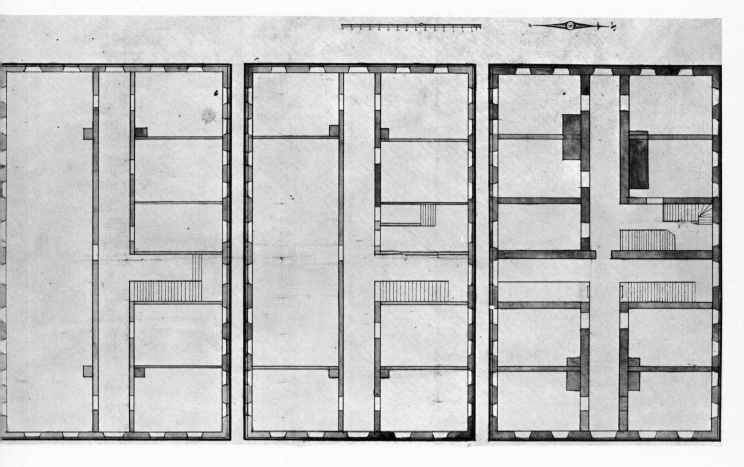

30. Undated Plans of the Second Single Brothers' House, Bethlehem

structure.[79] These were put into place on June 24, 1748, according to the diary, which reads in translation as follows: ". . . Today also two beautiful big stones, a kind of marble, were mortared into our house, in the one which stands above the door on the north side the following verse has been chiseled: 'May the young men's activity rebound to the praise of the Trinity.' VATER, MUTTER, LIEBER MANN-HABT EHR VOM JUENGLINGS PLAN. And on the other one which stands above the south side, a sun dial above which these words have been chiseled 'Praise to the (wounded) side.' Gloria Pleura and above it a star and quite at the bottom the year numerals."[80]

Earliest prints of the building are not sufficiently detailed to show the use of shutters. Indications of these do appear, however, on the more detailed early nineteenth-century views of the structure. One would conjecture that from the time of its erection the building had shutters on at least the first floor for the usual reasons of security and heat conservation.

Although the house was the largest then erected in the community, the growing number of brethren and the increasing activities in trades and crafts soon necessitated an enlargement of their still new building. Thus, by 1762, an annex was built to the east. This appears on a 1766 map in the Unitas Archive at Herrnhut. This annex was presumably demolished in 1854 to make way for the building known as Main Hall of Moravian College. All information indicates that this 1762 addition was a low wooden building of little architectural consequence.

Six years after the 1762 date, a second annex was added but no information fixes its exact location. This is presumably the wing to the west of the 1748 structure which appears in a drawing made around 1836 by Samuel Reinke and in the Grunewald lithograph of c. 1830. This annex was, in turn, demolished to make way for the present West Hall of Moravian College when the latter building was erected in 1857 or 1859. The belief that this addition was placed to the west of the 1748 building is corroborated by the existence of two ink line drawings now in the Bethlehem Moravian Archives (Plates 31, 32). Plate 31 shows the south elevation of the original building

with the proposed addition, architecturally identical to the 1748 structure, to the left of the elevation, which would place it to the west of the original structure in terms of the present college plan. No basement windows are shown to the right of the 1748 section indicating further that this elevation is the south side, since the ground slopes downward to the south and west in this entire area. Moreover, the existing vaulted rooms at the east end of the first or basement level are shown on plan. The use of the term *jetziger*, "present" or "at present," (Plate 32) in several places affirms that these plans show contemplated changes to an existing building. Moreover, they form an invaluable source of information for the identification and use of certain rooms in the building at that date. Thus, in the basement (Plate 31) one finds that the bakery was located in the northwest room and occupied six hundred square feet. Across the hall, in the southwest corner of the structure, was the kitchen.[81]

On the floor above, starting in the northwest corner and reading east, the first room is simply identified as one of the brothers' rooms. Next to it was the musicians' room, next to the stair area. Another brothers' room follows and in the room at the northeast corner was located the saddler. The cobbler was situated across the hall, on the south side next to a room for European brethren and by the cross-hall that led to the south entrance. On the west side of the cross-hall was the doctor's room, then the glazier, and in the southwest corner was the glovemaker's room.

On the third floor the northwest room was given to a Br. Hoeger. Br. Weber was in the next room, and Thom. Bartow was assigned a small room which was partially taken up by the stairs. No use is given to the first room east of the stairs, but the room in the northeast corner served as the pastor's or sacristan's room, while across the hall, in the southeast corner, was situated the superintendent, followed by a long room of a thousand square feet which was used as a hall for dining and services. Flanking it was a room in the southwest corner of the structure assigned to Arbo.[82] Presumably there was no con-

79. Translation from *ibid.*, May 27, 1748:
. . . went across the Ferry to fetch some stones for our New House, into which one can make some writing, came home again in evening and brought nice stones along for that.
80. *Ibid.*, June 24, 1748. The translations of the inscriptions used here are those from Hamilton, *Church Street*, pp. 18–21.

81. These locations are affirmed further by the physical evidence of the structure, as revealed by archeological investigation.
82. This is presumably John Arbo, who was a leader of the community and whose name is inscribed in several of the architectural and engineering books now in the Bethlehem Moravian Archives.

templated change to the floor above this, for a plan of it is not included.

Plate 32 not only shows the changes in room use, but also indicates for the first and second floors, at least, the use to which the rooms in the new annex were to be put. Aside from the bakery on the first floor of the 1748 building, the new wing was to include a bread room, a living room for the baker, and, in the northwest corner of the wing, the future bakery. Across the hall from it was to be the room of the kitchen brethren or cooks, the stove room, a small kitchen, and a second kitchen room next to the *jetziger Küche* or present kitchen. South of the room of the kitchen brethren was to be the future new kitchen, and south of that the dining hall.

The floor above the new wing was to contain the warden's room, the warden's bedroom, and a room for one of the brothers. Across the cross-hall was the pastor's or sacristan's room, which would be moved from its spot in the northwest corner of the third floor. Next to it, in the 1748 structure, the brothers' room of the existing plan was to become another pastor's or sacristan's room, while the musicians' room was to be put to use as another brothers' room. There is no indication of what was to become of the musicians. All the other rooms in the 1748 section on this floor continued the same use as shown on the other sheet. Other rooms added in the wing included a superintendent's room, flanked by two small bedrooms, and a chamber for the glovemaking shop, next to the glovemaker's room in the 1748 building. The southern part of the wing contained two more rooms, i.e., a classroom and at its extremity a new chapel room.

The use of the third floor was to be essentially the same as shown on the companion sheet.

The fourth floor shows three of the five rooms on the north side of the structure to be used as boys' rooms, while one of the others was assigned to David Zeisberger, and the other was for the use of the tailor. The entire south side of this floor was to be used as a dormitory. There is no evidence that this contemplated wing was ever brought to fruition. The building that the Grunewald lithograph shows is a low, two-story structure, with a gable roof. Other than these two wings, the Single Brothers' House remained in a relatively untouched condition until 1814, when it ceased to be their home and was taken over by the young ladies' boarding school. At this time, in order to adapt it for its new purpose, the

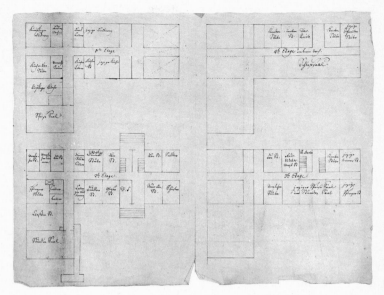

31. Undated Ink Line-Drawing of Proposed Wing of the Second Single Brothers' House, Bethlehem

32. Undated Ink Line-Drawing of the Second Single Brothers' House, Bethlehem, Showing Proposed Addition and Room Uses

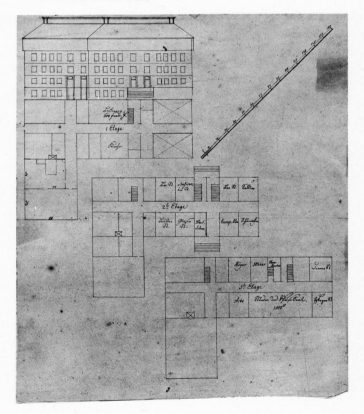

interior and exterior were completely changed and refurbished. It is presumably at this time that the windows were enlarged from about four feet in height to approximately five feet. Although the first- and second-floor windows on the south side were probably also enlarged at this time, the third floor openings were left unchanged. This would possibly indicate that the recently removed double-level porch on the south side of the building was erected at this date also. Moreover, the roof and dormers on this side were likewise left undisturbed. With the enlargement of the windows, the red brick arches were torn away and the defaced stonework was concealed by a smooth coat of stucco, more in keeping with the urbanity of taste of the early nineteenth century. This was then marked off in an ashlar design. The stucco on the south façade was removed some years ago, but the pargetted surface remains on the north façade. The windows on this façade may have been further enlarged, presumably during the summer of 1859 when West Hall was being built west of the 1748 building, since the uniform lintels one now finds on the structure are nineteenth-century in origin and are undoubtedly an attempt to make them of equal size with the newer building.

The building today still contains a number of very interesting vestiges of its eighteenth-century origin. The large vaulted basement storage rooms to the east are still intact as are the windows and window frames in that area. The large strap hinges on the doors to these rooms and a large portion of hardware in other sections of the building are also preserved. In the ground floor kitchen area one can still see the massive form of the fireplace and the ovens. Indications of other fireplaces are also in evidence upon close scrutiny of the walls. The two levels under the roof have escaped most of the heavy remodeling that the main floors received in 1814 and later. Consequently one can see much of the original timber work in the attic, beautifully mortised and tenoned, and the small original stair leading to the belvedere.

The close of 1748 saw the addition of two new stone structures to Bethlehem's skyline—the second Single Brothers' House and the eastern addition to the Bell House. In 1749 the western addition was completed to the same structure. It is also known that the summer months of that year witnessed the erection of a stone residence—probably one of the earliest, if not the earliest, single-family residence in the village.

This went up on *Ladengasse* (Market Street) for Timothy Horsefield, "late of Long Island."

OLD CHAPEL
(Erected, 1751; Extant)

With the erection of a new chapel building in 1751, connecting the *Gemeinhaus* with the 1749 extension of the Bell House, the number of known major stone buildings in the community rose to seven as opposed to two extant before the erection of the second Single Brothers' House. In addition, the new chapel was one more link in defining the space of Bell House Square which was completely closed on three sides the following year by the erection of the northern wing of the first Single Brothers' House.

By 1751 there were at least two hundred persons living in Bethlehem and hence *Der Saal* or chapel in the *Gemeinhaus* was by that time too small to accommodate all the individuals of the community for worship at one service. Thus it was that on February 1, 1751, plans for a new two-story stone chapel were examined and adopted. Ground was broken for the building on April 5, 1751, and the masons began to work immediately. Timber for the structure was floated down the Lehigh from the Gnadenhuetten (now Lehighton) sawmill as had been done when the second Single Brothers' House was commenced in 1748. The building was finished by July 9, and the next day at noon Bishop John Nitschmann dedicated the structure, after the customary meeting and love feast for children had taken place at eleven o'clock (Plate 33).

The new structure connected the east end of the north side of the *Gemeinhaus* with the west end of the extended Bell House. It measured thirty-two by sixty-six feet, and parts of the two older structures mentioned supplied walls for the new building. The basement of the chapel was planned to serve as a large dining room for married people, but this was not opened until February 8, 1752.[83]

When erected, one of the features of this new chapel was that the actual sanctuary could not be entered directly from the outside, although there were two doors to the married couples' dining room from the outside. The chapel's main entrance, which

83. *Bethlehemisches Diarium*, Moravian Archives, Bethlehem.

33. Undated Nineteenth-Century Photograph of the 1751 Bethlehem Chapel, Victorian Corpse House to the Left

was for the exclusive use of the clergy and the males of the community, was located at its south end and communicated with the second floor hall of the *Gemeinhaus*. A second entrance, now walled up, permitted women and girls to enter directly from the first floor of the Bell House.[84] Directly above this was another small door that connected with the second floor of the Bell House and provided access to a narrow gallery that ran along the north end of the auditorium. According to Hamilton, this was used chiefly by aged and infirm women.[85]

The two outside entrances were on the north and south sides of the structure, near the *Gemeinhaus*. These gave onto a small vestibule or *Vorhalle* and it is possible that from this cross-hall a flight of stairs connected the chapel with the dining hall below, although no trace of any such stair exists today.[86]

The structure was originally roofed with red clay tiles that were removed in 1753 when it was found that the underlying limestone shelf gave insecure support to the building. The latter fact had been discovered during the building period, and for that reason the large ribbon buttresses, which contribute so effectively to the architectural quality of the structure, were erected, three on the west side of the building and one on the east side. Some years after the heavy clay roof tiles were removed in favor of wooden shingles, there was still apparent concern for the stability of the structure, and solid masonry walls were at that time run across the dining hall area in the basement, engulfing the simple pillars that had formerly supported the upstairs chapel. According to Howland, this dining space was

so cut up that the area was abandoned as a dining hall.[87] The fact that this cross-wall was the second such is shown on the Grossert plan of 1897 (Plate 34) and is indicated by its thinner section and the absence of a doorway to give entrance into the space on the other side of the wall. Hence the conclusion that the other cross-wall is the original forming an entrance vestibule.

In the original arrangement of the interior of the chapel, the communion table stood on a low platform at about the center of the west wall. This was usually covered with a black cloth. Along the north end of this wall was a bench for the wives of the ministers and the single sisters who were the heads of the women's "choir." The south end of the same wall was reserved for the bench that accommodated the male dignitaries of the church. As was the custom in Germany, backless benches for the congregation ran north and south, i.e., lengthwise. At the southern end these were occupied by the boys and men, the boys sitting on the front rows. At the northern end of the room sat the girls and women. Several rows of benches were also placed east and west across the chapel under the gallery along the north wall. In later years this was the area in which the girls from the school in the Bell House sat as a group. On the south wall was a small gallery containing the organ, the musicians, and the singing choir. Between the windows on the west wall (how many were there originally is not known because of the mid-nineteenth-century addition at that end) were hung paintings by the Moravian preacher-artist, John Valentine Haidt, sometime after 1755. These supposedly depicted a series of scriptural scenes.[88]

With the completion of the present Central Moravian Church in 1806, the chapel lost its use for worship services in favor of the new and larger structure. Thereafter it served the community in a number of ways. For a while it was the chapel of the girls' school, and much later it became the archive

84. This would be at the northern end of the east wall.
85. Hamilton, *Church Street*, pp. 18–21.
86. The most northern of the windows on the east side of the chapel, the basement area, was later converted into a door. This is now a window again, as is the other former door on the east side of the building. However, Grider's drawing of 1854 shows this doorway at the northern extremity of the east side as it must originally have appeared. There must also have been a doorway for service purposes from the western extension of the Bell House, from what would have been the kitchen, into the dining hall in the chapel area, otherwise, food would have had to be taken from this kitchen in the Bell House outside and through the east door of the chapel building to the dining hall. It is not very conceivable that the Moravians would have tolerated such inconvenience. If such a door originally existed, this would mean that there was communication with the west end of the Bell House extension to the northern end of the east side of the chapel on three levels, i.e., the basement, the first floor, and the balcony.

87. Howland, "Moravian Buildings of Bethlehem," p. 244.
88. John Hill Martin, *Historical Sketch of Bethlehem in Pennsylvania with Some Account of the Moravian Church* (Philadelphia, 1872). Martin quotes Dr. John Schopf, *Incidents of Travel in 1733–34*, p. 42, as follows:
> We attended at their devotions in the church. This is built with the same disregard to ornamental architecture as the rest of the town. About twenty paintings representing the principal passages in our Saviour's life are hung about the walls, but that it should not appear that they were placed here with a view to ornament the building . . . they are without frames of the simplest kind.

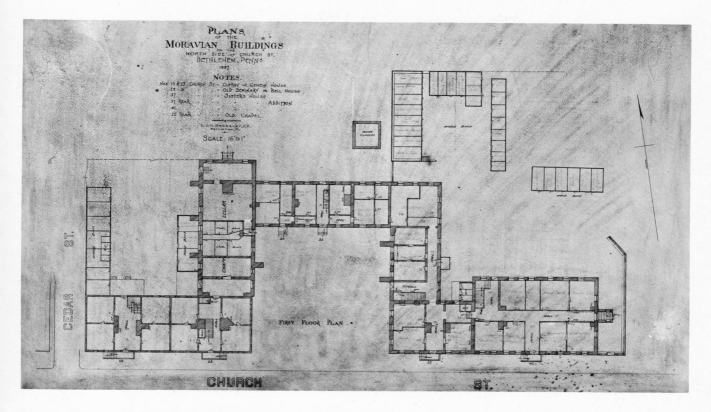

34. Grossart Plans of the Bell House Court Buildings, Bethlehem, including the *Gemeinhaus*, Old Chapel, Bell House, and Single Sisters' House, dated 1897

room of the Moravian congregation, which must have caused some changes in the interior. In 1827 it was "remodeled" to adapt it to its new use as a hall for concerts given by the Bethlehem Philharmonic Society. Some changes on the interior probably occurred in 1859 when the new organ, still there, was installed. Extensive alterations, inside and out, appear to have occurred in the year 1865, when the north end of the building was demolished and the present rectangular façade and vestibule were created, thus giving a new exterior entrance to this north side of the building (see Plate 33). In the alteration process, the original old north balcony was removed and the doors into the Bell House were walled up.

It is, indeed, to be deplored that the mid-nineteenth-century Moravians felt so little of the distinctive quality of their heritage of three-dimensional history that they allowed the 1751 chapel building to be mutilated for convenience by this new entrance in the architectural style of the latter age.

It is mild, however, in its mutilating force when compared with the treatment afforded Bethlehem's eighteenth-century apothecary building. The true story of Bethlehem's eighteenth-century apothecary building is relatively unknown today, a testimony to the vagaries of history and the insensitivity of man who remembers only that which he chooses to recall.

APOTHECARY
(Erected, 1752; Demolished, 1862)

The history of the Bethlehem "drugstore" begins in 1742 with the arrival of John Adolph Meyer, a member of the First Sea Congregation.[89] Meyer was to serve as the physician for the colony and was the

89. Levering, *Bethlehem*, p. 107. The *Seegemeine*, i.e., Sea Congregation or Ship Congregation, was the name given to the groups of colonists as they migrated from Europe to the Bethlehem colony, first on the ship *Catherine* and later on the *Irene*.

first such accredited professional person in the Lehigh Valley. He had studied in Europe under his father, who had also been a physician.[90] After arrival in Bethlehem on June 21, 1742, Meyer wasted little time in organizing the medical services of the community, for it is noted that in July, 1742, eight men and seven women were appointed as nurses under his direction. Some were employed as assistants in the dispensary and some were used in collecting and preparing medicinal herbs and roots for the first pharmacy, which he set up in one of the rooms in the *Gemeinhaus*.

By the autumn of 1742, a number of small log structures were erected to serve various pressing needs of the community. One of these was fitted up as a small hospital to take care of sick men; ill women were accommodated in the *Gemeinhaus* where the apothecary was apparently then established. Although Dr. Meyer presided over this small dispensary, it is not known whether he actually transferred the apothecary from the *Gemeinhaus* to this log building at this time or not. Meyer served as the Bethlehem physician until January 3, 1744, when he was installed as warden of the new Nazareth community, nine miles north of Bethlehem. He also transferred his professional headquarters to Nazareth at that time. Taking Meyer's place in the Bethlehem pharmacy was John Frederick Otto, M.D., whose degree was from the University of Halle.[91]

In March, 1747, the extensive gardens, which appear on the Bethlehem map of 1766 (see Plate 5), were laid out with the provision that a portion was to be devoted to the growing of medicinal herbs for the laboratory and pharmacy. A medical conference held shortly before had decreed that special attention be given to the study of flora of the region, and men were appointed to collect herbs then known to have curative properties. These included various shrubs and plants, such as mandrake or May apple, snakeroot, sassafras bark, and berries.[92]

According to the 1766 map, that portion of the single brothers' garden devoted to medicinal herbs was the lot now known as 79 West Church Street. This is a long narrow plot divided on the 1766 map into a series of ten units, two by two, extending down hill from the south side of the present Church Street toward Monocacy Creek. In this garden were grown such medicinal plants as various mints, elderberry, mulberry, mandrake, snakeroot, dandelion, foxglove (digitalis), crocus, valerion, etc.[93]

Sometime after 1749, the doctor apparently moved his apothecary into his own building, for it is noted that in June, 1752, when the new shop on *Der Platz* was finished, that Dr. Otto "began to move the stock and outfit of his pharmacy from the room before occupied in the western wing of the girl's school building into the new quarters."

The new apothecary building was erected on *Der Platz* at the corner of a street since closed to provide space for the lawn immediately north of the Central Moravian Church. The façade (Plate 35) was graced with a central door and flanking windows on the first floor, with three windows across the front on the second story level. A single gable-roofed dormer was located on center. The roof had the characteristic change of pitch near the eave line to give the familiar "kick" at this point. There was also the typical upper and lower attic under the gable roof. Red brick, flat window arches may have been part of the original building. Although they do not show in this particular drawing, they could have been removed by the time the drawing was made. The late date of this source is indicated by the presence of such later structures in the drawing and also by the addition of a large four-light window to the right of the central door.

To the rear and east of the main building was a small one-story log structure that served as a stable. This was approximately fifteen by nineteen feet, while the pharmacy building itself was twenty by thirty-seven. The laboratory, which was located slightly to the north and east of the main structure, was a small building about twenty feet square. It is difficult to say whether the laboratory building was a stone or log structure for an indication of the building material in the drawing is not clear.

Note should be taken of the small, one-story wooden vertical battened addition to the north of the large stone structure, connecting that building with the *Kinderanstalt* or Old Economy House and

90. *Ibid.*, p. 121. Meyer was later ordained a presbyter in 1748 and also became the first warden at Nazareth, a post that he held between the years 1744 and 1746. Until 1749 he was stationed at the school and home mission on the farm of Antes in Frederickstown. He later lived in Philadelphia, where he practiced medicine during the Revolution, and died there.

91. *Ibid.*, p. 171. John Frederick was the elder brother of John Matthew, also a physician, who had been trained at Strasbourg, and who had arrived from Europe in 1750. John Frederick died at Nazareth in 1779, and John Matthew at Bethlehem in 1786.

92. *Ibid.*, p. 203. It was at this time also that James Greening and Owen Rice became assistants in the apothecary and the laboratory.

93. A list of these herbs taken from the doctor's prescription book, dated 1743, numbers approximately 104 items.

the apothecary laboratory. From a manuscript in the possession of Henry Rau of Bethlehem the following information about this addition can be gleaned:

In April 1839 the doctor sold the Drug Stock to me (Simon Rau) on Term of three years to pay with yearly interest as the town was increasing the inhabitants the demands for Drugs and Medicine also increased. And in less than three years I paid the stock and money loaned interest and principal. Said Drug Stock and money loaned of the Doctor amounted together to $1500. As business increased I needed more store room after prevailing to let me build a one-story building to the Drug Store between the House and Laboratory. This building was erected in the Spring of 1844. One year later an agreement was made that we should have the House and all buildings after the demise of both the Doctor and wife and payment was made in interest and principal after the decease of Mrs. Freytag to the Executor C. C. Tombler of the Estate. A few years later I paid for the Lot to Revd. P. H. Goepp who gave me the Deed as the Doctor held it under Lease. The price was named therein as the value or price about 175 dollars.

Although the property now occupied by the Bethlehem Chamber of Commerce is invariably pointed out by local citizens as the "old and original drug store" of eighteenth-century Bethlehem, this is not true, since an article by Rau[94] states that his father or grandfather tore down the "old and original drug store" structure in 1862 to erect a new residence and an adjoining apothecary building. Moreover, the Moravian Congregational Board has photographs taken about 1929 which show the drug store building and residence as they appeared at that time. Shortly after these pictures were taken the congregation of the Central Moravian Church demolished the building

94. Robert Rau, "The First Apothecary in Bethlehem," *Transactions of the Moravian Historical Society*, XI, 62–63.

35. Undated Watercolor of the Bethlehem Apothecary of 1752, with the *Kinderanstalt* to the Left

immediately to the north of these two structures as well as the residence. The drug store of 1863 was moved into the void created by this demolition. The space created by this moving and destruction of the 1863 residence was converted into the present green lawn just north of the church.

In the thirties, an architectural firm "earlied up" the façade of the building to the Georgian mode. Thus, despite popular misconception, Bethlehem has not had its "old and original drug store" since 1863. Bethlehem lost its eighteenth-century apothecary building over a century ago.

INDIAN HOTEL
(Erected, 1752; Demolished Early 1800's)

Despite the large number of eighteenth-century structures that survive in the community, the apothecary shop was not alone in disappearing from the scene. Perhaps one of the more interesting structures, sociologically if not architecturally, that no longer stands was the *Indianer Logis* or Indian Hotel. This added to the accommodations for visitors already available in the community at the Crown Inn across the river. Since the life of Moravians in their village was constantly involved with the Indian, it seems reasonable to believe that the Indian Hotel was erected to give shelter to these *naturliche Männer*, or natives, and to keep the Crown Inn free for traveling colonists. It is interesting to note that the cloth workers suggestions to incorporate this structure into proposals for a new fulling mill, bolting mill, and tawing mill came only six short years after the erection of the building, and only two years after a log chapel had been erected south of the hotel, presumably for Indian use (see p. 13). The reason behind these suggestions can be found in the carrying out of long-range plans by Moravians to remove all Christianized Indians resident in Bethlehem to nearby Nain, which were consummated on October 18, 1758.

There is early evidence of the almost constant presence of Indians in Bethlehem in the eighteenth century. In 1745 there are a number of references to them in the Congregational Diary.[95] Since the Moravians came to America chiefly to Christianize such heathen, it is not surprising to learn that a special

Indianer Logis had been built soon after the Bethlehem settlement had been founded. Foundations for the structure were begun August 14, 1752, and by October 25 of the same year, the building was ready for occupancy. The site was on the west bank of Monocacy Creek, due west of the industrial concentration on the opposite side of the creek bank.[96]

Of stone, it was fifty-one feet long by approximately twenty feet wide and one story high.[97] Little is known of the structure's appearance save as it is viewed in the elevation for the proposed new fulling mill (see Plate 28). As shown on this plate, it was a rectangular structure with a door on center, approached by two steps, with four windows flanking the entrance, two to a side and evenly spaced across the façade. A stone water table surrounded the building at the first floor level, and if one presumes that the floor plan shown on the same manuscript is the original plan, each of the rooms flanking the central hall and entrance vestibule had at least two windows on the entrance façade and probably two on the opposite wall.[98] The south wall was blank, probably backing a fireplace, but a window or door was probably originally on the north side in an off-center position.

The roof, probably of tiles from the kiln up the creek, is shown as a gable in the elevations although the plan shows it hipped. The latter, of course, may indicate a proposed change that would make it architecturally more pleasing in its role as a one-story wing of the new fulling mill.

Little is known of the subsequent life of the structure save that it was demolished in the early nineteenth century when a nearby spring rose in the cellar threatening the foundations. Portions of the tile paving were visible, however, at least until the 1860's.[99] According to Levering, a log building sixty-three by fifteen feet, containing a chapel, was erected

95. They started a blockhouse, which was finished by August 17, and on July 7, they are noted as finishing a cabin. Congregational Diary of Bethlehem, I, Moravian Archives.

96. It was first erected as a temporary dwelling for Indians from Friedensheutten, a Moravian settlement for Christianized Indians, not far distant from Bethlehem, to house them until they could be located elsewhere. Later, before the Sun Inn was erected, it became a lodging for white travelers who found it impossible to cross the Lehigh at night to the Crown Inn. It therefore early replaced the log guest house of 1743 as the only place of lodging for travelers on the north side of the river in the years before the erection of the Sun Inn.

97. Levering, *Bethlehem*, p. 258, incorrectly notes its dimensions as 52′0″ x 40′0″. Three manuscript sheets in the Bethlehem Archives which show it also vary. One notes its width as 20′6″, while another indicates it as 21′0″, and a third as 20′0″.

98. See floor plan, Plate 18.

99. William Cornelius Reichel, *Memorials of the Moravian Church* (Philadelphia, 1870), p. 23.

just south of it in 1756, but this was removed in 1758 to the nearby Indian village of Nain.[100]

STORES

(First Store Erected, 1753; Demolished, c. 1890)
(Second Store Erected, c. 1763; Extant)
(Third Store Erected, 1794; Demolished, 1920's)

The growth of the Bethlehem community can be partially calculated by the opening of the village's first store, approximately a year after the *Indianer Logis* had been erected. The fact that the store operation was a flourishing part of this unusual community is attested by successive moves to ever-larger quarters. To the alert eye, the second store building on Market Street can still be readily recognized as an eighteenth-century structure in proportion, bulk, and scale, despite the mutilating changes succeeding generations have dealt it. Like the eighteenth-century tannery still standing in the Monocacy Creek valley, this second store structure enjoys an undeserving anonymity in today's Bethlehem. Although the third store structure was lost to the community in the earlier part of this century with the erection of the present Hotel Bethlehem, the second store building remains, awaiting the moment of recognition and opportunity to tell its story.

In the spring of 1753 it was finally decided to make commerce an official branch of Bethlehem's economy because of the increasing demand for manufactured articles from Bethlehem, not only on the part of Bethlehemites, but also the settlers and Indians living in the vicinity. It was Spangenberg who felt the greatest need for such an addition to the economy.[101]

After some deliberation it was decided to locate the store in a new building to be erected adjacent and west of a structure that was already standing in 1749. As stated earlier, Timothy Horsefield of Long Island moved to Bethlehem on November 8, 1749, and "took possession of a new stone house that had been built for him during the summer outside [*sic*] Bethlehem beyond the graveyard" (Plate 36).

This addition to the 1749 structure (Plate 37 showing some Victorian changes) was erected in 1753 and remained standing, later serving in various capacities other than a store, for approximately a hundred and thirty-seven years. It is noteworthy that when it was demolished around 1890 it was the wing that was destroyed and not the original 1749 structure itself.[102] It is known that work was commenced on

100. Levering, *Bethlehem*, p. 258. Nain was the village for Christianized Indians situated northwest of Bethlehem. In order to get the Indians out of Bethlehem and to follow the 1742 plans to establish such a settlement near Bethlehem, the chapel of the village was dedicated October 18, 1758, and the Indians took possession of the village at that time. The settlement was short lived and was broken up by government order, the buildings being sold and removed to Bethlehem by April 13, 1765. One of these still stands on the west side of Heckewelder Alley in Bethlehem.

101. The following excerpts are from Erbe, *Herrnhuter Kolonies*, pp. 70–71. In a letter to Zinzendorf, Spangenberg wrote on May 7, 1753:

Up to this time a Plan for this had always been lacking. Now our neighbors push us into it, and we find it necessary ourselves in order to enable our big household to continue to exist. We must always have some money on hand, to be able to purchase iron, powder, glass, salt, and other such items: We also can never raise as much fruit, flax, and such things, also never raise as much farm stock as we consume. So we must sell some of our hand-

work, especially from the handcrafts, to our neighbors and also keep them in the habit, to bring their things to us for sale, so that we must not get them from other places. But if they cannot get the necessary wares from us, they will drive to the city (Philadelphia) and then we have to see where we can get what we need. . . . There are 200 different articles, which could be for sale in a store, of which 180 are made by our Brethren and Sisters themselves to be furnished for the store. 20 or 30 articles could be purchased wholesale and afterward again sold at retail.

He further wrote to Johannes von Watteville:

. . . as soon as the store is completed, we will entirely separate the stock which properly belongs to our Economy and that which is only for sale. There is no intention of buying wares on credit, nor sell to others on credit. That would bring about too much trouble and hardship and nothing but loss would result in the end. No, may the Saviour guard us against that! This is rather the idea: we wish to place in the store what we make ourselves for what the people ask for and sell it either for cash or wheat, butter, flax, hemp, and similar wares to others. Everything that the storekeeper receives from our Economy, will be his account, he will pay it back in raw products for a set price for example, if he received 1 dozen hats at 5 sh. each after four weeks, he will either put down the hats or the money for hats sold and the remainder in raw products. Then also when something has to be purchased, as for instance tea, sugar, coffee, rice, glass, and such, that indeed will not amount to too much and we will also see to it, that we can purchase it for cash.

A memorandum of Spangenberg dated June 1, 1754, states:

I have decided to erect a Store-Building up on the mountain. This building, I hope, will have your blessing. It is not intended to be extensive but only to sell articles made by our Brethren themselves, and for the purchase of those items which we badly need in our Economy.

102. This earlier building still stands at what is today 42 West Market Street and is marked with a bronze plaque as the site of the first store of the community, despite the structure's having served not as the first store but as the residence of the storekeeper, Timothy Horsefield. The building is much changed; the shed-roofed dormer is gone, the limestone walls have been pargetted over, and the windows changed. The entrance door has been shifted to the opposite side of the façade from its original place.

the building on November 6, 1752. After some delay the structure was finished by July, 1753, and was ready for occupancy by July 17.

According to the Inventory Record of 1759 of the Unity Director's Board, "The Store building, 67 feet long, 27 feet wide, two stories high, has 10 rooms, 2 cellars, and 1 kitchen. Valuation: 450 pounds." To judge from the size of the building, noted on a 1766 map of Bethlehem as "Boemper" and "Horsefield" houses (see Plate 5), this footage included the length of the earlier 1749 building. If one assumes that the new western addition of 1753 was approximately the same size as the 1749 structure, as the 1766 map seems to indicate, then the new addition would have been approximately thirty-three-and-a-half feet long.[103]

According to an undated but early photograph, the 1749 structure (Plate 36) was constructed of native limestone with the characteristic red brick arch over each of the windows. The entrance door was to the right in the street façade. This was flanked to the left by two windows, three windows being spaced evenly on the second floor level. A large cove cornice, presumably lime plaster, finished off the meeting of the gable roof with the masonry wall of the building, and a single shed-roofed dormer graced this side of the gable between the second and third windows of the second floor. Unlike most buildings of the eighteenth-century in Bethlehem, this smaller structure had only one attic under its roof. On the basis of other buildings in Bethlehem during this period, the 1753 addition was probably also of native limestone, roughly ashlared, with the usual red brick flat arches over the windows (see Plate 37), and the plaster cove cornice was continued along the front of the new building. The 1757 view of Bethlehem shows the 1753 addition with five windows along its southern or main façade, while a 1793 view of the community shows only four windows along this façade. Both views picture three chimneys, spaced evenly along the peak of the gable roof, one at each end and one in the middle. According to the 1793 view, the new addition had an entrance door at the extreme left of the façade to balance the entrance door of the 1749 building at the extreme right of that structure. It is likely that each of these build-

ings had a floor plan similar to those found in many of the larger "choir" houses as well as in some of the smaller structures, i.e., an entrance giving on a hall that was flanked by two rooms, equally or nearly equally dividing the first floor area. The second floor would have been arranged roughly like the first, save for a small room at the top of the stair which gave the second floor three rooms. Such a plan would account for the ten rooms mentioned in the inventory record of 1759.

Timothy Horsefield held many positions in Bethlehem but was known best for his long tenure as the proprietor of the store, a position he took when it was opened and one which he held until John Francis Oberlin, who had arrived from England on the Moravian ship *Hope* in late October, 1761, took over as storekeeper about 1763.[104] Horsefield died on March 9, 1773, approximately a decade after being relieved by Oberlin as storekeeper and upon his decease, Henry van Vleck, a merchant, is known to have taken up residence at the Horsefield house in February, 1774.

As early as 1785, Heckewelder had proposed a new store site because of the growing business of this facet of the Bethlehem economy and on February 13, 1792, it is known that the Elders' Conference referred a plan to the *Aufseher Collegium* for the erection of a new store building. It was also proposed at the same time to turn the old store building and so-called Horsefield house adjoining it into an adjunct to the Sun Inn. Finally, on February 16, 1792, the site for the new store was chosen "next to Joseph Horsefield's house."

Plans for the building were finally approved on August 2, 1792, and the store contents were moved into this new structure before it was completed in 1794 (Plate 38). By August 30 of that year, it is known that the building was near completion and that John Christian Reich, assistant storekeeper, had moved into it.

The structure that Reich occupied was a three-and-a-half story building, with double chimneys and three gable-roofed dormers on its gable roof. An early photograph shows that it had eight shuttered windows to a floor on the street façade arranged in

103. The hypothesis that this 67-foot length includes both the old and the new structures is reinforced by the statement that the building has "10 rooms, 2 cellars." A 33 by 27-foot structure would be too small to have that many usable rooms on only two floors and would not necessarily contain two cellars.

104. Oberlin and his family eventually returned to Europe after he had served as storekeeper for eighteen years. Levering, *Bethlehem*, p. 514. On February 26, 1781, Christian Renatus Heckewelder replaced Oberlin as storekeeper. Christian Renatus was the brother of the Moravian missionary, John Heckewelder, who translated the Bible into several Indian dialects.

36. Undated Nineteenth-Century Photograph of the Structure Erected in 1749 for Timothy Horsefield as a Residence on Ladengasse in Bethlehem

37. Undated Nineteenth-Century Photograph of the First Store of Bethlehem, Erected Adjacent to the Horse-field House in 1753 and Demolished *circa* 1890

38. Undated Nineteenth-Century Photograph of the Third Store of Bethlehem, Erected in 1794 and Demolished in the 1920's

a three-three-two rhythm, with the main entrance in the center of the first floor on the long side of the structure facing the street. The general scale of the building, the relation of the solids to voids, and the lack of a double attic under the roof are architectural characteristics that belie the date ascribed to it by scholars. This is the store building Levering identified as the second store of the community. However, more recently uncovered documentary information indicates that it was probably the third store, the second having been located on Market or *Ladengasse*, as was the first, a little to the west of the first building.

If one accepts the descriptive information that the 1753 building added to the 1749 structure is the first store building, one is then faced with the problem of identifying why a second building, farther west on the same side of the street, is noted on the plan of 1766, as well as on John Ettwein's memorandum for a new plan for Bethlehem, dated February 16, 1791, as *Laden* or store, in both cases. On the map of 1766, the accepted site of the first store is identified as "Boemper's" house with "Horsefield's" house adjoining it. On Ettwein's manuscript of 1791 the Horsefield house is correctly noted as then being the residence of "v. Vleck" and the first store is still noted as "Boemper." However, the structure on the northeast corner of Market Street and the extension of the street now known as Heckewelder Street, proposed in Ettwein's 1791 memorandum, is another building, noted on both maps as a store. It is significant to note that this particular structure does not appear on the Bethlehem map of 1761. One is, therefore, drawn to the conclusion that the building was erected sometime between the years 1761 and 1766.

It has been noted that John Francis Oberlin became storekeeper about 1763. It is also known that three years later, the first store site is listed as Boemper's house. It is, therefore, very probable that the store operation was moved from its original site at what is now 42 West Market Street to what is now 68 West Market Street, presumably at the time Timothy Horsefield retired and John Francis Oberlin took over his duties as storekeeper in 1763. This would make the store structure erected "next to Joseph Horsefield's house" on *Der Platz*, occupied by 1794 and later incorporated into the fabric of the Eagle Hotel, now the Hotel Bethlehem, not the second store building of the community, as Levering concludes, but actually the third store structure.

The second store building that appears on the 1766 and 1791 maps still stands. It is further identified by an early picture in the collections of Historic Bethlehem, Inc. (Plate 39). Although much changed at the time of this early photograph (and changed still further today), the building most certainly had a central hall plan, with flanking chimneys, and characteristic upper and lower attics under the gable roof. The central door on the south façade was flanked by two windows on either side, and the second floor had a window centered directly over the entrance.

The building still shows vestiges of the early pargetted surface of the south façade, with ashlar indications scratched into the surface. This type of wall finish was characteristic of the early years of the nineteenth century and can also be seen in photographs of the Central Moravian Church and the second Single Brothers' Choir building of 1748.

WATER WORKS AND ITS SYSTEM
(*First Building Erected, 1754; Demolished, 1761*)
(*Second Building Erected, 1761; Extant*)

Almost coinciding with the erection of Bethlehem's first store building, the establishment of an effective pumping and water distribution system in 1754 establishes this community as one of the earliest in the colonies to provide such services. The frenzy of building activity that the village had witnessed since its founding created a profusion of structures of major and minor importance housing large segments of the community. With the thoroughness usually associated with Germanic peoples and such foresight as witnessed in John Ettwein's new plan for the settlement of 1791, it is not surprising that such a water distribution system was planned and successfully carried out. The stone structure of 1761, a replacement for the first pump house, is perhaps the smallest eighteenth-century structure that reflected the architectural characteristics associated with the large "choir" buildings on Church Street. With the neighboring tannery building, it forms one of the few extant tangible links with Bethlehem's eighteenth-century industrial concentration.

Bethlehem claims to have had the first water works in America (or at least in Pennsylvania) to successfully use a pumping system. The history of this water works and its system is inextricably entwined with the history of the community, for it was the

39. Undated Nineteenth-Century Photograph of the Second Store of Bethlehem, Erected *circa* 1763 on Ladengasse, the Dormered Structure at the Left

never-failing abundance of cool, clear, sparkling water which first drew the Moravians to this site. For many years this spring on the banks of "Menagassi" Creek served as the principal source of water for the community. Before the erection of the first water works, distribution of water was made by appointed handlers or carriers. Godfrey Haberecht was the first individual appointed to that office in July of 1742.[105] He was followed by a Mr. Schnell, who in turn was followed in 1748 by a man named Hussey. After him came a Mr. Wittke, who was the last person to fill this office. It was Hans Christian Christiansen, who arrived in New York aboard the ship *Irene*, on the evening of September 24, 1751,

who was destined to change this system. Trained as a millwright, he had been born near Hadersleben in Holstein, which was then under Danish rule. It was he who commenced the erection of the first water works in the spring of 1754.

A frame building nineteen by twenty-two feet was erected a few yards east of the oil and bark mill. This timber structure was to house the machinery for the pumping system. Water was led from the spring house either by a mill race or wooden conduit, as Rau calls it, into a cistern. The cylinder was five inches in diameter and the pump was made of lignum vitae.[106] According to Levering, John Boeh-

105. Robert Rau, "First Water Works in America: Historical Sketch of the Bethlehem Water Works," *Bethlehem Daily Times*, February 21, 1877.

106. Rau got his detailed information from Gilbert Bishop who had had charge of the water works. He was the grandson of Charles David Bishop, whose father, John David Bishop, had apprenticed to Hans Christian Christiansen.

ner, a West Indian missionary and one of the pioneers of Bethlehem, was visiting at the time Christiansen began his water works project. Boehner apparently had some knowledge of pumps and made a model of the pump and the necessary connections. In preparation for the piping system a collection of hemlock logs was drifted down the Lehigh River from Gnadenhuetten in March, 1754.[107]

Things were sufficiently advanced by June 21 to demonstrate the feasibility of the plan by forcing the water "as high as the houses around the square in the town above, to the astonishment and joy of all." With this success the machinery was perfected, a separate water wheel was built, and the pipes were laid. To receive the water, a large wooden water tower was erected between the two log structures that housed married couples.[108] Also a large tank was built in the Bell House Square farther east on Church Street. Water was successfully forced into the wooden tower on May 27, 1755, and exactly a month later the flow into the tank in the square began.[109] The water works proved to be one of the great visitor attractions in the community. It must, indeed, have been fascinating to watch the undershot water wheel, powered by water from the spring house, set into motion the hydraulic pump that in turn pumped the water into the wooden tower above the water works building.

A sheet in the Unitas Archive, in Herrnhut, East Germany, titled in translation "Explanation of the Water Works in Bethlehem," contains the following notations (translation):

a) The water wheel is 18′ high

b) the barrels, two feet four inches high, the diameter in the clear of four inches. The iron 5/4th of an inch thick.

c) The lead pipes, which go only halfway to the tower, are 2½′ diameter in the clear, the lead 1½ quarter inches thick.

d) Below from the water works to the tower, the water rises perpendicularly the diagonal length is 320′; the tower itself is 32′ high. Total: 352′.

e) The perpendicular height, which the water has to rise, must be 94′.

The water works system was successful as reported by Spangenberg on January 13, 1759, and in Appendix 2 of the Unity Directors Board X, 145, he says: "This Water Works is now approaching its fifth year and so far has not required any further repairs, except for occasionally the leather on the buckets and the barrels gets worn off." The value of the works at that time is recorded to have amounted to one hundred pounds.

The use of wooden pipes must have proved unsuccessful since Christiansen began in 1761 to improve upon his first success and to construct larger, more powerful machinery to satisfy the needs of the growing community. This new plan was perfected by Christiansen in conjunction with a man by the name of Marshall and with John Arbo. The new plan called for a new two-and-one-half story building. This is the structure that still stands in Bethlehem essentially unchanged from its original form (Plate 40). Architecturally it follows the example set in 1744 by the first Single Brothers' House on Church Street in that it was constructed of native limestone with a series of red brick arches over each of the windows. According to Rau the building was originally covered with red tiles.[110] The 1793 view of the village indicates that the roof originally had a small jerkin head on the west side which is now gone. Main entrance to the building was presumably on the south side. This is now a window. A photograph of the structure, dated c. 1860's (Plate 41) shows this present window as a door, with four overlights and a large heavy wooden lintel above, topped by the ever-present red brick arch.[111]

The building was presumably always heated, since the 1790 view shows a chimney in the center of the structure.

Barge boards that increase in width as they descend from the apex of the gable roof to the eave line are one of the subtle architectural features of the building. With the exception of the introduction of sliding garage doors on the west side, the making of the south door into a window because of the rise of ground level, and the removal of the tile roof and the jerkin head to the roof, the building remains essentially as it was when first erected.

It was not until July 6, 1762, that the new pumps began the first flow. According to Rau's description of this new or second water works, the machinery consisted of three single-acting force pumps of

107. *Ibid.* Gnadenheutten was on the Mahoning River and was an Indian mission near the present Lehighton, Carbon County.
108. These were situated on the site of the present Central Moravian Church.
109. According to Erbe, *Herrnhuter Kolonie*, p. 76, this first water works served as the model of the later water works in Philadelphia.
110. Robert Rau, "Historical Sketch of the Bethlehem Water Works," *Bethlehem Daily Times*, February 21, 1877, p. 4.
111. This door is now a window because the ground level in the area along the Monocacy Creek has risen approximately three to four feet in the last hundred years.

40. Undated Nineteenth-Century Photograph of Bethlehem Oil Mill, Right, and the Water Works, Left

41. Undated Nineteenth-Century Photograph of the Bethlehem Water Works, Looking North

four-inch calipher and eighteen-inch stroke worked by a triple crank. These were forged by the resident blacksmith, Steven Blum, and geared to the shaft of an undershot water wheel, eighteen inches in diameter, two feet clear in the buckets. The head of water was two feet. On the water wheel shaft was a wallower of eighty-three round, which geared into a spurwheel of fifty-two dogs attached to the crank; each of the three piston rods was attached to a frame or crosshead, working in grooves to give them a motion parallel to the pumps. The crossheads were of wood as were the parts containing the grooves for guides. The works were calculated to raise the water seventy feet, and this was subsequently increased to a hundred and twelve feet. The rising mains were now made of gum wood as they were subject to greater pressure, and the other pipes were of pitch pine. According to Rau the entire cost of the building, with roof tiles included, was five hundred and fourteen pounds, sixteen shillings, and five pence. The above-mentioned pitch pine mains had to be renewed as early as 1769 by a second set of such pipes brought from Pocopoco in Monroe County. The shingle-roofed wooden tower that stood between the two log "choir" houses of the married couples continued to serve as the distributing reservoir.[112]

By about 1790, from the Bethlehem tower, water flowed into seven central reservoirs: (1) a cistern in the center of the Bell House Square opposite the Widows' House on Church Street; (2) the apothecary, which is today the site immediately south of the present Chamber of Commerce Building; (3) a wooden tank that formerly stood on Market Street, east of Main Street;[113] (4) one of the farm houses; (5) the Sun Inn on Main Street; (6) the rear of the Brothers' House; (7) and what was then the school area in Willow Square behind the Church Street *Gemeinhaus*.

From the Bell House reservoir, lead pipes carried water to the Old Chapel, the Sisters' House, the Widows' House, and the stable to the east of the Widows' House. From the Brothers' House cistern, there were connections to their stable and hattery, and from the farmhouse cistern connections led to the stables and to the "milk cellar." By 1796 all of the pitch pine pipes had been given up, and lead pipes had been substituted in the entire system.

With the commencement of the Central Moravian Church in 1803, the old wooden water tower between the two log houses of the married people was removed, as were the houses. The tower was supplanted by a second tower of local sandstone, situated on Market Street, which served the community until 1832 when Christiansen's system was completely overhauled. It was in this year that the old oil mill, also a product of Christiansen's genius, became the central point of a new water works system. It was also in this year that the second tower on Market Street became superfluous, and a new set of pumps were constructed by a Philadelphia concern replacing the original Christiansen pump, making the eighteenth-century water works of Bethlehem a thing of history.

KINDERANSTALT
(Erected, 1754; Demolished, 1869)

The attention drawn in 1754 to the new pump house and successful water distribution system seems to have focused the eye and mind of the recorders away from the large stone structure concurrently abuilding on *Der Platz* above the Monocacy Creek valley. This structure, despite its size, more permanent building material, and construction on a site that helped to more clearly delineate the actual boundaries of the square has had little written about it. Perhaps it was the lack of specific use, save to serve the needs of an ever-growing community, that consigned the structure to relative oblivion and varied occupancies throughout its span of existence. The *Kinderanstalt*, of all the larger Bethlehem structures of the eighteenth-century "choir community," enjoys the distinction of having less known about its construction than almost any other large building erected in Bethlehem in the eighteenth century, with the possible exception of the girls' boarding school. No master craftsman's drawings of it survive, nor are any lengthy and repetitive references made to its construction in any of the Moravian archival material such as one meets concerning the second Single Brothers' House. With the apothecary to the

112. A very deceptive view of this water tower, by "old Mr. Oerter," is in the collections of the Moravian Historical Society at Nazareth, Pennsylvania, which shows the tower as though it were attached to the west side of the easternmost of the two choir houses. This is purely an elevation drawing and plans in existence indicate that the tower was behind this house and east of the nearby second log house for married couples. The Oerter water color shows a completely wooden structure in three sections gently tapering toward the top on which was a weather vane in the form of a fish.

113. These first three were finished by 1766.

south, the farm buildings to the northwest, and the locksmith, blacksmith, nailsmith, and pottery buildings facing it from the opposite side of *Der Platz*, it commanded a place of prominence in the village. For this, it deserves separate attention and inclusion in any list of noteworthy structures of this eighteenth-century Pennsylvania settlement.

The project for the building primarily known as the Old Economy House or *Kinderanstalt*, also referred to as the Boys' House, the Men's House, etc., was broached by Spangenberg as early as March, 1753.[114] It was planned to serve as an apartment house as well as to house some of the crafts of the community.

On April 2, 1753, the foundation lines were staked off, and by June of that year it was decided to merely finish the walls of the cellar because of the pressing need for hands to reap an abundant harvest. In the spring of 1754, however, construction was begun again, and the building was completed and moved into by September 30. On February 20, 1755, a few short months after its completion it became the home of the "boys' institute" and was occupied as a boys' school until the spring of 1759 when that school moved to Nazareth, nine miles north, to a new economy building (later known as Nazareth Hall), the cornerstone of which had been laid on May 2, 1755.

114. Levering, *Bethlehem*, p. 283.

Because of the growing needs of the girls' school, this educational institution was moved on June 8 from the Bell House to the *Kinderanstalt* after it had been vacated by the boys. It is presumably at this time that the building received the name *Kinderanstalt*, as opposed to the old girls' seminary headquarters at the Bell House, which was then spoken of as the Old *Kinderhaus*. At an unknown date, not too distant from this date of removal from the Old *Kinderhaus*, the girls' seminary moved back to the Bell House and this large stone building on Main Street was then converted to a building of private dwellings and received the name "Family House." At a later date, with population shifts, it became filled with parsons pensioned by the church and given the name "Economy House."

During the course of the Revolutionary War, the structure served as a jail for prisoners of war; on September 2, 1777, it housed approximately two hundred and sixty British soldiers. Three families living in the three apartments in the building were forced to move out to accommodate them. After serving various other uses, the building was demolished in 1869 to make way for a new Moravian Publications Office.

To judge from a drawing of the structure in Levering's book, as well as the photograph of a watercolor in the collections of Historic Bethlehem, Inc., it had an architectural character similar to the

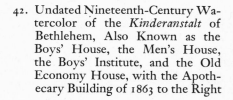

42. Undated Nineteenth-Century Watercolor of the *Kinderanstalt* of Bethlehem, Also Known as the Boys' House, the Men's House, the Boys' Institute, and the Old Economy House, with the Apothecary Building of 1863 to the Right

east wing of the Single Sisters' House on Church Street (Plate 42). It was thirty by sixty feet in dimension, constructed of stone, and three stories high. There were the usual upper and lower attics under a gable roof; only the lower of these was lighted by gable-roofed dormers. The crest of the gable was crowned by three evenly spaced chimneys, their placement being dictated by the use originally intended for the building. The entire north section of the first floor was occupied by the cabinetmaker and joiner's shop, while the corresponding southern section of this first floor was devoted to the warden's room and a conference room for the affairs of the settlement.

On the second floor, the north and middle sections contained four dwelling rooms, while the south section was left as one large room for any purpose for which it might be needed. The third story was used as a dormitory. The basement had large masonry vaults on the western or street side of the building, and the eastern half of the cellar housed the linen-weaving room at one time. There were two front entrances to the building with passages running through the house, dictating two rear entrances as well. Also, there were corresponding passages on the second floor. Communication between these was effected by means of a balcony on the east side of the structure.

There was an even fenestration pattern of five windows across the west façade (and also presumably the east façade) on the third and second floors, while the first floor alternated the pattern of doors and windows. The north and south elevations had the usual two windows per floor evenly spaced across the ends of the building. Although Levering's sketch does not indicate brick arches over the windows, this was such a strong architectural characteristic that it seems almost safe to assume that they were originally part of the architectural character of the structure along with the native limestone of which the building was constructed. Records do not indicate whether the building was roofed with red tiles or whether it had wooden cedar shakes such as those that covered the house of the single brethren on Church Street.

SUN INN
(Begun, 1758; Extant)

The Crown Inn had been catering to travelers to Bethlehem since 1745. Also, the Indian Hotel of 1752 helped alleviate the growing problem of overnight guests in the area, but by 1754 it was evident that more commodious and convenient accommodations were necessary. Thus, while work progressed on the establishment of the first store, while the pumping system and water distribution system successfully distributed its water for the first time throughout the community, while a new saw mill was erected to replace an earlier one, and while a score of other projects in the settlement were completed, the question of a new inn remained urgent but unresolved. Finally, designs were approved in 1758 and the completed structure was first used in 1760. Noting the length of time involved between the first mention of a new inn in 1753 and its final occupancy, one is aware of the importance attached to the new inn in the minds of the community leaders. Once opened, the Sun Inn quickly developed renown that extended throughout the colonies—a fame based not only on hospitality but cleanliness of accommodations, excellence of service, and completeness of cuisine and wine and spirit cellars.

The Moravians who settled Bethlehem in 1741 were sufficiently remote from travel routes at that time that there was no need for an inn or hostelry in the village.[115] As the tide of settlement moved farther northward and the area became more populous it was increasingly evident that such a facility would be needed in a short time. Accordingly, in July, 1754, they first gave consideration by committee to the erection of such a building.[116] By this time Bethlehem was on a direct line of travel from the Carolinas to the Massachusetts Bay area, and the population of the village was approximately four hundred. Nothing came of the committee's consideration at that time, and it was not until February of the following year that they again gave further thought to a new inn. It was to be located just outside the closed community's boundaries.

Finally, in the autumn of 1757 preparatory steps were taken with actual construction work scheduled to commence on the building the following spring. In January 1758, the unknown master craftsman's plan as submitted was accepted (Plate 43), and

115. The Crown Inn was already on the south side of the Lehigh River, built on land purchased from William Allen in 1745. A squatters hut on this tract had been enlarged, and in May of 1745, it had been opened to travelers. In 1794, the inn became a farmhouse, and in 1854 it was demolished to make way for a railroad station.
116. William C. Reichel, *The Old Moravian Sun Inn, Bethlehem, Pennsylvania, 1758* (Philadelphia, 1893), p. 8.

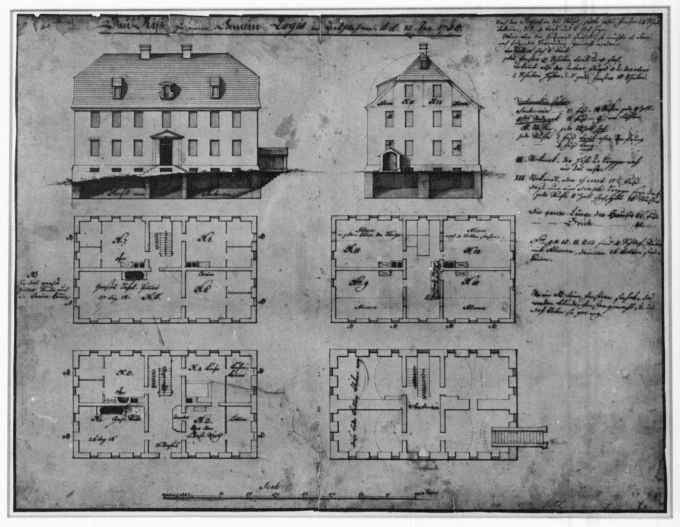

43. Plans and Elevations of the Sun Inn, Bethlehem, dated 1758

ground was broken in the first week of April of that year. The site that was chosen was "situated on the road leading to the tile kiln, and opposite the Monockasy and the quarry." By the end of May the cellar had been excavated and walled out. Work dragged intermittently on the project. For one reason or another there were many interruptions, and it was not until March 24, 1760, that the first inhabitants moved in.

In June of the same year, application was made to the court at Easton to entertain travelers and to sell beer and cider. Finally, on September 24, the first travelers were entertained, although the building was not completely finished and equipped until the spring of 1761. These first guests at the inn were the beginning of a long line of visitors, including the great and near-great, who frequented the rooms of the inn. Some of the famous visitors to the Sun Inn

during the later eighteenth and early nineteenth centuries include the following:

Governor Hamilton, June, 1762
Sir William Johnson, Baronet, June 29, 1762
Governor John Penn and Brother Richard, July, 1765
General Gage, September, 1772
Governor Richard Penn, May, 1773
Governor John Penn, 1774 and 1776
General Gates, December 17, 1777
General Sullivan, December 18, 1777
John Adams and Lyman Hall (Georgia signer of the Declaration of Independence), January 25, 1778
General Armstrong, March 11, 1777
General Schyler, May, 1777
William Ellery, Rhode Island Delegate to the

Continental Congress, June, 1777
William Whipple, New Hampshire Delegate to the Continental Congress, June, 1777
General Mifflin, July 25, 1777
Generals Greene and Knox, August 23, 1777
General LaFayette, September 20, 1777
John Hancock, Samuel Adams, James Duane, Nathan Brownsen, Nathaniel Folsom, Richard Law, Elyphalet Dyer, Henry Marchant, Henry Laurens, Harnett, Benjamin Harrison, Joseph Jones, John Adams, and William Williams (all delegates to the Continental Congress), stayed and signed the registry of the Sun Inn on September 22, 1777

During the first six months of 1778 the following guests signed the registry:

General Greene
General Gates and family
Ethan Allen
Baron Steuben
Pulaski
General Conway
Generals Lewis and McIntosh
Governor Morris
Monsieur Gerard, Minister Plenipotentiary of France, and Don Juan de Mirelles, Spanish Gentleman of Havana, November 25, 1778
General George Washington, July, 1782
The Marquis de Chastellux, December, 1782
Commodore Barry, of the Ship United States, June 7, 1803.[117]

The original drawing (Plate 43) for the inn is an interesting and valuable record of the typical Germanic architecture erected on the edge of this Moravian village in the eighteenth century. The sheet shows four floor plans, from the basement to the third floor, and two elevations, an east or end elevation and a south or longitudinal elevation. One also sees in both of these elevation drawings a cross section of the cellar area below grade. The title reads, in translation, "Plan of a Community Lodging House in Bethlehem, 12 January 1758." The German script

to the right of the sheet yields the following information: "As far as the preparation of the house is concerned, every window shall have 24 window panes, each four wide and six high. Should this, however, be too many, then the following calculations must be followed: each window pane should be ten inches high and eight wide, and each window three panes wide and five panes high. Then the lower window sash will be three and the upper window sash will be two panes high and each window will have fifteen window panes."

A general description of the heights of the stories follows. The cellar or *Souterrain*, as it is called on the drawing, was to be twelve feet high. From the floor to the surface of the ground there were to be eighteen steps, each nine inches. The first floor was to be ten feet nine inches high, and there were to be sixteen steps leading to the next floor. These were each to be seven-and-one-half inches high with each step one foot wide and four feet long. As far as the second floor is concerned, the unknown master builder noted that the room height and the steps should be the same as the first floor. The third floor or "garrett" was to be eleven-and-one-half feet high. To get to this garrett level he noted that there should be a simple stairway, that each step should be eight inches high, and that there should be sixteen steps in all. The over-all dimensions of the structure indicate that the entire length of the house was to be sixty-six feet and the width was to be forty feet. To the notes are added: "Nos. 9 and 10, 11 and 12 are four bedrooms with alcoves and in these could be placed sixteen beds." He then noted that windows marked with a "B" should be false windows and in the attic or loft windows should be left out entirely.

Starting with the floor plan at the lower right of the sheet, one notes the cellar floor. This is a simple central plan with a wide access hall in the center, flanked by two rooms on either side. In the lower right room is an access stair to the outside. The curved dotted lines on the plan indicate vaulted rooms. The note to the left mentions that these cellars could be left unexcavated and cleared later.[118]

117. No rates are known to the author for 1803, but in 1762 they were as follows:

Dinner	1 Shilling
Supper	6 d.
Breakfast	6 d.
Night's Lodging	6 d.
Shave	6 d.

118. Bethlehem tradition states that there is a tunnel leading from this basement under the city to the cliff along the banks of Monocacy Creek. The author has no substantiation for this, but he has seen what is supposed to be the walled-up entrance of the tunnel from the Monocacy Creek cliff. It is not now known what use the tunnel, if it exists, originally served. See James B. Laux, *Brother Albrecht's Secret Chamber: A Legend of the Ancient Moravian Sun Inn of Bethlehem* (Lititz, Pennsylvania), 1914, for a delightful story involving this tunnel.

To the lower left of the sheet is the plan of the first floor of the building. One notes that the main entrance of the structure is on the south or long elevation. This created an off-street entrance or inn yard, since the short end of the building faced the main thoroughfare. In the eighteenth century this road led from the Lehigh River to *Der Platz*. A central hall twelve feet wide can be noted on the plan. To the left was a coffee or common room, twenty-four by sixteen feet with a large open fireplace. Behind this, on the same side of the building, was a three-room apartment with a closet. On the other side of the structure on the same floor was the landlord's office with a counter letting onto the *Vorhaus* or entrance hall, and adjacent were quarters for the landlord. In this business space a tile stove for heating the area can be noted. Behind the landlord's office was the large kitchen with its big fireplace, probably with a great chimney bonnet over it. To the side of the kitchen was a pantry room.

Moving upstairs to the second floor, one notices first, at the front of the building, the large chamber thirty-seven by eighteen feet with open fireplace. This, presumably, was the main social hall of the hostelry. The remainder of the floor was divided into three three-room apartments, of which the two to the rear are shown to have had tile stoves. On the next floor or garrett, four large rooms flanked the central hall. The notes indicate that four beds could be placed in each alcove, thus making a possible total of sixteen beds on the top floor, and each of these rooms was to be heated by a tile stove. In the center hall there is an indication of some sort of stair to the upper attic or loft.

One notes that the elevations are architecturally characteristic of this Germanic settlement. Of special interest is the gable roof with its graceful cant or change of slope at the eave line, as well as the jerkin at either end of the gable. Chimneys are placed on the interior of the structure, as opposed to English building tradition in the middle colonies, which placed them on the ends. Typical also of eighteenth-century building in Bethlehem are the shed-roofed dormers instead of those with gables. Of particular interest, however, is the dormer over the main entrance. This has strong indications of a baroque influence in the curved top as well as in the scroll motifs that flank the opening.

Looking to the utilitarian entrance on the end elevation of the structure, it is interesting to note the characteristic herringbone pattern of the door

which one still finds in many buildings in Bethlehem and especially in those on Church Street. The boards in such doors are rabbited, mortised, and tenoned into each other and into their frame to create an exceptionally solid portal. Such doors were common in seventeenth- and eighteenth-century Germany.

An inventory of May 4, 1762, indicates that four hundred and thirty-seven pounds, two shillings, nine pence were spent in equipping the house, of which one hundred and fifty-seven pounds, one shilling, three pence was spent for furniture.[119]

Despite its illustrious past, the Sun Inn today remains an almost unknown structure in the United States. Much modified, it still exists at 79 South Main Street. Although the main entrance remains in the same location, the roof line has been changed considerably, additional floors have been added, and the entire stone building has been brickcoated.

The Sun Inn and another structure, erected in 1768 to house widows of Moravian missionaries, contrast the manner in which historic structures survive the vicissitudes of time. The considerable alterations and shoddy neglect of the Sun Inn have reduced the once famous hostelry to a blighted state. The Widows' House, still in Moravian care, has more of its original fabric intact and is perhaps less changed than any other structure in Bethlehem.

WIDOWS' HOUSE
(Erected, 1768; Extant)

With the erection of the Widows' House, the Bell House Square complex now came as near to completion as it was ever to be, a state that is indeed formal when one views the Bell House from the second floor center window of the Widows' House. Visually, if not actually, the structures that face each other across the intrusion of present Church Street interact as a cohesive whole, creating a successful urban complex of considerable beauty and standing as a prime example of the eighteenth century's capa-

119. This included three English and three German beds, six single bedsteads, six double blankets, and twenty-two single striped and woolen rugs. These furnished the traveler's chambers. Equipment in the inn also included kitchen utensils and the contents of the larder and cellar. In the cellar were two gross of tobacco pipes, twenty gallons of Madeira, ten gallons of Teneriffe, two quarter-casks of white Madeira, one hundred and nine gallons of Philadelphia rum, sixty-four gallons of cider royal, four hogsheads of cider, and a barrel of beer.

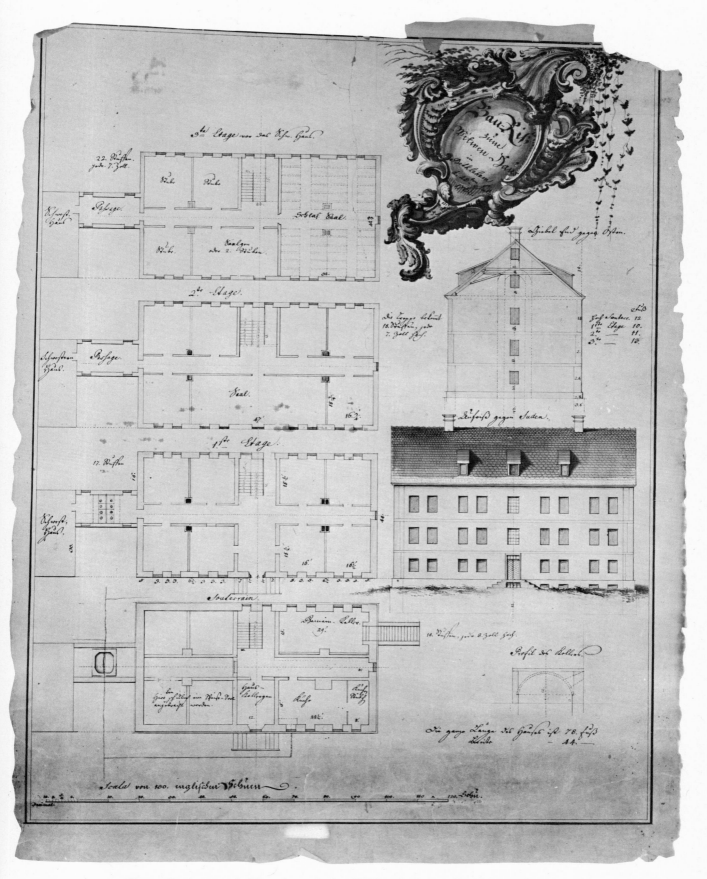

44. Plans, Sections, and Elevation of the Widows' House, Bethlehem, dated 1760

bilities in the planning and control of a community's environment.

Nazareth was the seat of the first Widows' House of the Moravian church in America. It was here that the widows of the various Moravian missionaries lived after the deaths of their husbands. This particular "choir" had been formed in the spring of 1755, but by 1760 the building at Nazareth was too small. It was, therefore, proposed through the Congregational Council at Bethlehem that a building be erected for this group in that city, adjoining the Sisters' House.[120]

A beginning was made as early as 1758 when a donation of fifty pounds from the widow of James Burnside started a building fund for the building. On May 29, 1760, after discussion in the general church council, the Board of Elders finally committed itself to the new structure.[121] The original drawing, still in the Moravian Archives, undoubtedly was made as a result of this meeting for it carries the date of July 23, 1760 (Plate 44).

This plan called for a façade three stories high in place of the two-story elevation later erected. The gable roof shows only one set of shed dormers in the lower register, although the end elevation clearly indicates an upper window above the framing. A floor could thus be laid at this level to create a lower and upper attic. Note should be taken also of the subtle "kick" at the eave, the characteristic architectural refinement of all Moravian structures in Bethlehem.

From the drawing we learn that the building was to be forty-four by seventy-eight feet, the exact size of the structure later erected. A profile of the cellar shows that a vaulted or arched construction was in-

tended, while notes on the adjoining east end elevation indicate the height of the basement was to be twelve feet, that of the first floor ten feet, the second eleven feet, and the third thirteen feet.[122]

According to the basement plan it was thought that "perhaps a dining hall could be made here," i.e., the rooms in the front left corner of the structure as one faces it. Note that this area was shut off by a partition wall across the hall which would have undoubtedly required changing the wall storage unit shown on the plan to an access door if such an idea were carried through. The dining hall would have been flanked by the kitchen, the larder, and a small "house cellar" across the same side of the building. Contemplated across the longitudinal hall was a congregational cellar.

A typical plan with a central entrance hallway bisected by a longitudinal hall was suggested for the first and second floors. The various areas were evenly and symmetrically divided, and the lack of open fireplaces undoubtedly indicates the planned use of tile stoves to heat the rooms.[123] The "choir" chapel was to be located in the center section of the south side of the second floor, while a smaller hall was to occupy a similar position on the third floor. This latter floor is of particular interest in that the *Schlafsaal* or dormitory occupied the entire eastern half of the structure, while the remainder was given over to three private rooms and the aforementioned small work or common room. The sleeping room could accommodate fifty widows according to notes on the plan.

Of special interest are the inside toilets in the narrow wing shown on the first floor plan, half of them for use by the occupants of the adjoining building. This first floor toilet feature served as "passage" on the second and third floors and is of special interest since it connects each floor with the smaller building marked *Schwesternhaus* or Sisters' House. This, plus the note that this is an elevation facing south, leads to but one conclusion: the proposed site of the Widows' House was on the north side of the present

120. The widows then living in Bethlehem resided in the house for married people, i.e., the log house on the site of the present central Moravian church, as well as in the so-called "Clergy" house and in the nursery. See John W. Jordan, "Historical Sketch of the Widow's House at Bethlehem, Pennsylvania," *Transactions of the Moravian Historical Society, Nazareth*, Vol. IV (1895). It should also be mentioned that the main body of the Widow's Choir had removed to Nazareth from Bethlehem in 1755 to occupy one of the two original log cabins of that community. Before that date they were not organized as a "choir"; they had no building in which to live but found quarters wherever space was available. Levering, *Bethlehem*, p. 285.

121. Hamilton, *Church Street*, p. 26, quotes from the *Protocoll der Aeltesten Conferenz*:

We are unanimously resolved to begin in earnest with the erection of the Widow's House. All of the brethren who are masons and can therefore be of particular help in this, e.g. Schober, Neibert, are to assist in it. Brother Lawatsch is to supervise this building, but Hoeger will continue in his present duties. We appeal to the married People's Choir, both here and in Nazareth, to make common cause of this and to offer all possible aid.

122. An accompanying note to the effect that the stairway was to have eighteen steps, each seven inches high, undoubtedly was meant to be taken with modification, for a notation on the first floor shows seven steps indicating, with a ten-foot ceiling height, that the risers would have to be slightly higher.

123. Attention should be called to the end elevation showing the divided chimney flues that unite in the attic to form one exterior chimney. One can still see such an arrangement in both the Widows' House and in the last addition to the Single Sisters' House.

Church Street east of the Bell House court, instead of the south side of that street facing north and on an axis with the Bell House group, where it was actually erected. The Sisters' House noted on the drawing would, therefore, be the 1744 building erected for the single brothers and the structure that they vacated for use by the single sisters when their second building was completed farther west in 1748. This is the site used in 1773 for the eastern addition to the 1744 building erected by the growing Single Sisters' Choir.

Plans for the widows' building were postponed and it was not until convocation of the synod in 1766 that work actually got under way. On December 2 of that year, Sisters Werwing and Huber, who were the chaplains of the Widows' Choir, came from Nazareth to select the site. According to Hamilton, they chose a location in the "congregational garden" opposite the Bell House.[124] About a month later, plans were approved. The building was to be forty-four by seventy-eight feet long. Brother Carl Schulze was put in charge of construction, Andrew Schober and Martin Schenck were the master masons of the job, and Tobias Hirte was the master carpenter.[125] These men were master mechanics who had worked at other settlements of the church.

The cornerstone was laid on April 27, 1766, and by September 21 the rafters were raised and the roof was covered with cedar shingles from Philadelphia instead of the red clay tiles, which seem to be indicated on the elevation drawing. Because of financial problems, work dragged and it was not until October 11, 1768, that the structure was finally completed. The following day the widows left Nazareth in a body at 7:00 A.M and arrived in Bethlehem at 10:00

A.M., after a trip presumably made on foot. At the Sun Inn they met with church officials who welcomed them in the name of the local congregation, and from there they marched in a body to the new "choir" house on Church Street. There the entire "choir" of thirty persons, with the clergy of Nazareth and Bethlehem as their guests, took their first meal in the new house. This was followed at 2:00 P.M. by a love feast held in the new dormitory after which, under the guidance of Bishop Nathaniel Seidel, they were led to the new chapel of their building. Its dedication ended the opening services.

There is no stated cost of the structure, but Jordan has compiled a list of contributors of money, labor, and materials made between June, 1776, and June, 1779, which amounts to one thousand pounds.

Outwardly the elevation of the building followed the pattern set by the first Brother's House, which was occupied by the single sisters at the time of the erection of the Widows' House. Again, native limestone was used, and the correlation of the structure with its neighboring buildings across the courtyard in the Bell House group had been taken into consideration by use of red brick arches over each of the windows. Like those buildings, the structure was two stories high (instead of the three originally planned), with an upper and lower attic under a gable roof rather than the usual gambrel roof. Like the first Brothers' House, the lower register of dormers were gable roofed, but the upper register consisted of long shed dormers spaced between those on the lower level. Unifying the design was a coved plaster cornice, forming an easy transition from roof to façade along the longitudinal side of the building. At some unknown date the original roof hip or jerkin at the western end of the building was removed, as was that on the *Gemeinhaus*, creating the plain gable roof that crowns each building today.[126] On the exterior, evidence of this former hip is noticeable by the line at which the original limestone stops under the window of the upper attic. Above this, pargetted brick clearly indicates the later addition and change in form.

Howland feels that there were five windows on the western or gable end of the structure.[127] If one compares this building with the master craftsman's drawing for the Sun Inn, the second and fourth windows, which are blind, were probably so originally

124. Considering the Moravian tradition for planned settlements, it seems highly improbable that the site was chosen by chance when the site later occupied by the 1773 addition of the Sisters' House was decided against, for the erection of the Widows' House created the fourth side of the Bell House Square. Thus, even today, despite the square being bisected by heavily trafficked Church Street, one gets a visual relationship between the Bell House group and the Widows' House, especially from the vantage point of the second floor central window of the Widows' House looking across and over Church Street to the Bell House court. Moreover, the length of the Widows' House, i.e. seventy-eight feet, is exactly equal to the space between the eastern end of the *Gemeinhaus* at the west side of the court and the western side of the Sister's House on the east side of the court. Thus, the planned open square tradition was carried forth. Unfortunately, the eastern addition to the Widow's House of 1794–95, as well as the 1773 addition to the Sister's House, have tended to destroy the unity of the concept as has the interjection of Church Street.

125. Howland, "Moravian Buildings in Bethlehem," p. 255.

126. Framing in the upper attic still indicates the position of the hip running originally to the coupled chimneys from the east wall.

127. Howland, "Moravian Buildings in Bethlehem," p. 256.

since the above mentioned drawing also indicates several blind openings on the eastern end of that structure.

The plan, as erected, contains a central hall with a stairway at the far side of a lateral hall that runs lengthwise through the building at the approximate center of the structure. Howland presumes that the four quarters created by these dividing halls were originally single large rooms or apartments. If one is to judge from the 1760 plan for the building, this need not necessarily be so since this earlier plan indicates a division of rooms into smaller units similar to those found in the building today.[128]

Although the lack of open fireplaces on this plan indicates the use of tile stoves for heating, openings similar to fireplaces were incorported into the halls of the structure when it was finally built.[129] Opening into the lateral hall there is a small opening in the back of each chimney. The Moravian schoolhouse in Berks County had a similar arrangement for heating the classrooms from the central corridor in order not to disturb classes.

The great brick chimneys with brick web between are a major exterior architectural feature of the structure. In the upper attic the two chimneys are corbelled toward one another as they near the roof. Beneath the roof peak they are brought together by an arch that forms the continuing web between the two chimneys above the roof line.

Of all structures in Moravian Bethlehem, the Widows' House is the building that has perhaps changed the least (Plate 45). In contrast, the Bell House group has had much of its window sash, frames, and hardware replaced over the years. In the Widows' House, however, with the exception of the papering of the walls and a few added partitions, there is a great sense of the building as it was originally built. The stairs in the structure have the same characteristic monumental relationship of riser to

tread found in many other Moravian buildings. The newel posts are square with rounded edges, and the handrail is very functionally rounded to fit the curve of the hand. The steep flight from the lower to the upper attic is of special interest for its excellent workmanship. With no handrail, the beauty of the stair lies in the solid oak stringers with the same grooved line along each side of the rounded corners, which one can find on the newel posts of the stair on the floor below. There are no risers, but only treads rabbited into stringers. The building also has its original thick, wide, red pine floor boards. In addition, many of the doors retain their original long strap hinges and box locks.

While the lower attic served as the *Schlafsaal* where all the members of the "choir" slept, the rooms on the lower floors were used for work and daily living. It is probable that the *Saal* on the second floor was set aside for love feast or worship purposes.[130]

It was very likely to provide room for a new chapel that the twenty foot addition was started to the east of the structure in May 1794. This was finished the following year. There is obvious physical evidence on the exterior of the building to show this addition. The stonework, for example, is not as carefully laid up as that of the earlier part of the building. Howland feels that the long lateral hall originally terminated with an entrance door to the chapel in the new addition at the east end of the building. He goes on to suggest that the chapel originally only took two thirds of the new area, basing this hypothesis upon the fact that the north-

128. Undoubtedly there are certain additions in partitioning that are later than the original structure. Howland bases his premise of single large rooms in each quarter of the building upon the relatively thin, hollow sound of these partitions as against the more solid and thicker partitions of the hall walls. This would not necessarily indicate that these partitions were not original but only that they are not load-bearing.

129. Various reasons put forth for the existence of these include heating the hall, but these openings are too small to permit much of a fire, and moreover they are placed exactly opposite each other which is contrary to good planning if they were to be used for heating purposes.

130. Two sources offer proof that there was a chapel in the original part of the building. The first, *Bethlehemisches Diarium*, October 12, 1768:

At two o'clock in the afternoon the love feast was held in the dormitory. The service began by the trombone playing the following verse from the little tower:
"God bless your arrival and your entrance as well."
The brethren and sisters of the helpers' conference had been invited . . . after the guests had left the whole choir proceeded to the meeting room for its consecration.

The "dormitory" translates from *Schlafsaal* while "meeting room" translates from *Versammlungssaal*. The little tower referred to is probably the tower on the Bell House. The second source, Jordan, "Historical Sketch," *Transactions*, IV, is as follows:

A memorable day in the history of the Widows' House was the visit of General Washington on the afternoon of July 25, 1782, while en route to Newburg, New York. He called with Brother Ettwein, was introduced to Sister Werwing, the deaconess, inspected the chapel, and was served with cake and wine, and in May 1791 his friend, Alexander Hamilton, was also an interested visitor.

45. Undated Nineteenth-Century Photograph of the Bethlehem Widows' House as Erected

ernmost hall partition is thin and the south one is slightly thicker and seems to be of stone. If this is true, the new meeting place for chapel would have been not much larger than one of the rooms in the earlier part of the building.

The basement of this section indicates that there were other reasons for constructing the addition. There are two brick-paved rooms in the basement, the one on the north containing a brick oven while the one to the south, which opens into the garden, was presumably used as a laundry, since there is a fireplace tall enough to hold a large kettle in the center of the east wall. Moreover, this is flanked by two brick fire boxes with small kettles originally built into them, although only the one to the right is still in place. These spaces were simply washing, dyeing, or soap-making utility areas. There is no connection between this basement and the one under the original house, which has a large arched twelve-foot opening under the entrance hall, the original use of which is not known.

In 1889 an annex measuring forty by eighty feet was built to the south of the original building, connected to the original structure by a short wing or "hyphen" of wood. Although of stone, this late-nineteenth-century addition has architecturally little in common with the eighteenth-century structure. Fortunately, the latter is large enough to visually negate this unfortunate rear addition from the Church Street side.

GIRLS' BOARDING SCHOOL ("OLD CASTLE")
(*Erected, 1790; Demolished, 1856*)

Like the *Kinderanstalt*, relatively little is known about the structure erected in 1790 to serve as a boarding school for the young ladies of the community. In a sense, the structure was archaic when erected, for the contacts during the Revolution and the many non-Germanic visitors whom that strife brought to flood Bethlehem streets and buildings drastically affected the community; the village, although still confined to Moravian dwellers, was never again as insular and continental in outward character as it had once been. The Central Moravian Church of 1806, in its quasi-Federal character, is perhaps the most significant evidence that the Germanic mode of building in eighteenth-century Bethlehem was a thing of the past. It is, therefore, possible to say that the girls' boarding school structure was probably the last example of Bethlehem's non-Georgian tradition

in building. Thereafter Bethlehem slowly accepted the overwhelming influences of architecture in the English tradition, and the character of the continental origins of the Moravians disappeared in the structures that they now erected.

The Moravians always had a compelling interest in the education of the youth of their community and particularly that of the young girls. As early as May 4, 1742, the Countess Benigna, daughter of Count Nicholas von Zinzendorf, had established a school for girls in Germantown, Pennsylvania. It continued to operate there until it was reorganized at Bethlehem on January 5, 1749.[131] Headquarters were then established in the building later known as the Bell House, which had been finished in October, 1746, supposedly to provide housing for married couples.

The girls' school stayed in this building until it outgrew its quarters. After permission was obtained from the Bethlehem Elders' Conference on August 16, 1789, as well as permission of the Session of the General Conference of Elders on August 22, which stated that the monies for the erection of any new structure must come from the school account, not out of the congregational treasury, and that the building should be stone rather than frame, two sites were taken into consideration. One was that of the cow stable and log kitchen belonging to the Single Sisters' House, but when the single sisters promised to remove the two buildings and generally to improve the area of their garden, it was decided to place the school on the hill behind the Bell House.

Approval of the plans for the new building were obtained on September 11, 1789. These called for a one-story building of stone, forty by fifty feet in size, consisting of four large rooms on the main floor, with a basement under the entire building to be used as a refectory and cellar and an attic for a dormitory that would accommodate a maximum of forty to fifty students. The building was originally planned to be gable-roofed, similar to that of the eastern extension of the Single Sisters' House, but in November, 1789, it was decided to cap the building with a gambrel so that shorter timbers could be used to span the roof and to make available even more room under the eave line of the building[132] (Plate 46).

131. Levering, *Bethlehem*, p. 533.
132. *Ibid.*, p. 549. Members of the building committee consisted of the following: Joseph Horsefield; John Christian Hesse; John Heckewelder; John Andrew Heubner, principal; James Cruckscheinck, steward and bookkeeper; John Schropp, warden; and Paul Meunster, warden of the village.

After collecting building materials through that fall and winter, the cornerstone was laid with appropriate ceremony on May 2, 1790, by the new school principal, Jacob van Vleck. Although finished by the autumn of 1790, it was not occupied until spring of the following year, when on April 12 the building was formally dedicated. It served as the boarding school until approximately 1816 when it became a private dwelling for the next forty years. In 1856 it was demolished to make way for the new brick parochial school building that still stands on the spot.

Reproductions of watercolors in Levering give clues to the outward appearance of the building and the possible interior plan.[133] Typical of Moravian architecture and Germanic architecture in general, there were two attic levels under the gambrel roof (with an even rhythm of fenestration on both short-end elevations consisting of two windows per floor flanking the end chimneys). The gambrel roof contained an upper and lower register of shed-roofed dormers of which there were three in the lower register on either side of the building with alternating dormers of the same type in the upper register, two to a side. There was an even rhythm of five windows across the south façade, and since the ground slopes considerably at this point, there was presumably an equal number of full windows below these with a door in the center leading from the building, giving this south exposure a full two-story appearance.[134]

The north side shows a one-story building with a central doorway flanked by evenly spaced windows, two to a side. There are two asymmetrically placed smaller windows shown to the left of the doorway. Such asymmetry is unusual. One or both of these may be later additions, though the interior stair arrangement may have dictated the placing of one or both of these windows. Such openings could have provided light on landings where the stair would have returned upon itself if it were arranged in this manner. To judge from the exterior relationship of the entrance door and the placing of the windows on the north façade, one probably entered the building

133. The original was executed in 1892. *Ibid.*, p. 550.

134. The exact arrangement of the lower level of the building on this south side is unknown because of the placement of certain outbuildings in these watercolors which hide the first floor of that side of the structure.

46. Undated Nineteenth-Century Watercolor of the Bethlehem Girls' Boarding School Building, Referred to as the "Old Castle"

at a level between the basement and the main floor, descending a series of steps to the basement or ascending a short flight to the main floor before continuing to the attic dormitory.

Although visitors marveled at the large store structures of the Bethlehem community, it was the industry of the settlement which offered the most lasting impression. As history relegates the common man to oblivion, so has been the fate of most smaller structures of Bethlehem. While each of the large "choir" houses and other structures of importance gathered its surrounding share of small buildings, it was the industrial community clustering on the banks of Monocacy Creek which gave birth to an impressive score of small buildings, mostly wooden but sometimes even of stone, wherein the raw materials were turned into finished products for the use of Bethlehemites and dwellers of the satellite Moravian communities in the vicinity. The rough wooden walls of the small log structures, and the red tile, thatch, or shingled roofs undoubtedly gave the community a texture and color that it lacks today, despite the large concentration of surviving eighteenth-century structures (Plate 47).

OTHER BUILDINGS, INDUSTRIES, AND CRAFTS

The basis for Bethlehem's industrial community was established in Herrnhut, its precedent in Europe. Unlike most Germans coming to Pennsylvania in the eighteenth century, many Moravians had an artisan's calling rather than a background in an agrarian economy. As early as 1747, according to a letter of Cammerhof's on file at the Unitas Archive in Herrnhut, there were as many as thirty-two different types of crafts and industries active in Bethlehem.

By 1756 a memorandum of Boehler's for a conference in Bethlehem states that this number had grown to forty. These are outlined in a diaconal report as follows:

1	Tanner	11	Waggoner
2	Tawer	12	Nailsmith
3	Dyer	13	Blacksmith
4	Clothmaker	14	Tinker and Tinman
5	Clothdresser	15	Locksmith
6	Woolcomber	16	Gunstockmaker
7	Wool Sorter	17	Turner
8	Butcher	18	Cabinetmaker
9	Millwright	19	Cooper
10	Hatmaker	20	Saddletreemaker
21	Saddler	32	Clockmaker
22	Shoemaker	33	Glover and Breeches-maker
23	Tailor		
24	Weaver	34	Baker
25	Stockingmaker	35	Brewer
26	Maker of gold lace, etc.	36	Bookbinder
27	Soapmaker	37	Meal Grinder
28	Mason	38	Sawyer
29	Carpenter	39	Fuller
30	Brickmaker	40	Oil Presser
31	Potter		

[The following were later added:]

41	Organ Builder	45	Tar Refiner [at Gnadenhuetten]
42	Silversmith		
43	Saltpeter worker	46	Innkeeper
44	Forge [artisan]	47	Silkworm Culture [attendant]

Those industries and crafts originally located in some of the "choir" buildings swiftly outgrew their quarters on Church Street, and an industrial quarter, localized along the banks of the Monocacy, gradually arose in the community. By 1758 there were approximately fourteen industrial buildings in Bethlehem.[135]

The first building for the blacksmith shop was begun on January 1, 1743.[136] This was a log structure that the smithy occupied until 1750, when a newer building of stone was erected immediately to the east and slightly south of the original structure.[137] The second building was a one-story stone structure forty-six by twenty-five feet in dimension which was shared by the locksmith and the nailmaker. An extension was added in 1761, and a second story was added to the entire structure in 1763.[138] The nailsmith's shop in this structure was short-lived, however, for in 1754 the nailsmith moved to the log building that first had been used by the potter. This was a small building only seventeen by twelve in size and presumably one story.

In this building the tinsmith also had his shop in 1759, where he made such finished articles as sprinkling cans, coffeepots, candlesticks, lamps, little

135. Erbe, *Herrnhuter Kolonie*, p. 62. Moravians were trained from fairly early youth for certain trades and crafts. Youths were assigned to the type of work they desired and for which it was felt they had the most aptitude.
136. Congregational Diary of Bethlehem, Moravian Archives, p. 1.
137. This then was one of the row of structures that grew up on the western side of *Der Platz* and helped define the open space on this boundary.
138. Levering, *Bethlehem*, p. 390. It was in this building that the first wrought iron nails were made at Bethlehem.

47. Undated Nineteenth-Century Oil of the Monocacy Creek Industrial Community of Bethlehem, showing the Oil Mill, Water Works, Pottery, Tannery, and Other Buildings

bowls, sieves, noodle funnels, sausage makers, coffee mills, children's spoons, beer mugs, nutmeg graters, whistles, lanterns, etc.

In 1750, when the smithy moved from his log building of 1743, the hattery of the community was established in the earlier wooden structure. This building was fifty by eighteen feet in dimension, and the hatters shared the building with the wagon maker's shop. This building had originally been much smaller than the above-mentioned dimensions, but had been lengthened in February, 1745, when the press for wagons, carts, and plows became so great that the industry had to enlarge.[139]

In 1742 a small log house had been erected for the carpenters and joiners. This structure was connected to the first log cooper's shop, and together they measured approximately sixteen by twenty-four feet. According to inventories of the carpenter's shop of the 'sixties and 'seventies, he worked with pine, walnut, oak, poplar, and cherry. In 1774, for example, he had seven walnut chairs in his shop; in 1780 a new commode or low chest of drawers and one arm chair. The following year a footstool appears on the inventory, and in 1785 one commode with headpiece, eight chairs, and one grandfather chair can be noted. In 1780 the inventory also lists two coffins. The wood-turners jointly occupied this 1743 log structure until 1754 when they moved into the ground floor of the Single Brother's House. It was in this portion of the shop that the many spinning wheels that were in constant demand throughout the surrounding countryside were made.[140]

A tile kiln had been early set up in the vicinity of Bethlehem, north of the community proper, on Monocacy Creek and near the "Burnside House." It was at this kiln that the red pottery roof tiles were made that once covered many of the buildings of Bethlehem. The first tile stove in Bethlehem was set up in October 1742, in the chapel of the *Gemeinhaus*. These tiles had not been made in Bethlehem but in the kiln of Ludwig Heubner, the potter "in the swamp."[141]

When Heubner moved to Bethlehem to become the potter, he built his first oven and wheel for turning out pottery in a small structure, probably of log,

between the log buildings occupied by the carpenter's and cooper's shops. In 1749 a more pretentious pottery building of stone was erected which was thirty-two by thirty-five feet in dimension. Brick ovens or clay kilns were usually built beneath their own shed roof shelter. The nailsmithy took over the first pottery building in 1754.[142] It was presumably this building that was converted into a dwelling for widowers in 1758.

According to Erbe, the pottery enjoyed unexcelled renown and was well known as far away as Philadelphia. It shared the facilities of this stone building with the stocking weaving industry.

The inventories of many of the crafts and industries throw considerable light on the character of the community and the commodities available to its inhabitants. The tobacco factory, for example, carried not only ordinary snuff but "good snuff." Also listed were smoking tobacco, fine chewing tobacco, and coarse chewing tobacco, including small rolls from Philadelphia and Virginia Twist.

The saddle maker's shop in the Single Brothers' House lists all sorts of saddle trimmings, plush, brass trimmings, silk trimmings, cord whip sticks, leathers of all types, ladies' saddles, saddle trees, and ladies' pouches. Both the instrument maker's inventory, signed by the secretary and musical director, Emmanuel Nitschmann, and that of the organ builders of Nazareth and Bethlehem, Klemm and Tannenberger, list many types of planes and saws for the making of musical instruments.

The glovemaker's shop in the decade of the 1770's not only lists many pairs of gloves but a number of pairs of pants, and the shop used such materials as sheep skins, deer skins, "brain skins," linen, and silk.

The glazier's and painter's inventories of the 1770's and 1780's give clues to the paint colors used in eighteenth-century Moravian Bethlehem; whiting and lampblack were available, as well as English red and Venetian red. Moreover, they carried both a supply of small leaded windows and stock size window lights, ranging from eight by ten inches and nine by seven inches, down to six by eight inches.

Through the inventory of the bookbindery, we learn that they used marbleized end papers and covered their books with sheepskins and red leather. Among the books, bound or unbound, included in

139. Congregational Diary of Bethlehem, Moravian Archives. The shop at that time shared the building with the smithy.
140. Levering, *Bethlehem*, p. 389.
141. *Ibid.*, p. 145. "In the swamp" refers to Faulkner's Swamp, an area south of Bethlehem.

142. This is undoubtedly the building that had its roof blown off in a storm of April 2, 1745, as recorded in the Congregational Diary of Bethlehem, Moravian Archives, 1745, p. 9.

the inventories of 1772 are *London Sermons*, *Berlin Speeches*, *Pennsylvania Addresses*, two volumes of *Extractions on Matthew*, both German and English spelling books, and catechisms and New Testaments in English and in German.

Unfortunately little is known of the physical aspects of the all-important sawmill in Bethlehem. According to the Congregational Diary, a Walt Becker arrived from Menessing on May 4, 1744, to erect the sawmill, which he actually began on May 26.[143] By June 23, it apparently had already broken down because "Gotthard D——" is noted as having come to repair it.[144] It is further noted in the same Diary that the mill was working again by June 26. The exact life span of this first sawmill in Bethlehem is not known, but it is known that in January, 1756, steps were taken to start a sawmill again in Bethlehem to replace those then in use at the Moravian settlements of Gnadenhuetten and Christiansbrunn. The masons started on June 9 and the building was completed in September. On September 21 the sawing of lumber began again in Bethlehem.

According to Erbe the dimensions of the first building were sixty-six by twenty feet and it was valued at three hundred pounds.[145] Although no known representations of the first sawmill exist, a stereoptical picture in the archives of Historic Bethlehem, Inc., shows what could possibly be the second mill. This is a wooden, clapboarded structure of rather nondescript architectural character.

Several other undated manuscript documents exist in the archives which throw some light on the operation of the sawmill and some other buildings in its vicinity. Whether these refer to the first mill or the second mill is not known. One manuscript notes that the sawmill referred to was sixty-six feet long and twenty feet in breadth. This is a plan of a mill wheel showing the water wheel and two notations on where the wagon or carriage was to stand. This was probably for the first mill. A second manuscript shows a similar plan including an elevation that indicates the relationship of the water wheel to the various gears of the machinery and the placement of the vertical straight saw that shaped the boards.[146]

While the erection of the tannery and the grist and fulling mills was important to the economic growth of Bethlehem, the sawmill was also badly needed. After it was in operation, it contributed perhaps more than any other industry to the growth of the community. One need only to tour the twenty or more eighteenth-century Moravian buildings still extant in Bethlehem to note its usefulness to the growing community—the random width floor boards, the single width doors with exterior leafs in herringbone pattern, the solid stair stringers, and the chamfered posts. It is further known that eighteenth-century Bethlehem also supported a wheelwright, a cartwright, a joiner's shop, a carpenter's shop, a cabinetmaker's shop, and a spinning wheel maker's shop. All would have drawn upon the sawmill for materials. Considering its importance, it is somewhat surprising that information concerning the building is scant. This can perhaps be attributed to the existence of other mills in the vicinity upon which Moravians depended until they opened their own.

Other archival material shows a plan "for a dwelling house to be added to the sawmill beside the old dwelling house." This was a new building to be erected at an unknown date, to be about twenty-two feet along the front and twenty-five feet deep. Its elevations and plans indicate that the various rooms were to be heated by tile stoves and that a large open fireplace was to be placed in the kitchen area in the center of the house.

143. *Ibid.*, p. 3.
144. *Ibid.* This probably refers to the same Gotthard Demuth who was in Bethlehem in April, 1743, to assist Henry Antes with the erection of the Grist Mill. Demuth was then living in Germantown, Pennsylvania.
145. The year 1745 saw the erection of another sawmill in Gnadenthal and one at Gnadenhuetten, each connected with a cornmill. The mill at Gnadenthal is known to have been 44 by 42 feet and to have been valued at £230, with an overshot wheel in contrast to the undershot wheel "otherwise customary in the province."

146. The eighteenth-century book of illustrations of various mechanical mill buildings by Johann Scopp, signed by John Arbo, is one of the few volumes of an engineering and architectural nature in the Bethlehem Moravian Archives known to have been in the possession of an eighteenth-century Moravian in Bethlehem. Arbo is known to have been the warden of the Brother's House as early as 1762, which office he held until his death on December 11, 1772.

IV

OTHER MORAVIAN COMMUNITIES

———•◆•———

I. PENNSYLVANIA

NAZARETH

The Moravians had come to know the Reverend George Whitefield in Georgia, and it was he who had offered Peter Boehler and other Moravians in that settlement their passage to Philadelphia when they decided to leave Georgia because of hostilities with the Spaniards and their initial lack of success with the natives. Whitefield was interested in building a school for Negro children in Pennsylvania and purchased five thousand acres at the "Forks of the Delaware" from William Allen, of Philadelphia, on May 3, 1740. It was to this "Barony of Nazareth," so-called because of certain seignioral prerogatives of the baronies of Great Britain and Ireland associated with the land through deed from William Penn, that Whitefield invited his Moravian religious confreres to erect a building for him[1] (Plate 48). A

1. Joseph Mortimer Levering, *A History of Bethlehem, Pennsylvania 1741–1892, With Some Account of Its Founders and Their Early Activity in America* (Bethlehem, 1903), p. 44.

cabin of unhewn logs was under roof by June, 1740, to replace the first rude shelter with which the Moravians had protected themselves from the elements. Because of rain and difficulty with building materials and hired workmen, September saw this stone building only to the doorsills. The hired workmen were discharged, and by permission of Whitefield's agents, the brethren erected a two-story hewn timber house in which to pass the winter. When Whitefield returned to Philadelphia in November, 1740, Boehler journeyed to the city to report conditions in Nazareth and found Whitefield distant, apparently disposed to resent the Moravians because of a previous difference of opinion on the doctrine of predestination with the Moravian missionary Hagen while in Georgia. Renewing the discussion with Boehler, Whitefield met the same difference of opinion and as a result angrily ordered the Moravians to leave his land. It was at this juncture that Nathaniel Irish, a miller of Saucon Creek, offered to act as agent to acquire the five hundred acres of William Allen's land for the Moravians which became the site of Bethlehem.

48. Undated Nineteenth-Century Photograph of the Whitefield Structure in Nazareth, Pennsylvania, Intended as a School for Negro Children

With the death of his business manager, William Seward, Whitefield was sufficiently financially embarrassed that he was unable to continue his Nazareth plans, and on July 15, 1741, the purchase of the tract was announced by the Moravian church in Europe. The fact that Nazareth was closely tied with Bethlehem during the eighteenth century is amply borne out by all accounts. A 1757 map of Old Nazareth clearly indicates the rather developed settlement that existed in the area at that date.[2]

The heart of Old Nazareth was laid out as an irregular square, east and somewhat south of where New Nazareth was laid out, in 1771, around a central open plaza. Surrounding Old Nazareth were a series of fields, dotted here and there by isolated structures distinct from the cluster of buildings that comprised the center of the community. Old Nazareth itself consisted of a *Gemeinhaus*, fifty-six by thirty-six feet, flanked to the south by a structure noted as a *Familienhaus*, forty by thirty feet (which was removed by 1771), with its separate small kitchen building, sixteen by sixteen feet. A long narrow cow stable, one hundred and seventeen by twenty-seven feet, formed the southern side of the quadrangle of buildings, southeast and perpendicular to the previously mentioned structures. This had been newly erected at that date (1775). A similarly long barn, one hundred and fifty-six by twenty four and probably one of the earliest structures erected at the site to judge from its reference in 1775 as the "Old Barn," formed the eastern side of the quadrangle at a slightly obtuse angle from the *Gemeinhaus* (Plate 49). Another barn, one hundred and thirty by thirty-four feet, formed the northeastern side of the space, while northwest of it stood a small bakery and weaver's house, forty by thirty feet. Both of these bordered the north side of the road to Easton. Behind the "Old Barn," a series of small buildings housed a washhouse, thirty-eight by twenty-six feet (removed by 1771); a pigsty, sixteen by twelve feet; milkhouse, thirty-two by eighteen feet; smithy, twenty-one by twenty feet; and the smithy's coal shed, fifteen by fourteen feet. While some of these structures may have been of stone, it can be rather safely presumed that most of them were of squared log construction similar to the Married Brother's House and water tower, which stood on the site of the present Central Moravian Church in Bethlehem.

Behind the *Gemeinhaus* a vegetable garden was planted, and immediately south of it was a kitchen garden. A flax house, fifteen by fourteen feet, stood somewhat removed and south of the smithy, in the corner of a large meadow running south and east of the settlement.[3]

Surrounding the garden meadow and settlement was a large tract of approximately a hundred acres, thirty-nine of which were fallow in May of 1775, the remainder being seeded. North of the settlement was a large orchard, on the upper edge of which was the nursery, the stone structure begun by George Whitefield.[4] This was the building that Whitefield had invited the Moravians to Nazareth from Savannah to help finish. In 1757 this two-story double-attic gambrel-roofed structure looked over a garden to the north and was flanked to the south on one side by two smaller wooden structures noted as a kitchen and a Widows' House.[5] An avenue of trees ran northwest-southeast between the garden and the nursery building, while north of the garden and orchard, a second large area of almost a hundred acres had about thirty-three acres newly seeded, about fifty-five fallow, and the remainder in meadow and woodland.

In the midst of a third large cleared area northwest of the nursery and orchard stood the Manor House, a limestone brick-trimmed building approximately ninety-eight feet long and forty-six feet wide, erected in 1755 by the Moravians as a residence for Count Zinzendorf. This grand double-entrance structure was two stories high with a jerkin-headed gambrel roof covering its upper and lower attic.[6] To the south, a two-hundred-foot area or green gave the structure the setting that still distinguishes the building today. North of the building was a formal garden area, two hundred by four hundred feet, divided into eight plots, two by two. Due east of the south side of the residence, in a wood on the edge of a cleared area, was the burial ground. Isolated in a gully formed by a spring stood a building where roof tiles were made. This was due south of the

2. The writer is indebted to Walter Peters of Nazareth for prints of this 1757 and later eighteenth-century maps made by Byron M. Schmidt for Warren L. Boeing, Sr., who presented the copies to the Nazareth Moravian Historical Society, January 26, 1939.

3. All of these structures have disappeared. One obviously aged structure still extant in the general area may be the children's house.

4. This structure was enlarged in the nineteenth century and certain heavy Victorian trim was added to unify the two parts.

5. One of these is probably the small stone building known today as the Grey Cottage.

6. Zinzendorf returned to Germany and never lived to return to the New World Palace the Moravians had built for him. During the nineteenth century and earlier part of the twentieth century, it served as a boys' school. Today it is an apartment house.

49. Sketch by Rufus Grider of Some of the Structures in Old Nazareth, 1854

residence, close to the road to Bethlehem, southwest of the square and in the heart of Old Nazareth.

On January 19, 1771, a plan for a new town was laid out, centered slightly south and east of the residence later known as "Nazareth Hall." Two streets, sixty feet wide intersected at a square, two hundred feet wide and three hundred and forty feet long, with a water tank in the center. A secondary east-west street, forty feet wide, ran parallel and south to that intersecting the square. Sixty-nine lots were proposed and forty-four were laid out. Each was seventy feet wide and varied in length from one hundred and forty to two hundred and ten feet. A lot, two hundred and eighty by one hundred and seventy, immediately east of Nazareth Hall and on the square facing it, was given over for the future erection of a Single Sisters' House. Lots 28 and 29

were given over for the immediate erection of a log inn. Also during 1771, Peter Worbass, carpenter, built a stone house on Lot 38, while Jacob Christ, hatter, also built a stone building on Lot 23. The next year, Lot 22 was given over to the erection of a stone community store building. The village saw no more major buildings constructed that year, but 1773 witnessed the erection of a Single Brothers' House, a stone building erected on Lot 35, while nailsmith Melchior Christ, baker Wenzel Bernhardt, and harness maker August Schloeser built houses on Lots 24, 27, and 37, respectively. Bernhardt's building was log, Christ's and Schloeser's were structures of unknown materials. John Leisher, sexton, and Dr. Joseph Otto added to the growth of the community in 1774 by erecting stone dwellings on Lots 26 and 33. No further building is recorded until 1779 when

John Beitel, brooch maker, added another structure to the village on Lot 25. This seems to have started a second flurry of building activity, and the following structures were erected in Nazareth between 1780 and 1784:

1780—John Michael Kern,
      potter   Lot 30   Stone structure
1781—Jacob Eyerle,
      blacksmith   Lot 31   Stone structure
1781—William Henry,
      gunsmith   Lot 32   Stone structure
1782—John Dealing,
      silversmith   Lot 34   Stone structure
1782—Azarias Smith,
      shopkeeper   Lot 4   Unknown material
1782—John Martin Schenk,
      mason   Lot 3   Stone structure
1783—Christopher Myretetus
                  Lot 5   Stone structure
1783—Christian Giersch
                  Lot 20   Stone structure
1783—John Godfrey Belling,
      tanner   Unknown material
1784—Single Sisters' House
                  Lot 2   Stone structure

Most of the stone structures erected were one-and-a-half story buildings of native limestone, with flat brick arches over doors and windows and the same ample proportions to be found in similar structures still extant in Hope, New Jersey (Plate 50). Known exceptions to this were the two-and-a-half story building erected for the Single Brothers' and the larger Single Sisters' House (Plate 51). As if the erection of the large stone building for the single sisters signified the cessation of construction activity in the community, little or no structure of note was erected until after 1790, when Owen Rice built a stone house on Lot 40, and Frederick Schafer erected another next to it on Lot 39, in 1791. Thereafter, building activity seems to have ceased once more until it renewed strength in 1819 with the erection of the principal's residence of "Nazareth Hall,"—a boys' school. But the eighteenth-century Germanic building tradition was broken by this time and the structure erected in 1819 was stylistically in the English Federal tradition. The traditional limestone building with brick-arched windows and doors gave way to construction entirely of brick, thus tolling the death knell of a building tradition characteristic to the community and introducing a new building tradition whose alien roots were couched in the ever-broadening English inheritance of the colonies.

50. Sketch by Rufus Grider of Single Family Residences in Nazareth, 1855

51. Undated Nineteenth-Century Photograph of the Single Sisters' House, Nazareth

The date and the reason for the founding of Lititz have been set forth as December 2, 1742, and an address by Zinzendorf. John George Klein, a farmer, heard Zinzendorf speak in Lancaster and was sufficiently moved by his remarks to allow the erection of a log church on his property in which itinerant Moravian ministers preached from time to time.[7] By September of 1746, as a result of a meeting in Klein's house to consider the erection of a *Gemeinhaus*, Klein donated three and three-quarters acres of his land in an area that is now part of the town. The cellar was dug in November, 1746, and the cornerstone was laid the following March 29, but it was not until May 24, of 1748, that the structure was finally occupied.

The building that was erected was a one-story gambrel-roofed structure with an upper and lower attic and a double row of dormers. The upper slope of the roof had jerkin ends, and two symmetrically placed chimneys pierced the ridge.

From this beginning the Warwick Country Congregation of the Moravian church was founded on February 9, 1749, with eleven members. Within the year, the congregation had increased to thirty-five. When Klein offered his 491-acre farm to Zinzendorf in 1755 for the founding of a church settlement, Zinzendorf's ambition to organize such a town in the area was satisfied and the proposed new town was named Lititz the following year.

The new town was surveyed and laid out in lots on February 9, 1757 (see Plate 7). The plan called for a main street, running southeast by northwest, which took its direction from a stone house that Klein had erected a short time before. According to a map in the Bethlehem Archives dated December, 1759, there were sixty-six lots, in groups of six, with cross alleys between, at the extremities of the town and two groups of eight lots flanking another cross-alley in the center. The latter led to a *Platz* or main square, around the south side of which the church and "choir" buildings for single sisters and single brothers were to be placed, although on this map the central lot was to be the site of the *Gemeinhaus* with a 736-foot-long lot behind it leading to the cemetery. A much more interesting map in the same archive is undated but could be earlier since it concerns

itself with an entirely new town and makes no note of existing structures or surrounding farms. The general plan is essentially as indicated on the dated map, with a long main street, a central square as a focal point for major structures, and a cemetery to one side of the square. On the side opposite the cemetery, a *Gemeinhaus* was to be placed flanked by eight two-story houses, four to a side. These were to face eight similar houses on the opposite side of the main street and a church was to balance the composition of the square opposite the *Gemeinhaus*. From the latter, a "Corpse Road" was to lead to God's Acre, and separate paths for the single sisters and the single brothers were to radiate like spokes to the cemetery from opposite sides of the church. The Single Brothers' House was to stand next to the church on one side, and the Single Sisters' House was to be placed in a similar position on the other side (Plate 52).

The entire town was to occupy nineteen acres, with the exception of the cemetery. The most noteworthy aspect of the plan is a number of openings between groups of houses marked, in translation, "gate." A translation of the latter part of the notes on the map explains this as follows: "N. B. If each house had its yard in back enclosed by a wall, a wall would thus extend around the entire town." Had this plan been carried through, the United States might well have extant today a rare example of a medieval-like walled town on its eastern seaboard. Such protection would have been desirable, for the year 1755 had seen complete destruction of Gnadenhuetten by the Indians, and 1763 saw further Indian massacres and incursions.

The manuscript under discussion gives further insight into plans for the town in the individual structures planned. An elevation for a private dwelling is titled in translation, "A Project for a one-story house. See Ground Plan below," which states further: "In the roof where the bay-window is, a nice small room could be built in the middle of the house."

Of interest also are the double entrance halls and symmetrical plan of four rooms. The note below it states: "If someone wished to go to the expense, and built the kitchen and a cellar in the basement in the middle of the house, *one* chimney could serve for the entire house."

It is very probable that the structures erected for the single brothers and the single sisters were built about the same time. The fact that they were identical, at least as planned, is certain, for a master

7. Mary Augusta Heubener, *A Brief History of Lititz* (Mary Augusta Heubener, 1947), p. 5.

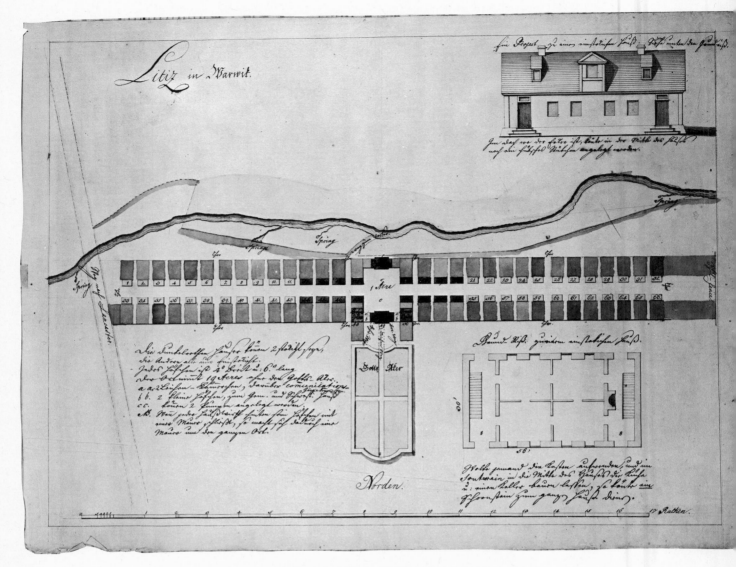

52. Undated Plan of Lititz, Pennsylvania

craftsman's drawing for them exists in the Bethlehem Moravian Archives. This is titled in translation, "Building Plan for Single Brothers' and Single Sisters' house in Lititz, January 6, 1758" (Plate 53).

These interesting proposed structures were architecturally characteristic of the eighteenth-century Moravians in their plan and façade symmetry, their upper and lower attics, and gambrel jerkin-headed roofs with shed dormers. They were to be rather small in scale, thirty-seven by fifty-seven feet. The basement of each was to be divided into four rooms, two to each side of the central hall. To the right, these are simply marked "cellar." Those to the left

were to be a kitchen with corner fireplace and a "kitchen room," probably a larder or preparation area. The cellar stairs were to have twelve-inch treads and eight-inch risers.

The first floor was to be divided in much the same manner as the basement, and tile stoves were to heat each chamber. On the second floor, two more chambers flanked one side, and part of the central hall was given over to a superintendent's room. The remainder of this floor was to be used as a *Saal* or common room. It is noteworthy that tile stoves are indicated in each of the rooms on this floor with the exception of the *Saal*.

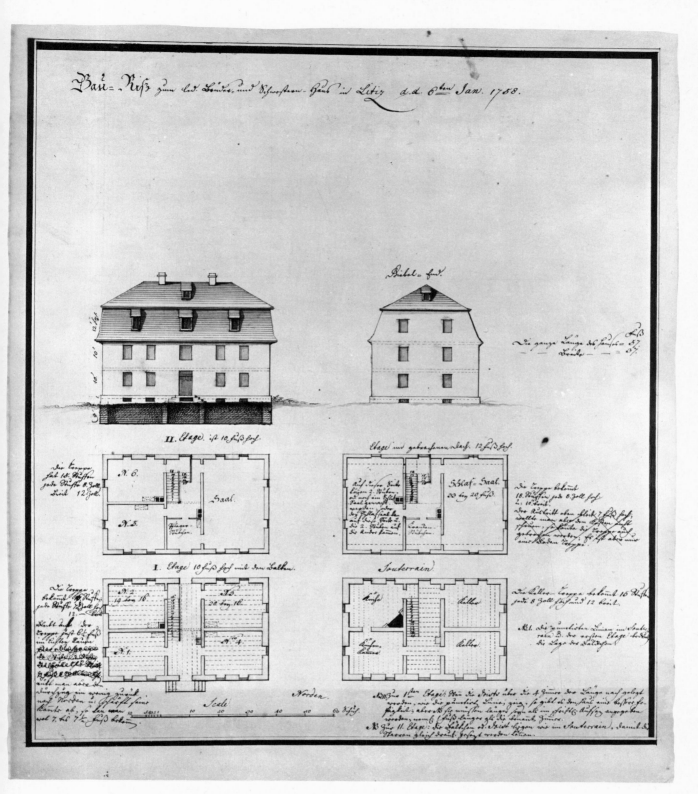

53. Plans of the Single Brothers' House and the Single Sisters' House, Lititz, dated 1758

The lower attic, also unheated, was intended for dormitory space, and an area equal in size to the superintendent's room below, and similarly placed, is noted as a sick room. The first and second floors were each to be ten feet high and the lower attic twelve feet.

Of particular interest is the attention given to good construction, as noted at the bottom of the sheet. The translation reads as follows: "N.B. For the first floor, if the joists are laid lengthwise over the four rooms, as the dotted lines show, it will give a better firmness to the house; but N.B. they must be longer than was stated in the written description, namely 1 ft. longer than the rooms signified. N.B. For the second floor, the beams or joists lie as in the basement, so that the rafters can immediately be set on them."

The church that was erected between the Single Sisters' House and the Single Brothers' House in 1787 was heavily remodeled in 1857 and seriously damaged by fire several years ago. To this building was added a second *Gemeinhaus* in 1763 which later became the church parsonage. The Single Brothers' House subsequently became the Sunday school building for the church, and the Single Sisters' House eventually came into use as a school building of Linden Hall Junior College. At least five other Moravian structures of eighteenth-century vintage survive in the town today, and perhaps more. The village ceased to be a closed, church-owned town in 1855; after that time lots were sold for $50.00 each, and the community was opened for development by non-Moravians.

CHRISTIANSBRUNN

Henry Antes, who seems to have masterminded many of the building activities of the Moravians, removed to Bethlehem from his homestead and mill in Frederick Township in June, 1745. A series of planned settlements were commenced on the Nazareth land north of Bethlehem at about the same time. Gnadenthal (Valley of Mercy) was started with the erection of a log house on January 13, and a larger house is known to have been commenced in September of the same year. The site of Zinzendorf's residence was planned at that time for a central village to be called Gnadenhoeh, and Gnadenstadt, another settlement, was planned north and east of it. The planned agricultural and dairy center of the

area, officially named Christiansbrunn (Christian's Spring) on August 4, 1749, in honor of Zinzendorf's son, Christian Renatus, was organized as a colony of single men on December 17 of that year. Christiansbrunn was located just off the Nazareth-Bethlehem road near Gnadenthal and was the southernmost settlement of the group of villages planned at that time for the Nazareth land.

All buildings in the above mentioned settlements have completely disappeared, save for the brewery, the only stone structure erected in Christiansbrunn. The beer for which Bethlehem's Sun Inn was so well known was brewed in this building. Despite the disappearance of the other buildings, the physical aspect of Christiansbrunn is known from nineteenth-century glass negatives in the Bethlehem archives. The structures were arranged in an "L" shape and, with the exception of the brewery, were constructed of wood (Plate 54). Closest to the road was a two-story gambrel-roofed chapel, with clapboarded sides and red tiled roof (Plate 55). The fenestration of the end elevation was evenly spaced across that side of the building, two windows per floor, with a single small window in the upper attic. Windows in the lower floor had nine over six lights, while those on the upper levels, including the two shed-roofed dormers in the lower slope of the gambrel roof, had six over six lights. To judge from the single chimney piercing the ridge at the left side of the building as one faced the back, the hall and stairs must have been on the opposite side of the structure, with at least the lower floor consisting of one large room.

Attached to the above building, but at a somewhat lower elevation because of the downward slope of the land from the road to the creek, was the laborers' *Gemeinhaus*. This was architecturally similiar and larger than the adjoining building, with three shed-roofed dormers on the lower slope of the gambrel roof and three windows per floor spaced across the long façade vertically in line with them. Like all other structures in the community, the building was set on a foundation of native limestone, in which the stereotomy was well developed, especially at the corners where the more regularly cut stones simulated a quasi-quoin effect. The building that, with the stone brewery, formed the stem of the "L," was similar to the first structure discussed but longer in proportion and, because of the topography, appeared as a one-and-a-half-story structure on the street side and a two-and-a-half-story building on the creek side. This was the Single Brothers' House. Archi-

54. Undated Nineteenth-Century Photograph of Christiansbrunn, Pennsylvania, with Stone Brewery Building in the Left Foreground

55. Undated Nineteenth-Century Photograph of the Chapel (Right) and the *Gemeinhaus* (Left), Christiansbrunn

tecturally, it had all the characteristics of the two buildings previously mentioned, i.e., gambrel-tiled roof, shed dormers, clapboarded sides, and stone foundation. On the road side, the rather pleasing façade presented two six-over-six-light windows flanking a central door (Plate 56). The latter had a six-light inset in the top of the door leaf. Three shed dormers were aligned vertically with the openings below. To the south or Bethlehem side of the structure, a wooden lean-to on a stone foundation, may or may not have been original, although it appears in all the later photographs.

The opposite façade repeated the arrangement of openings and windows of the street façade, save that the entrance was located in what would have been the basement level as viewed from the side and, like the boys' school building in Salem, North Carolina, the foundation stone rose to a full-story height on that side. The hall and stair area were obviously on center in the structure with the rooms on either side, probably arranged two to a side.

The brewery was aligned with the above building on its south side. The upper or road façade presented a door, with over lights and two six-over-six-light windows with brick lintels, from left to right as one faced the building. Unlike the other structures, it had a gable roof that was unrelieved by dormers, with two chimneys at each end of the ridge. On the downhill or creek side, the façade presented an even rhythm of openings and windows, indicating a vertical circulation area located to one side of the structure.

Aside from a collection of small sheds, one other building deserves mention, and this was a small gable-roofed structure north and east of the complex already discussed, which served as the cobbler shop in the community. Reminiscent of some of the earliest private dwellings in Salem, the building was clapboarded with vertical siding in the gable end. Windows were six-over-six-light and the door was placed to one side of the building (the same side as the chimney), possibly indicating that the interior might have been a single room. Such spaces were often divided, however, by a vertical molding-edged board partition such as Franklin describes in his paper on the Germans.

The life of Christiansbrunn as an organized community was short. It was closed on April 1, 1796. Blaming intemperance "to a deplorable extent," Levering says: "This was the most prominent evil in the declining establishment of the single men at *Christiansbrunn*, which finally sank into decadence that became hopeless."[8] After this date, the farm and more important industries were put in the charge of more competent men, and "several of the deteriorated bachelors were given a mere asylum there under watchful restraint." Thus, the excellence of the product that made the settlement noteworthy finally caused its abandonment and eventually its consignment to other uses.

OLEY AND NAIN

The fact that the Moravians were active throughout Pennsylvania is attested by the continual entries in the Bethlehem Diary referring to new buildings and settlements at different locations. As early as 1752, the Moravians had at least thirty-five sites in the Pennsylvania colony where at least a schoolhouse was functioning. During the 1745–46 period, there are at least twelve diary entries relating to school buildings at at least seven different locations. How many of these structures survive is not known. One, however, deserves note and this is the Moravian schoolhouse built in the Oley Valley, west of Reading, in what is now Berks County, probably in the late 1740's. Unfortunately, this structure fell into ruin within the last decade and has now completely disappeared.

Architecturally the construction of the building determined its interest. Not only was it half-timber, but it made use of wattle and daub like buildings at Ephrata instead of the more commonly found brick nogging. A sketch of the structure, made in 1855 by Rufus A. Grider, a Bethlehem artist, showed the building with a pent roof between first and second floors, completely encircling the building. Fenestration used the familiar six-over-six-light windows irregularly placed across the façades of the structure to accommodate the framing timbers. The apex of each gable was sheathed by vertical boards, as late as 1855, and the expanse of the roof was broken only by the massive central chimney. The entire structure was approximately forty-one by thirty-one feet.

In plan, the central door gave on a hall that was flanked by two rooms of about equal size to a side. Of special interest were the two large fireplaces that faced each other across the wide central hall. Openings from the back of each of these allowed the ad-

8. Levering, *Bethlehem*, p. 540.

56. Undated Nineteenth-Century Photograph of the Single Brothers' Choir Building, Christiansbrunn

57. Photograph of the Log Indian Chapel as It Appeared in Bethlehem, 1866

joining rooms to be heated by iron or tile stoves, thus providing heat where needed but allowing the fires to be fueled without disturbing the occupants of the rooms.

A settlement that also deserves passing mention is the Indian village of Nain, which was situated at an unknown site within the present confines of West Bethlehem. The site is known to have been selected on January 9, 1758, but it was not until October 18 of the same year that we learn of the dedication of the chapel to serve this community of Christianized Indians. The village was destined to be short-lived; it was closed by government order in November, 1763, because of Indian troubles in the neighborhood and the unfortunate association of some of the inhabitants of Nain with various nearby incidents. It is interesting to note that two years later the log structures of Nain were sold at public auction, and six of them, including the chapel, were dismantled and moved to Bethlehem and re-erected on the south side of Market Street (Plate 57). These were gradually destroyed until only one remains, disguised in stucco, on Heckewelder Street.

The latter structure gives evidence of the small scale of these buildings. To judge from old photographs, the chapel differed from the private houses only in having an extra window to one side of its main door which balanced two others on the opposite side of the door. All the structures were one and one-half stories, with central chimneys of ample proportions, much like the Lick-Boner House of Salem in North Carolina.

Further insight into the far-flung settlements in the Moravian story can be gained through the reconstructed village of Schoenbrunn in the Tuscarawas Valley of Ohio. It was to this valley that the Moravian missionaries David Zeisberger and John Heckewelder of Bethlehem led a group of Christianized Indians. Schoenbrunn was laid out in a "T" plan with a log *Gemeinsaal* at the head of the "T," flanked by a log school and sixteen log houses that were used as dwellings for the Indians. Subsequent villages were established in Ohio by the Moravians at Salem, Gnadenhuetten, New Schoenbrunn and Goshen, all situated along the Tuscarawas River below New Philadelphia.

II. NEW JERSEY

HOPE

Hope, New Jersey, had its beginnings when Anna Abigail and Samuel Green sold their thousand-acre farm to the Moravians. The Greens had become acquainted with the Moravians through the missionaries who frequently passed in the area and stayed with them. The actual purchase of the farm was arranged through the Reverend Nathaniel Seidel on March 7, 1769. With the removal of Peter Worbass and his family to the tract the same year, settlement had begun.[9]

Worbass is known to have erected a log house, similar to that of the Greens, which was also log. Both structures were undoubtedly small buildings, probably typical of the house plan used by Germanic settlers of the area, i.e., a *Küche* or hall-kitchen with fireplace and *Kammer* on the first floor, and *Stube*, a single large room, on the second floor.

Typical of the Moravians, the scheme was to make this settlement as self-sufficient as possible and as soon as possible. Hence, Hans Christian Christiansen, designer of Bethlehem's water works, was asked to work with Philip Maifel, a master mason, and Joseph Grotz, a master carpenter, on an income-producing flour mill. By 1770, this was completed and operating. Although most of the structure was given over to the milling operation, at least one floor and an area around a large fireplace on the lowest level were put to other uses. The latter reputedly served as a smithy and the former as living quarters for the miller. The mill had four sets of stones and a thousand-foot-long mill race that was cut through slate, at times to the depth of twenty-two feet. This three-and-a-half-story limestone structure still stands as the largest building in the village.

Shortly after the erection of the mill, two farms were developed, one south of the village and another to the north. The latter farm is known to have had two log or frame barns, since disappeared, in an area set aside as a cow-yard. It is further known that a third barn constructed of stone, which still stands,

9. Unless otherwise noted, all information concerning Hope derives from *The Moravian Contribution to the Town of Hope, New Jersey*, published by the Hope Historical Society in 1955. The writer is indebted to Mrs. F. C. Van Horn, president of the society at the time a field trip was made to Hope, for making the source material available.

was added shortly thereafter and that a stone house was erected in 1775 on this tract. The house, which also still stands, bears out the typical *Küche-Stube-Kammer* house plan, with a fenestration rhythm of window, door, window, window across the façade (Plate 58). One window and the door gave light to the *Küche*, while the other two lighted the larger *Kammer*. In the upstairs *Stube*, a window in each of the gable ends of the house lighted the single room. In the upper attic, light and ventilation were similarly arranged. Red brick arches over the windows carried on the characteristic Moravian approach to exterior architecture, although one finds limestone window arches in the village also.

Bricks for arches, chimneys, and other uses came from the brick and lime kilns located slightly north and west of the settlement. It was Stephen Nicholas, kiln operator and builder, who was responsible for the second stone house erected in the village. This house undoubtedly followed a plan similar to that just described. It still stands, changed and enlarged, on what is now Hickory Street.

Greenland was the name finally adopted for the community in May, 1770, by Christian Gregor, John Loretz, and Hans Christian de Schweinitz, when these members of the Provincial Helper's Conference visited from Bethlehem. With the naming of the community, the village seems to have prospered. In 1771 a small building of wood was erected to serve as the community store. This was managed by Frederick Leinbach, who had already been alloted four lots of his own near the mill. Shortly thereafter a cemetery, *Gottes Acker*, was laid out on a ridge southwest of the town. After the community was recognized and named by the church, however, the site of the cemetery was moved from the ridge to a site closer to the road that ran southwest from the community.

In 1773 three major structures were added to the community. What must have been a half-timbered building was erected for use as a tannery near the stream southwest of the mill. Frederick Blun was the tanner in charge. Above the mill, a distillery and brewery building was erected at about the same time. Little is known of this structure, save that it was at least two stories high, since it is known that living quarters were situated on an upper floor and that the lower-level windows had iron bars.

58. Twentieth-Century Photograph of Two-Story Single Family House at Hope, New Jersey

Finally, 1773 also witnessed the erection of the community inn and its outbuildings. Of prime interest is the fact that a room or *Saal* in the building served as the community's church for eight years. Where services had been held before this time is unknown, but commonly they were held in private houses. Even in 1773, the community was small; only nineteen persons were scattered throughout fifteen buildings. It must have impressed the Moravian church leaders with a sense of stability, however, since authority was shortly given to make it an *Orts Gemeine* or regular closed church-community. It was surveyed by J. W. Golgosky on November 25, 1774, and a plan was laid out. In a decision by lot, the name was then changed from Greenland to Hope on February 8, 1775.

No new structures are recorded until 1776, when Adolph Hartman erected a dwelling and smithy, and Mr. Leinbach built a new stone store building, with living quarters above the store, just east of the earlier one. There is the possibility that several private dwelling houses were erected about this time, but there is apparently no definite record of them.

The War for Independence naturally affected the community, and it was not until 1780 that a new industry can be noted. This was housed in a building erected along the mill race and was the first of two sawmills subsequently built in the community. Heretofore, the Moravians at Hope had relied on an outside source to supply their cut-lumber needs.

Finally, a *Gemeinhaus* was begun approximately twelve years after the Moravians began the Greenland, now Hope, experiment. The cornerstone was laid on April 2, 1781, and the structure was dedicated November 8, 1782. This building, which now serves as a bank, was a two-and-a-half-story structure in the familiar grey native limestone used for all stone buildings in the community. It had six very large windows on the second floor and four on the first, with two wide entrance doors, one for men and one for women. These gave on a hall with the wide and ample staircase to the *Saal*, characteristic of Moravian buildings. The first floor contained an apartment for the pastor and a room used as a boys' school.

The decade of the 1780's saw considerable industrial development in the community. John Schenk, a nailsmith, opened a shop in 1782, and the next year, Lewis Moeller, a potter from Salem, North Carolina, erected a building near the tannery to produce his wares. The same year, the inn apparently was discontinued, and the building became a girls' school run by the single sisters.

Building continued with a dwelling for J. Hartman which was erected in 1785; and in the same year, John Weinland built a combination saddle shop and dwelling. In 1787 a stone wagon shop was erected by Mr. Koenig. This may be the structure still standing behind the flour mill. Mr. Colver, storekeeper, built a stone dwelling, and another went up for Mr. Whitesell, who was assistant at the sawmill. William Hessler opened a linen-weaving shop in 1788; and in 1790, a potash industry was added to the lengthening list of industries in the community. An oil mill was set up in the lower part of the sawmill in 1791, and in that same year Mr. Ricksecker started clothmaking and dyeing and at least three more buildings are known to have been erected. The population of Hope, which had reached a peak of 100 in the village and 47 in the surrounding area in 1790, then began to decline, and by 1799 only 84 of the 147 remained.

The last major Moravian building to be erected in Hope was built for the Single Sisters' Choir in 1796 and dedicated on April 11 of that year. The single sisters occupied the structure on July 8, and the boarding school for girls was opened in it on August 1. Situated across the street from the *Gemeinhaus*, and slightly south of it, the original building was of the same native limestone as the *Gemeinhaus*. It was two stories high, with a characteristic upper and lower attic under the gable roof, limestone arches over the windows, and two windows per floor on the gable end, with the exception of a single window in the upper attic. This building comprised only the southern end of the present structure. The present northern addition may have been added to house a school for boys, known to have been opened on November 16, 1796, in this structure. Investigating members of the Provincial Helper's Conference, visiting Hope in 1799, recorded eight empty houses and the abandoned girls school.

The Moravian church in Europe had always contributed to the maintenance of Hope. Zinzendorf's death and the accompanying complex financial problems, the decline in population, the subsequent increase in economic instability, and unsettled conditions in Europe have all been noted as reasons contributing to the abandonment of Hope by the Moravians. Whatever the reasons, the Moravians agreed to sell Hope to Nicholas Kramer and Abraham Horn of Northampton County, Pennsylvania, on September 22, 1807. The total acreage was about fifteen thousand, and the selling price was $48,000. At a last service on Easter, April 17, 1808, the congregation was declared terminated; and the various members were relocated in other Moravian centers, such as Nazareth, Bethlehem, and Salem, North Carolina.

III. NORTH CAROLINA

WACHOVIA

In 1749 the British Parliament passed an act that recognized the Unitas Fratrum as "an ancient Protestant Episcopal Church" and granted it privileges enjoyed only by the Church of England in the English colonies. Shortly thereafter, the governing board of the Unity of the Brethren decided to start a new settlement in North Carolina and sent Bishop Augustus Gottlieb Spangenberg, in the company of other Bethlehemites, to survey acreage belonging to John, Earl of Granville. On August 7, 1753, the Earl conveyed 98,985 acres to the Moravians in nineteen separate deeds. *Der Nord Carolina Land Und Colonie Establissement* was formed to finance the enterprise and the name Wachovia or *Wachau* was given to the land, after the name of an estate of the Zinzendorf family in southern Austria.[10]

Fifteen men were picked to make the settlement trip to Wachovia; eleven were to remain and four were to return to Pennsylvania to serve as advisors and guides for future settlers. Bernard Adam Grube and Jacob Loesch, both ministers, were chosen to lead the group, and the latter was also to act in the capacity of business manager. Most of the remainder of the party were chosen from Christiansbrunn, from among those who were skilled as shoemaker, carpenter, cooper, millwright, tanner, tailor, surgeon, baker, farmer, etc., to help insure success for the venture.

The group left Bethlehem on October 8, 1753, and, after a laborious trip, took over an empty one-room log hut on November 17. This hut, abandoned by a squatter, was the beginning of Bethabara.

BETHABARA

The name Bethabara, or House of Passage, itself indicates that the Moravians perhaps never looked on their first settlement in North Carolina as a permanent venture, although none of the source material alludes to this point of view. However the brethren thought of their settlement, they wasted no time in starting to work, as their diary indicates:

Nov. 19th, Monday. After morning prayers the axes and hatchets were sharpened, and other tools made ready for use. . . . We began to build a bake-oven, so that we might again have bread, of which we have had little lately. Our food has been largely pumpkin broth and mush, which has agreed with us very well.

The Brn. Nathanael and Jocob Loesch measured off eight acres of land, which is to be cleared at once, so that wheat can be sown. Others began to gather the dead wood, and build bonfires. The grindstone was set up, a cooper's bench and wash-trough made. The Brn. Gottlob, Nathanael, and Grube laid a floor of clapboards in our cabin, for the better protection of our goods. In the evening Br. Grube held singstunde (Hour of Song) and evening prayer.[11]

To judge from diary entries, the brethren, like most settlers, looked to the clearing of land, the sowing of seed, and the purchase of animal stock before much thought was given to buildings. "Dec. 19th. We are not to undertake any building just yet, but push the clearing of land, that as soon as possible we may be able to eat our own bread."[12] Early in 1755 plans were finally made for a cornmill, and trees are noted as having been felled for it. This was, therefore, presumably a log structure like many of the first industrial structures in Bethlehem, as pegged timber structures required considerably more shaping, joining, and other exacting carpentry.

Further note is made on January 3 that several of the brethren built a stable and others sawed and

10. Adelaide Fries, *The Road to Salem* (Chapel Hill, 1944), pp. 44, 53. See also Chester Davis, *Hidden Seed and Harvest: A History of the Moravians* (Winston-Salem, 1959), p. 40.

11. E. M. Eller, *The Houses of Peace* (2nd ed.; Winston-Salem, 1952), p. 84.

12. *Ibid.*, p. 86. All subsequent quotes from the diaries have been taken from Eller, Part III. Note: *The Records of the Moravians in North Carolina*, translated and edited by Adelaide L. Fries, and published by the State Department of Archives and History at Raleigh, North Carolina, make available the day-to-day recordings of the Moravian settlers in North Carolina as noted in diaries now in the archives of Southern Province of the Moravian Church in America.

planed clapboards, both clues to the growth of the community and to the methods of construction. Shortly thereafter, January 7, ground was cleared and a small dwelling staked off "near the spring." The next day, the felling of logs for the new house was started, but further work on the building was delayed in deference to further preparation of land for the planting of wheat. Construction on the cabin, intended primarily to house the many guests the Moravians had, was presumably resumed immediately after the planting, for not long after this one notes that the cabin was completed in two days time—"of wide rails laid like logs, and has a small fireplace, so that in case of need we can lodge [at one time] two sick guests." Thus the community began; orchards were planted, roads laid out, and fences set.

By May 22 we know that a two-story Single Brothers' House was well under way, for the diary notes: "Today we finished laying the floor in the second story of our new house. Br. Nitschmann has helped with it all this week, and has also made a table for our assembly room."

The fact that a smithy was in operation is evidenced by an entry of July 22 that "a so-called Dunkard or Bearded Man came to the smithy." Earlier note had been made that "Two Brethren made nails to fasten the boards on the mill dam." By mid-September we know that a mill, suggested above, is under construction. "September 17. Work at the mill continues. Today the frame was raised, and we sang several verses to the Saviour as we laid the foundation of the building in His name, placing our names under the sill at the southeast corner."

In November, 1755, seven married couples, ten single men, and five wagon drivers arrived from the North. The men were lodged in either the original hut or a later dwelling and the married people on the first floor of the apparently unfinished Brothers' House. Partitions were made at that time of tent cloth and later replaced by boarding.

An entry for February, 1756, tells us that construction continued on the mill, the length of time involved in its construction leading one to assume that this was a stone rather than a log structure. One notes for the first time that a *Gemeinhaus* was under construction, as well as a tailor shop, and that "Boards were made; stones hauled for a pottery . . . a wash house for the Sisters begun; candles, shingles and bedsteads made. . . ."

By March 5 the *Gemeinhaus* was sufficiently finished to allow the married people to move into it, freeing the now completed Single Brothers' House

for occupancy by members of this group. At the same period in 1756, the erection of a sawmill occupied much attention and the potter's shop was finished. Indian unrest in the neighborhood had led to the erection of a palisade around the settlement, the mill, and the cemetery. The protective fence around the settlement was irregular in shape and took advantage of the walls of several houses to form part of the barrier. There were at least twelve structures inside the stockade and several others nearby. In addition to the main gate, a secondary gate on the southwest side opened onto a path leading to "God's Acre."

The *Gemeinhaus* was to the right of the main gate as one entered the stockaded area and the Single Brothers' House was apparently directly across from it. Scattered around the compound were about twelve other buildings, at least six of which were dwellings. Others probably contained some of the crafts then known to exist in the settlement, such as the shoeshop on the southwest side of the compound near the second gate.

According to Adelaide Fries,[13] the stockaded mill during the period of the Indian unrest in 1755–56 had a row of eight log cabins near it which had been erected by refugees, the back walls of the cabins forming one side of the palisade, while the other three sides were built of boards sawed at the mill.

Bethabara continued to prosper during the latter part of the eighteenth century, eventually containing all the crafts and industry buildings associated with Moravian "place congregations," whether they were in Pennsylvania, New Jersey, North Carolina, or elsewhere, the concentration of residential and trade buildings comprising a village that was surrounded by farms. With the founding of Salem, as chief center of the Moravian Wachovia tract in 1766, Bethabara's star slowly but surely diminished. Today, it is situated in the outer suburbs of Winston-Salem. The original stockade is gone, as are all of the village structures, save one or two small stone buildings, now much changed, which were probably the original pottery and brewery of the settlement. The one outstanding monument to this once busy center which still remains is the church, consecrated November 28, 1788, at a time when Salem had already completely overshadowed its earlier neighbor.

As shown in an early drawing in the Wachovia Historical Society Museum, the stone walls were pargetted and marked off in an ashlar design reminiscent of the practices associated with the opening

13. Fries, *Road to Salem*, p. 75.

[113]

years of the nineteenth century. The building alternated two fully arched windows and doors on the side now facing the highway, with two arched windows on the gable end, similar single windows being repeated above the first floor on that side. At the opposite end of the gable roof, an octagonal bell tower, with concave conical roof topped by weather vane, crowned the peak. Immediately adjacent to this gable end of the structure, a slightly smaller gable-roofed section continued, with four flat-arched windows evenly spaced across what is now the street façade, the characteristic use of red brick that helps make Moravian architecture colorful and distinctive.

BETHANIA

Three miles from Bethabara, the site of the second North Carolina "place congregation" was chosen on June 12, 1759, by Spangenberg, his wife, and several of the brethren. The establishment of this second village was proposed by Michael Hauser, Sr., who had fled to the stockaded mill area during the period of Indian unrest and chose not to return to his isolated farm. According to Fries, the site picked was on the road that passed by the mill at a place called Black Walnut Bottom.[14] By June 30 lots had been laid out and the name Bethania or Bethany had been chosen for the town. Three other Moravian families joined the Hauser family to start the settlement, and the congregation was organized on April 13, 1760.

Papers relating to Bethania are relatively few in the Southern Province Archives of the church, but they do include a plan dated 1766 and references to a *Gemeinhaus* and a general store. The present church dates from 1809 and to the author's knowledge, no eighteenth-century structures of the community survive in the present village.

FRIEDBERG, FRIEDLAND, AND HOPE

These communities were the three "country congregations" established by the Moravians in the eighteenth century in North Carolina and are but three of the many such establishments set up by Moravians in other parts of the colonies and abroad. They consisted of little more than a series of farms surrounding a meeting house.

14. *Ibid.*, p. 78.

The Friedberg Society was organized on February 4, 1770, mostly by families from Maryland and Pennsylvania. The congregation was organized in April of 1773, and the first church was consecrated March 12, 1788. This was subsequently replaced by a second building in 1827.[15]

Friedland was settled by families from Broadway Plantation, now Waldoboro, Maine. They were Palatines who had not originally been members of the Moravian church but were formally organized as a "country congregation" on September 3, 1780. A church building existing at the site was erected as late as 1847.

Hope, the third North Carolina Moravian "country congregation" was organized as a society by English-speaking settlers mainly from the earlier Carroll's Manor, Maryland, in November, 1776, and the congregation was organized in August of 1780. The major portion of the few items relating to Hope in the Salem Moravian Archives are from the nineteenth century.

SALEM

Active planning of what was to be the central town of Wachovia commenced upon the arrival of Frederic William Marshall in 1764. Marshall had been appointed *Oeconomous* or chief executive of the new town by church authorities in Germany. After several months of searching, a favorable site was located on February 14, 1765, on a ridge about six miles from Bethabara. A plan with a central square, drawn in Europe, called for the main structures to be grouped around it with streets radiating like spokes of a wheel from the square. This was unsuitable for the site chosen, and it was Marshall who guided the development of the final plan. Correspondence between John Ettwein and Marshall, who was then in Pennsylvania, sheds light on the care Moravians gave to the planning of their towns and, at times, the conflict between formal plans and utilitarian ideas. In a letter from Ettwein to Marshall dated August 6, 1765, this is especially clear: ". . . Br. Reuter's idea of a straight street through the town and your idea that one should not sacrifice convenience to appearance can readily be reconciled. Whether the long street, on leaving the town, con-

15. North Carolina Historical Records Survey, *Guide to the Manuscripts in the Moravian Church in America, Southern Province* (Raleigh, 1942), p. 34.

tinues or turns right or left, is of little moment; the way to the lower entrance of the town will probably be able to run straight for a long course, after Br. Reuter looks for and finds the right line. . . ."

And in another Ettwein letter to Marshall of November 20, 1765:

Regarding the plan of the town, we in the Conference are agreed how it should be. (Br. Reuter will give you his thoughts on your letter separately.) Regarding the Square, we all thought it too long; because none but two-story houses will be built on the Square, the place in the middle is made to appear so much larger than if three- or four-story houses were built around it. Besides, if it were shorter it would be more even and level. It is not only for lack of lime that we do not wish to build high houses, but I do not regard it as advisable because of the high wind-storms in this country. Last summer many large, strong trees were broken off on the Salem ridge. . . .[16]

The actual construction of the community began on January 6, 1766. "Monday, a dozen Brethren partly from Bethania, partly from Bethabara, took a wagon and went to the new town site where in the afternoon they cut down the trees on the place where the first house was to stand, singing as they worked. . . ."[17] The plan actually laid out ran a main street along the crest of the ridge that formed the heart of the site, with secondary streets parallel to it on both sides. Cross streets were placed at regular intervals creating a gridiron plan for the town. The central square, which was to be the heart of the village, was eventually chosen on this high ground only after thoughtful deliberation involving many months.

Appropriate ceremonies attended the laying of the foundation stone for the first house on the main street on June 6. Local stone that could be conveniently broken to proper size was used, and the pieces were laid in clay. Because of the scarcity of lime for mortar, this method of foundation construction was adopted, and walls were built thick for strength. At the suggestion of Marshall, half-timber construction was recommended for the superstructure chiefly because of the lack of a sawmill and the expense of hauling wood from Bethabara. Heavy timbers were used for the frame work, the spaces between being filled with hand-split lath wrapped in a mixture of straw and clay to form a cylinder of the proper size. These were then slipped into the grooved sides of the framing and pressed down to create a solid wall the thickness of the framing. Although comparable to brick nogging in warmth, the durability of such "dutch bisquits" left something to be desired, and as signs of washing out later appeared, a coating of lime-plaster or the application of clapboards helped solve the problem. Since the Moravians started making bricks in Salem as early as the late summer of 1766, only the earliest structures erected were half-timbered with mud and straw between, and the more durable brick early replaced that method of filling the spaces between the framing members.

Such was the method of construction of the Single Brothers' House, one of the earliest large structures to be erected in the community. Although the foundation stone was laid in 1768, the building was not consecrated until December 27, 1769. The essentially medieval half-timber construction that was adopted as the building system for the structure spaced the upright timbers of the framing two to three feet apart, with diagonal bracing placed where needed. The interstices were filled with brick nogging. The square façade was developed with a system of three evenly spaced six-over-six-light windows, a typical door with overlights, followed by two more windows. The second floor fenestration repeated the first, a six-over-six-light window replacing the door of the first floor. Above the second floor, the gable roof covered an upper and lower attic. On the gable end, three windows were evenly spaced on the first and second floors. The lower attic had two six-over-six-light windows spaced between the end and middle windows of the second floor, and a smaller nine-light window lit the upper attic near the peak of the gable.

The entire structure sat on a foundation of local stone, with small cellar windows spaced under the windows of the first and second floors. A stoop, with steps on both the uphill and downhill sides, gave access to the main door. Because of the nature of the construction, a pent eave girdled the structure above the first floor to protect the exterior walls from the rigors of wet or freezing weather.

In 1786 a fifty-three-foot brick addition was made to the structure on the downhill side (Plate 59), which continued the foundation line of the earlier building. The entrance door off the square was at

16. Both extracts quoted in a letter from Frank L. Horton, director of research, Old Salem, Inc., Winston-Salem, to the writer, dated December 24, 1959. Br. Reuter referred to in the letters was Christian Gottlieb Reuter, surveyor and architect of some of Salem's earliest buildings.

17. Eller, *Houses of Peace*, p. 107.

59. Undated Nineteenth-Century Photograph of the Single Brothers' House, Salem, North Carolina, the 1769 Half-Timber Structure to the Right and the 1786 Brick Addition to the Left

that end of the addition closest to the earlier structure. This was followed by four evenly spaced six-over-six-light windows, each with a flat relieving arch similar to that over the door. Windows on the second floor were placed directly above those of the first floor, as well as over the door. The gable roof of the earlier structure was extended, and with the central chimney of the addition, a total of three chimneys, spaced roughly evenly over the mass of both buildings, punctuated the skyline. Foundation walls of the addition were two feet ten inches thick and constructed of local stone.

The basement was divided into two rooms approximately fifteen by thirty-six feet, each with a barrel-vaulted ceiling. Direct access was planned to the outside from the rear of the building. On the first floor, walls were eighteen inches thick between the two-feet-eight-inch windows. The entrance door gave on a ten-foot-wide hall. Perpendicular from it, an eight-foot-wide hall led directly to a *Saal* or common room that was twenty-two and one-half by thirty-five feet. Flanking this access hall were two small rooms. On the second floor a large *Schlafsaal* or dormitory occupied the space devoted to all three of the rooms and the access hall below. The only other room on this floor was a small area created by partitioning the end of the hall opposite the stairs which was twelve by thirteen feet.

The brick addition remained essentially the same before recent restoration but the original half-timbered building was clapboarded in 1825, at which time the pent presumably was removed, architecturally changing the aspect of the building considerably. These pent roofs were seldom renewed when deterioration occurred.

Although small structures continued to be erected, it was not until 1771 that the next major structure in Salem was built. This was the *Gemeindehaus*, erected on the square directly opposite the Brothers' House and consecrated on November 13 of that year.[18] The building is known to have been a large two-story, half-timbered structure with pent eaves,

a gable roof, and an upper and lower attic. It would have had two entrance doors on the main façade with a *Saal* or meeting room probably in the middle of the building. The consecration of this building would have signaled the birth of Salem as a Moravian congregation, touching off the commencement of the Salem Diary. According to Fries the structure was improved during the closing years of the eighteenth century when the pent eaves between the stories were removed, the entire exterior plastered, and the surface marked off in white in an ashlar design to simulate stone. With the growth of the girls' school, the building was destroyed in the first half of the nineteenth century to make way for a larger structure to serve the school.

The year 1771 also saw the erection of the first dwelling to be privately owned in Salem, despite the fact that Salem's *Aufseher Collegium*, the Moravian board that regulated the material affairs of the community, kept close supervision of the business that was transacted within its walls. This was the shop and dwelling of Matthew Miksch, former Bethabara storekeeper, who moved to Salem with his wife and daughter when poor health forced him to relinquish his Bethabara post.

The Miksch house and shop was built directly on the south side of the main street, just north of the square. Of log, its clapboarded street façade was broken by a herringbone-patterned "dutch door," with overlight and hood. To the right of this were a pair of six-over-six-light windows flanked by solid shutters. The north gable end had two windows on the first floor and one in the attic under the gable roof. The south gable was blank save for a small six-light single-sash window in the attic area. A red-tiled roof with gentle kick at the eave topped the structure, and a single central chimney crowned the peak.

As originally erected, the first floor was divided into a kitchen and a larger living room arranged on either side of the central chimney. The latter also served as a salesroom. A later wing to the rear added a *Kammer* or bedroom and part of the attic was finished as a bedroom for Martha Elizabeth, Miksch's daughter. This was heated by a tile stove. The remainder of the attic was used to store and dry-cure leaf tobacco. The sales-sitting room was heated by a five-plate cast-iron stove fired from the kitchen through an opening in the fireplace. Miksch erected a separate log outbuilding around 1782 or 1783. This was also used to store tobacco and to process it into finished products. It was divided into

18. Bethlehem sources refer to the community building in that village as *Gemeinhaus*, which Cassell's dictionary explains as "common, belonging in common to all." The same dictionary defines *Gemeindehaus* as "townhall." This could reflect a change of attitude within the Moravian church, from the strict communal organization of the earlier Bethlehem, which admitted of no private dwellings during its beginning years, to a more relaxed form of church communitarianism as reflected in Salem, a village of large "choir" structures but one in which the private residence was always present.

two rooms, and the smaller of these contained a fireplace.

Another small dwelling erected the next year in Salem was the Anna Catharina House, a small clapboarded structure slightly larger than the Miksch House. As restored by Old Salem, Inc., this little building, now in the garden behind the John Vogler House, was also clapboarded. Its street or east façade presents an a-b-a-a rhythm of window and door openings from left to right: the six-over-six-light windows are framed by single-leaf solid board shutters like the Miksch House. Unlike the Miksch door, no hood or overlights grace the entrance to this building, and the brick chimney that crowns the roof in a slightly off-center position is much more massive in proportion than the Miksch chimney.

Aside from developments above described, it is also known that a school for girls was founded in 1772 and that God's Acre, the cemetery, received its first interment in 1771.

About the same time, thoughts turned to a store building for the community to be erected on Main Street. A proposal in the Salem Archives indicates a building forty-four by sixty feet (Plate 60). The northern or uphill side of the structure was proposed as living quarters for the storekeeper and his family. An eight-foot-wide hall, running front to back through the structure, gave access to the store itself on the left and on the right to three rooms presumably for the storekeeper's use: a front chamber on the street fifteen and one-half by sixteen feet heated by a stove, a middle room nine feet wide, and a kitchen to the rear with open fireplace. On the store side of the building, entrance was planned for the extreme left of the structure as one faced it. The store room itself, thirty by nineteen feet, opened onto two smaller rooms behind with a stair between. Leading from this stair hall, a small wing contained a loading platform and a storage room with shelves, both with an attic area above. On the basement level, various storage rooms were provided for the store, while the residence side of the building, separated from the store on this level by an unbroken wall, contained a laundry room under the kitchen and an all-purpose cellar under the front chamber.

As restored by Old Salem, Inc., the structure has a dormer over the store entrance on the street façade, which could have contained a hoist-pulley at one time. The cream-colored exterior walls are parged and marked off in an ashlar design. As one faces the façade, three nine-over-six-light windows

with arch-headed openings and single leaf solid shutters light the store room, followed by a herring-bone-patterned entrance door. This is followed by two windows similar to the first three, with another door at the extreme right of the façade. The long, low proportions of the building, the small dormer against the expanse of the roof, arched window heads, and herringbone doors give the structure a distinct continental and non-English architectural character.

Like most Moravian towns, Salem had a problem with strangers—visitors and travelers—who stopped in their community because of the assurance of clean accommodations that Moravians offered and the excellent fare they provided. Hence, it is not surprising to learn that Salem, like other Moravian settlements, erected a tavern early, in this instance a frame building that was destroyed in the only major fire suffered by Salem in the eighteenth century. The foundations for a new tavern were begun in January, 1784 (Plate 61). Architecturally, it set the pattern for later construction in the community by being the first structure in the village entirely of brick. This was laid up in Flemish bond. The Germanic arched window heads were used above the six-over-six-light windows; however, the single gable-roofed dormer on the large expanse of the gable roof followed a scale and proportion seen in such earlier structures as the community store. The ample proportions of the structure indicate its Moravian origins, as does the warm but plain simplicity of its interior.

A central hall divided the structure. To the north of this, the gentlemen's room and more elaborately furnished sleeping rooms upstairs denoted a side of the building reserved for affluent visitors; the other half was given over to "publick" rooms and more simply furnished bedrooms. A wing to the rear of the main building housed the kitchen on a lower level. This congenial-looking room, as restored by Old Salem, Inc., has a slate floor, open-beamed ceiling, and two flat-arched fireplace openings side by side at the end opposite the entrance, one containing a bake-oven that is architecturally expressed on the exterior of the wing.

The use of brick and the general plan of the tavern, which was no different from other "ordinaries" of the South with the exception of the kitchen placement, and the plain, almost classic, porch that graces the front of the structure are elements that architecturally tend to cast it in the English tradition of

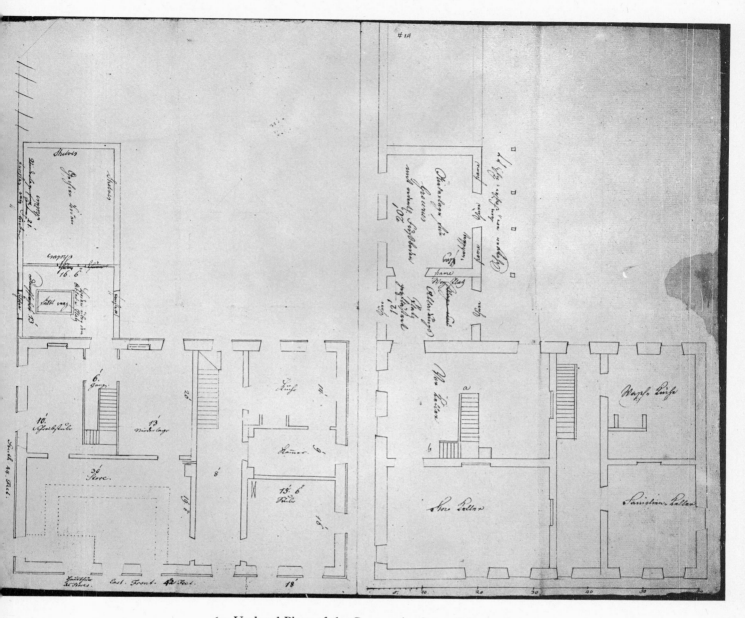

60. Undated Plans of the Community Store, Salem

61. Twentieth-Century Photograph of the Salem Tavern

the colonies rather than the Moravian Germanic building heritage of the town.

By 1780 Salem Square, the planned heart of the village, contained the half-timbered section of the Brothers' House on the northwest corner. Across the square, the *Gemeindehaus*, also half-timbered, faced the Single Brothers' House. At the southwest corner stood Anna Catharina's House, later moved back on the lot when John Vogler built his brick house in 1816. Between Anna Catharina's House and the 1769 Brothers' House stood the community store. In the decade of the 1780's, however, the square was destined to develop considerably. Tycho Nissen erected a small house similar to Anna Catharina's in 1782 at the southeast corner of the square. Between these two structures on the south perimeter of the square, G. Schober erected a one-and-a-half-story dwelling in 1785 across the street from Nissen's, and T. Bagge built a similar dwelling in 1787 across from Anna Catharina's. Major additions to the square were erected in 1786, however, when the single brethren added the brick addition to their house on the west side of the square, and the single sisters erected their lengthy building on its east perimeter next to Nissen's little house.

Following the example set by the new tavern two years before, the single sisters erected a brick structure, two stories high, with upper and lower attic under a red-tiled gable roof. The numerous dormers that now dot the roof may or may not be nineteenth century in origin, but the brick-arched window openings and the favorite herringbone pattern of the three entrance doors architecturally help to carry the continental Moravian character of the building. The building has long served as a dormitory for Salem Academy and College, an outgrowth of the girls' school opened in 1772.

Architecturally, the Lick-Boner House of 1787, erected on Salt Street north and west of the square, is a throwback to the earlier tradition (Plate 62). As restored by Old Salem, Inc., this little red-tile-roofed log structure has all the continental non-English architectural qualities associated with the Moravians and the earliest buildings erected in the community. Its single unshuttered six-over-six-light window on the street façade and its herringbone-patterned "dutch" door with overlight are the types of relatively small voids in the solid expanse of the façade with which one associated the essentially medieval character of the earliest Germanic building in this country, Moravian or not. A massive brick chimney

tops the gable roof on center. A later and slimmer brick chimney abuts the north gable end that is sheathed in finished, butt-jointed boards. A lean-to addition, of the same type of boarding and perhaps later, enlarges the structure and offers a second herringbone-patterned door on the street façade.

The 1790's saw the development of the north side of the square with the erection of the boys' school building in 1794 at the west end of this side of the square, butting on Main Street, and the *Vorsteher* House of 1797 just east of it.

Although a school for boys was started as early as 1771 (in the potter's house) and one for girls in 1772, the building erected in 1794 was the first permanent housing for the boys' school and was designed by the brickmaker Johann Gottlob Krause (Plate 63). The building has all the architectural attributes one associates with the late eighteenth-century Moravian building in Salem. Three stories high, with a center-hall plan, the basement or ground-floor level provided space for a storage cellar, a kitchen, and living quarters for the schoolmaster. The second floor was given over to classroom use, and the third floor provided dormitory space for the students.

The façade facing the square offered a pleasing rhythm of solids and voids across its surfaces. An English type of paneled door replaced the familiar herringbone pattern of earlier doors, but a series of overlights still gave the entrance complex its familiar format and the hall inside its much-needed light. Flanking this were four windows, two to a side, with the characteristic flat-arched opening, six-over-six-light sash and single-leaf solid shutters. The second floor presented five six-over-six-light unshuttered windows spaced over the voids below. From an eave immediately above them, the red-tiled gable roof reached to the peak unbroken by dormers or chimneys, the latter being placed on the ends of the structure.

The foundation of stone, pargetted and marked off in an ashlar design, carried around the building for the full height of the basement level. Brick, laid up in Flemish bond, formed the construction material of all levels above this basement floor.

On the gable end facing the main street, two widely spaced windows similar to those on the main façade punctuated the basement and first floors, while two more, closer spaced, gave light to the dormitory. These were flanked by two exceedingly small windows at this level, single-light over single-light, toward the eave lines. Two circular vent holes at the

62. Twentieth-Century Photograph of the 1787 Lick-Boner House, Salem, as Restored by Old Salem, Inc.

63. Undated Nineteenth-Century Photograph of the 1794 Boys' School, Salem

upper attic level ornamented this façade near the roof peak. Most interestingly, the bricks were laid in a quasi-diagonal Flemish bond pattern between the windows from the dormitory level and the roof peak.

The building became the Wachovia Museum in 1896 and was operated by the Wachovia Historical Society. In 1937 an annex wing was erected to house expanding collections. An early photo of the rear of the structure shows it to have continued the pargetted stone foundation around this side of the building, since the grade level was considerably higher on the side of the structure. The fenestration pattern resembles that of the basement level on the opposite side of the building with a central door flanked by four arch-headed window openings, two to a side. The door opening, however, was positioned between levels to bring it close to grade on the exterior. One entered an intermediate level or landing and descended to the basement or ascended to the classrooms. Above the door opening, an excessively large window area, four-lights high and as wide as the door opening, allowed its arched head to line up horizontally with the arched heads of the flanking windows, bathing the interior circulation area in floods of northern light.

According to plans in the Salem Archives, the *Vorsteher* House that went up in 1797 immediately east of the boys' school building was envisaged originally as a smaller structure than the one we see today. Plans called for a building forty-two by thirty-three feet. The structure was to sit on a stone foundation eighteen inches thick, and a center hall divided this basement level. The hall was flanked by four rooms, two to a side. Two of these were to be vaulted, while one indicates a corner fireplace on an outside wall, an element that helps account for chimneys at gable ends in later Salem Moravian buildings instead of the more characteristic placing of the chimney in the center of the roof. The upper floor was likewise arranged with a central hall flanked by two rooms per side, each side having a tile stove to heat one room and a corner fireplace to heat the adjacent room (Plate 64). The opposite side of the hall mirrored this arrangement. Above the basement level, the Flemish-bonded brick walls rose to the same height and proportion as those of the neighboring boys' school building. Unlike the latter, however, gable-roofed dormers seem to have been provided, although these also, like some other dormers in the community, may be later in origin.

Frederic William Marshall presented the plans for the Home Church of Salem in 1797, and it was finally erected in 1800 (Plate 65). This was planned for the northeast corner of the square next to the *Gemeindehaus*, the gable end directly facing the *Vorsteher* House. Marshall's plan was typical of Moravian church planning in that entrance to the sanctuary was placed on the long side of the building, with the benches to be placed parallel to the length of the structure. A balcony was to be constructed around three sides of the room; access to this balcony was from a stair in the southeast corner of the sanctuary and another stair in the vestibule area which was gained through a second entrance placed on the gable end of the church. The over-all dimension of the structure was to be forty-five by eighty-eight and one-half feet.

The elevation is of interest in that it divides the major elements of the design into almost equal parts (Plate 66). From grade to the eave of the gable roof was to be about twenty-six and one-half feet. The height of the roof was planned to be approximately twenty-seven feet, and the octagonal arcaded tower and attenuated onion dome of the cupola that was to cap the gable end of the edifice was to be approximately twenty-seven feet, with a ten-foot weather vane crowning the spire.

A large clock was planned for the apex of the brick gable façade. Immediately below this was located a large window with a pronounced arched head. Also, on this level of the façade, two very small windows were to flank the central window. Below, three larger windows, with arched heads as pronounced as those above, were to be spaced symmetrically across the façade; the center window had to be shorter to accommodate a gabled hood and an arch-headed door opening.

While the plan of the church is traditionally Moravian in concept, the exterior of the structure seems more English than Germanic in its architectural expression. Knowing that Marshall was the master designer for the structure and that he was apparently above average in education, it is conceivable that he could have made a conscious effort to Anglicize the design. It was Marshall who had insisted that the Salem Diary be kept in English, and it was for the first ten years of its existence. Whatever the reasoning behind the design, Salem Home Church, like Bethlehem's Central Church of about the same time, gives evidence of strong non-Germanic Federal architectural elements in its exterior design, most nota-

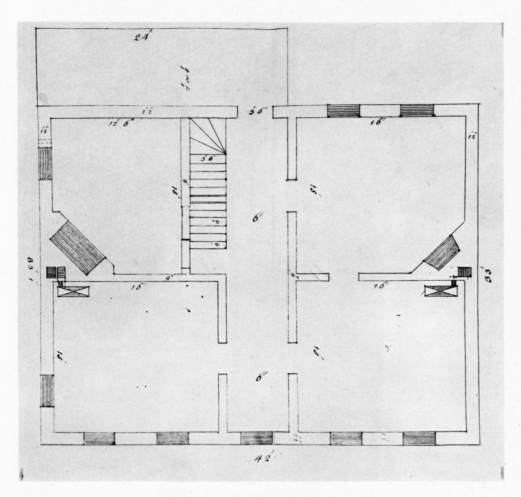

64. Undated Plans of the Salem *Vorsteher* House of 1797

65. Undated Plans of the Home Moravian Church, Salem, Attributed to Frederic
    William Marshall

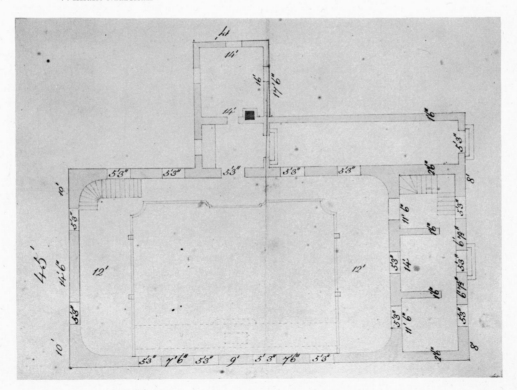

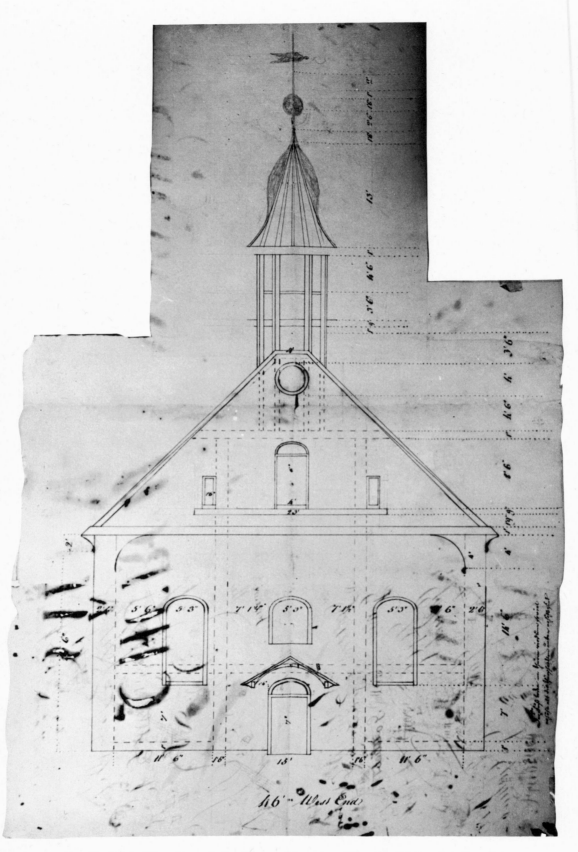

66. Undated Elevation of the Home Moravian Church, Salem, Attributed to Frederic William Marshall

bly in its cupola and especially in the intersecting mullions of its window arches.

A slightly more complicated architectural expression of such arched window openings can be seen in the Christoph Vogler House, also built in 1797. While maintaining its Germanic identity in its general proportions, the flat-arched window openings, the large arched door openings, the pattern of the doors themselves, and the size of the dormer in its relation to the roof expanse all seem to indicate a modifying of the Germanic architectural heritage of Salem.

As the nineteenth century dawned and Salem pro-gressed with the century, this dilution can be easily noted. The John Vogler House, of 1819, is basically a Federal house architecturally speaking, with its large windows, strict symmetry of façade, and slender gable chimneys. The same can be said of most of the private residences erected in Salem in the first two decades of the century. With the Timothy Vogler House of 1832, the exterior architectural expression of Salem seems to have swung almost, if not completely, into the English tradition, despite the fact that interior furnishings continued the brethren's Germanic heritage.

V

MORAVIAN RELATIONSHIP TO THE PENNSYLVANIA DUTCH

—◆·◆·◆—

The Moravians have always been a folk apart to students of Germanic culture in this country for the simple reason that they have been traditionally grouped with the so-called Pennsylvania Dutch, but upon closer investigation they prove to be sufficiently different in aspects of their culture to make this traditional liaison inexact. To the uninitiated, grouping the Moravians with the Amish or Mennonites is obvious. To those who claim a knowledge of these eighteenth-century pietistic Germanic sects, the inability to accept such a general grouping is equally obvious.

As has been stated earlier, the immigration of German-speaking peoples to this country divides itself into three parts, beginning with the late sixteenth-century migration led by Daniel Pastorius from Krefeld to settle what became Germantown, Pennsylvania, now part of Philadelphia. The timber and stone abounding in the area set the exterior architectural expression of the structures these people erected. Hides, wood, and bark probably sufficed for the more costly and unobtainable iron and glass in the earliest buildings. William Penn, in his *Tract of Information and Direction to Such Persons as are*

Inclined to America, recommended a one-story structure, eighteen by thirty feet, with partitions in a T form to create three rooms. This basic house plan can be found in the American colonies wherever German-speaking immigrants settled, and it is also found in surviving houses in German-speaking Europe. The Germanic cabin, as Franklin describes his typical example, consists of the larger common living-sleeping area and the cooking or work area; at times the larger space was divided to lend privacy to the sleeping area.

The second great immigration of German-speaking peoples started about 1709 upon the heels of not only political and religious oppression but a series of natural calamities, such as widespread crop failures and excessive cold weather conditions. These, coupled with Penn's trips to the Rhine-Pfalz to invite persons to his colony, initiated the mass exodus of those early years of the eighteenth century. This group, mistakenly called "Dutch" by the English settlers in Philadelphia because their port of embarkation had usually been Rotterdam, chose to settle on what was then the fringe of civilization west of Philadelphia. Here their first building efforts were characterized by many of the architectural forms to be found in later Germanic building in the colony, whether Moravian or not: basically a two-room *Küche-Stube* plan, usually with a board partition to create a *Kammer* or sleeping area as a third room; squared logs as building material; excessively few and small windows, mostly casement and parchment covered rather than glazed; a steep roof, often with two floor levels under the ridge, which terminated at the eave line by a change in direction creating a gentle kick; a large open fireplace on the inside wall of the *Küche* which placed the chimney near center at the roof peak; a pent roof extension on the eave side or, in a two-story house, circling the structure between the floors; and a general smallness of scale. A structure still standing in 1930 near Landis Store, Pennsylvania, as classified by Edwin C. Brumbaugh, well illustrates this architectural type. When the second generation Germanic immigrant built, he continued to follow the pattern established by the first settlers but substituted stone as his building material rather than using the squared logs of his settler father. Interestingly enough, he retained the encircling pent, originally conceived to protect walls that weathered badly. A good example of this type of structure can be seen in the Miller's House at Muhlbach, whose Germanic interiors have long been installed in the Philadelphia Museum of Art. One other architectural element to be noticed in this building is the presence of flat brick arches over the wall openings, a characteristic to be associated with many stone structures erected by Germanic builders.

Fort Zeller, in nearby Newmanstown, illustrates one more architectural element to be associated with the building efforts of these people and this is the diagonal batten-board door to be seen on the lower level. This structure also has the three-room plan noted elsewhere and is a fine example of the hillside cabin with entrances on more than one level—a building form that one finds rather frequently in the Pennsylvania Dutch counties.

It should be noted that the above cited examples are isolated today, as they were in the eighteenth century, as single structures in the wilderness. Herein lies a key to one of the major differences between the Moravians and the other sects that comprise the Pennsylvania Dutch. While the latter utilized many, if not most, of the architectural vocabulary one notes in Moravian structures, a vocabulary that is really paramount to Germanic vernacular building and not characteristic of any one Germanic group in eighteenth-century Pennsylvania, the isolation of the structures points to the agrarian extraction and milieu of the average Pennsylvania Dutch settler. These people were primarily farmers. They hailed predominantly from the farming districts of the upper Rhine near the borders of France, and the lack of desire on their part to remain in an urban center like Philadelphia well illustrates the strong attraction that the possession of land and the development of a farm had for them. Thus they could continue unhindered their religious practices and also were able to resume a way of life centering on personal ownership. This is amply verified, for example, by a check of street names in some of the larger towns in the Pennsylvania Dutch counties where English names predominate. It is only in the surrounding country that one finds names of universal German provenance.

The Moravians, however, hailed predominantly from southeast Europe, from the area of Bohemia-Moravia, later Czechoslovakia and Saxony. Geographically they were distinct from most other Germanic peoples coming to the colony. They were organized expressly as a group—a church-oriented, church-governed community that directed all of the actions, thinking, and activities of the individual in every facet of daily life while still giving him a freedom within the church framework. Of primary difference is the fact that the Moravians were of a much higher socio-economic origin than most other Germanic settlers in the colony. They had the backing, association, and leadership of not only a religious hierarchy but of the well-disposed nobility as well, chiefly in the form of Count Zinzendorf, his daughter the Countess Benigna, and others of the lesser German nobility. Moreover, the training and background of a majority of the group was of the craftsman class. Through the latter, the Moravians were able to establish, conduct, and develop the centers for their activities in the New World. Through this comes their greatest distinction, "the planned community." While the average Pennsylvania German took himself to the wilderness as a settler to clear the land for himself and his family alone, the Moravians migrated as an organized group and planned as a community before the actual act of settlement transpired. Their architectural contribution relies upon the same vocabulary used by non-Moravian Germanic settlers. It is only through the accent of this architectural vocabulary, chiefly in the communal disposition and relation of structures, that the Moravians can claim an especial distinction.

VI

CONCLUSIONS

———◆•◆———

Although the Moravians emphasized the trades and tradesmen, few names can be associated with the structures that they erected. This may seem strange until one realizes that the Moravians were and always have been a church-oriented missionary group. Church headquarters, then in Herrnhut, Saxony, now East Germany, had to give complete approval of plans at all levels of development, whether they were plans for entire villages or plans for single structures, before work could proceed. The transcendental point of view of the creators of these plans and the general anonymity that surrounds their building efforts in America in the eighteenth century contribute only an embarrassingly scant knowledge of the master craftsmen responsible for planning of these buildings and these communities and especially the association of particular names with specific structures. John Ettwein in Bethlehem and Frederic William Marshall and Christian Gottlieb Reuter in Salem can be designated the masterminds of specific actual planning activities in determining the layout of their respective communities. Ettwein's plan for a new Bethlehem gives ample evidence of his qualities in this direction. Marshall, who was the administrator of the Wachovia lands, drew a street elevation, now in the Salem Archives, to show at what level houses would have to be erected on Salem

Square in order to even the grade of the street from the Single Brothers' House to Reuter's House at the other end of the block. Reuter, who was a surveyor by profession, is responsible for the location of Salem Square in relation to the water supply. The Helpers' Conference minutes of April 8, 1766, record: ". . . concerning Br. Reuter's employ, particularly in Salem: he has been proposed by the Unity's Conference for building inspector. We would like to give him the oversight of laying out the town; building of houses on the spot and supervising the builders, paying them, etc. . . ." From this entry it would also appear that Reuter was the master craftsman in charge of all building activities in Salem.

Perhaps because of the earlier date of Bethlehem, fewer names can be associated with the creation and erection of specific buildings in that community than is possible at Salem. David Nitschmann as community leader appears to have masterminded the erection of the *Gemeinhaus*, since he is known to have been a master workman. Henry Antes, whose homestead and mill were located in Falkner's Swamp, Frederick Township, returned to Bethlehem in 1745, and it is he who thenceforth appears to have been the counterpart of Salem's Reuter in Bethlehem's building activities. As master builder, he is known, for example, to have been in charge of the erection of the grist mill and the fulling mill, with Gotthard Demuth as his assistant, and Charles Schaus and his son giving further assistance, at least as far as the grist mill construction is concerned. Antes also proposed extensions to the Single Brothers' House, and it was he who proposed the creation of six plantation settlements on the Nazareth lands.

John Arbo is another name that one should associate with building activities in Bethlehem although he cannot be definitely associated with any one building. In the three or four architectural and engineering books in the Bethlehem Moravian Archives, his name appears the most frequently. He is known to have been warden of the Brothers' House, a post that he held until his death, December 11, 1772.

To Hans Christian Christiansen of Holstein, who had emigrated to Bethlehem on the Moravian ship *Irene* in the fall of 1751, goes the credit of creating the first successful water works that distributed water to the community. He was apparently responsible for the mill works, in co-operation with John Boehner, the West Indian Moravian missionary then in Bethlehem, as well as the works of Bethlehem's oil mill. Brothers Schober and Neibert have been mentioned as master masons of the later building that was under the general supervision of Brother Lawatsch.

Although little is known of the persons in charge of the erection of the second Single Brothers' House, it is known that the two masons were from Lancaster. The Widows' House, however, is known to have been under the supervision of Carl Schulze during its construction. Andrew Schober and Martin Schenck are known to have been the master masons and Tobias Hirte the master carpenter.

As in the case of the second Single Brothers' House, outside workmen helped finish the Whitefield House at Nazareth, for it is known that four stone masons from Germantown were engaged to help Jacob Vetter on the project, and the woodwork in the structure was done by Anton Seiffert, master carpenter. Zinzendorf's retirement Manor House, which he never used and which served as Nazareth Hall School for Boys until its conversion to an apartment building, is the only other major Nazareth building of the eighteenth century extant, but no names can be ascribed to it to this writer's knowledge, although Peter Worbass, another master carpenter, is known to have worked in that community.

At Hope, New Jersey, the names of Philip Maifel,

master mason, Joseph Grotz, master carpenter, and Stephen Nicholas, builder and kiln operator, are all well known, but no specific structures can be ascribed to their efforts.

Frederic William Marshall's name is associated primarily with Salem, but the fact that he served in the capacity of General Warden in Bethlehem for several years before his departure for North Carolina gives rise to the possibility of linking his name to specific projects in both of these major Moravian centers of North America. He is known to have given the plan for Home Church in Salem, and the drawings in the Salem Moravian Archives are thought to be his. His notebook is also extant and gives evidence of a strong interest in things architectural.

Johann Gottlob Krause was a master builder whose name can be associated with a number of Salem structures. Starting life by learning the pottery trade, he then turned to brickmaking, then to masonry, and finally to contracting for entire structures. He is recorded as having planned at least one Salem structure that is now gone and is known to have been one of the two masons associated with the erection of the Salem Tavern, the first all-brick structure in that community. The fact that he had learned his trade well is evidenced by the boys' school building of 1795 with its interesting diamond design of dark headers in the west gable; the Christoph Vogler House of 1797 with herringbone designs in the gables and his own initials, "IGK," in one end; the bakery of 1800, with designs in its gables; and Dr. Vierling's house of 1802, the largest brick house in the community.

In addition to Krause, Melchior Rasp is known to have been a master mason who supervised all the stonework during Salem's earliest years, as well as that at Bethabara. Christian Triebel, a master carpenter, was responsible for the timbering of the first houses of Salem and Bethabara, including probably the Single Brothers' House. Johann Krause is known to have made doors, window sash, stairways, and other trim for most of the important Salem structures, notably between 1774 and 1795, if building records are to be believed. His name has also been identified with items of furniture in the community.

Joseph Ferdinand Bullitschek, a millwright, erected most of the earliest mills in Wachovia but is better known as an organ builder. Martin Lick, master carpenter, built a log structure in Salem in 1787 which is still standing. Johann Adam Wolff, a non-

Moravian, is responsible for having raised the timbered roof of Home Church in 1799. John David Blum's contract to build the inspector's house in 1810 is extant, and William Craig, another non-Moravian, is known to have contracted to do all the masonry work on the *Vorsteher* House.

The domination of the church, which dictated that permission be secured from church headquarters in Herrnhut before building activities progressed, can be cited as the chief reason for the excellent documentation of structures existing in Moravian communities, especially Bethlehem. These master craftsmen's drawings, possibly made in Europe, are often unrecognized works of art in themselves. The sheet of elevations and plans for the Bethlehem Widows' House, for example, is probably the finest extant, with the legend inscribed on a draped cartouche in one corner of the sheet and the whole polychromed in well-run water-color washes. The sheets containing plans, sections, and elevations for the last wing of the Single Sisters' House are especially well detailed and delineated, clearly showing the framing system, the circulation system, and the water disposal system. By and large, the drawings for the major structures of Salem seem to be less well delineated and to have had less artistic energies expended upon them. As a corpus of architectural records of eighteenth-century America, those of the Moravians can probably not be surpassed.

The architectural relationship between the Moravians and other Germanic peoples in eighteenth-century America has already been alluded to. Noteworthy is the "hardware" one finds in any Moravian community. In Bethlehem, at least, some of the earliest wooden latches still exist in the *Gemeinhaus* and the first Brothers' House. Strap hinges of wrought iron, cockshead hinges, palm latches, and box locks adorn the heavy door leaves, usually herringbone patterned on the exterior and with the interior surface more often a verticle single-board width than not.

Interior finish is characterized by whitewashed walls and clay tile floors or brick pavers, built-in wardrobe closets, and, occasionally, vaulted rooms such as one finds in the Brothers' Houses of both Salem and Bethlehem. In all Moravian structures, the stair proportion, the relation of riser to tread, approaches the monumental or public scale. Woodwork is characterized by a quality of ampleness and an attention to detail as observed in the section of a handrail, the form of which is dictated through the ease by which it can be grasped by the hand. Proportion and scale are the touchstones of Moravian building efforts that one finds uniformly successful. Proportions are generous, but the scale, while robust, has an intimacy and fineness one can associate only with the eighteenth century and possibly a new country. The open fireplaces are ample in proportion and the system of heating by adjoining tile stoves is a practice that one can almost say was unique with this group in the New World. It is interesting to conjecture the provenance of the corner fireplace that one finds only in Salem, but whatever it is, the force of this method did not reach other Moravian communities, nor had it been imported from Bethlehem.

A comparison of Moravian interiors in Hope, New Jersey, Nazareth, Bethlehem, and Salem—the only Moravian villages having appreciable eighteenth-century structures extant, indicates the common denominator of good scale and proportion in all despite later additions and changes.

A comparison of the exteriors gives a much more diverse picture. First, Bethlehem, being the oldest permanent Moravian settlement on this continent and the control center of the church, is the earliest and hence has closer architectural affinities with Europe than any of the other communities, thus making comparisons difficult. One must remember that Bethlehem's outward aspect was much more continental in the eighteenth century when many of its tile roofs, all of which are now gone, existed and when many of its steep gable roofs had "jerkins" at the ends, all subsequently removed. With the clapboarding of the log *Gemeinhaus* and the covering or removal of all other log structures in the community, the village lost much of the character that it must have had. Some of this character is retained, however, especially in the area of the Bell House Square, with the smallness of scale, the smallness of windows, and the tall ribbon buttresses. Only Ephrata Cloisters, also in Pennsylvania, gives the viewer an equally continental, medieval impact. A notable aspect of Bethlehem and other Moravian communities is the obvious fact that the Moravians adapted to the building materials at hand. Thus, Bethlehem is predominantly built of field limestone with brick and wood trim; Hope is an almost completely limestone village of a far colder color than Bethlehem; and Salem, where stone was scarce and clay plentiful, is a preponderantly brick community, although half-timber, as in the Brothers' House, was used at an earlier date as well as log. Nazareth, being closest to Bethlehem, varies the least in outward architectural expression and material.

If the architectural vocabulary is essentially Germanic, as demonstrated in the previous chapter, and the distinction of Moravian building efforts can be seen only through the accent given this vocabulary, wherein, then, lies the ultimate contribution of the Moravians to American culture? The answer to this can be primarily found by viewing the Bell House Court from the second floor center window of the Widows' House. From this spot, the complex of structures works as such a unified whole as to make any question that it is not a pre-planned complex entirely superfluous. This can likewise be observed in rudimentary form in Nazareth by facing the square on the side opposite the imposing structure erected for Zinzendorf's retirement. It can be noted to a degree at Emmaus, at Hope, at Lititz, and, barring the destructive qualities to the scale of the square by the college buildings in Salem, at Salem Square also. Having observed these, one is motivated to look more closely at the manuscripts one finds in the archives in an attempt to detect this same sense of completeness. One reads much about the courthouse squares of Virginia and the greens of New England, but none of these well-known early planning efforts are any greater than the planning efforts contributed by the Moravians in eighteenth-century America. Couple this with the continental non-English vocabulary of their architecture, and one realizes that the contribution of the Moravians is far greater than suspected at first meeting.

BIBLIOGRAPHY

Documentation of Moravian effort in America is un-usually ample. The secondary sources listed below are mostly based on the corpus of primary material to be found in the two main Moravian repositories in this country, i.e., the Moravian Archives of the Northern Province at Bethlehem, Pennsylvania, and those of the Southern Province at Salem, North Carolina. These consist, in part, of the congregational diaries that chron-icle the daily life of the respective communities and the daily records kept by each of the individual "choirs." In addition, the Board of Elders' proceedings shed light on some construction, as Bishop Hamilton notes, as do the collections of the Moravian Historical Societies at Salem and Nazareth.

Moravian centers in Europe, such as those at Herrn-hut, in Eastern Germany, and Neuwied-am-Rhein, in Western Germany, comprise further research centers.

Baldwin, Charles Candee. *Bethlehem and Ohio History*. Cleveland(?), 1892(?).

Beauchamp, William Martin (ed.). *Moravian Journals Relating to Central New York, 1745–66*. Syracuse, N.Y., 1916.

Beck, James Montgomery. *Bethlehem and its Military Hospital*. N.p., 1897.

Bethlehem Globe Times. *Bi-Centennial Edition*, June 24, 1942.

Bethlehem Globe Times. *Sesqui-Centennial Industrial Edition*, June, 1892.

Bethlehem, Pa., Moravian Church. *Regeln und Ordnun-gen der Brüder-Gemeine in Bethlehem, Pa., 1851*. Bethlehem, 1860.

Bethlehemisches Diarium, MSS. Bethlehem, 1741——.

Bolles, Albert Sidney. *Pennyslvania, Province and State*. Philadelphia, 1899.

Brown, William. *The History of Missions*. Philadelphia, 1816.

Brumbaugh, G. Edwin. "Colonial Architecture of the Pennsylvania Germans," *The Pennsylvania-German Society Proceedings and Addresses 1930*, XLI (1933), 1–60.

Buck, William Joseph. *History of the Indian Walk, Per-formed for the Proprietaries of Pennsylvania in 1737*. Philadelphia, 1886.

——. *William Penn in America*. Philadelphia, 1888.

Chandler, Joseph Everett. *The Colonial Architecture of Maryland, Pennsylvania and Virginia*. Boston, 1900.

Chastellux, François Jean, Marquis de, *Travels in North America in the Years 1780–81–82*. New York, 1827.

Chor-Diarium der Ledigen Brüder, MSS. Bethlehem.

Clewell, John Henry. *History of Wachovia in North Carolina*. New York, 1902.

Cranz, David. *The Ancient and Modern History of the Brethren*, translated by Benjamin Latrobe. London, 1780.

——. *The History of Greenland*. London, 1767.

Cressman, Austin M. (Comp.). *Historical Bethlehem, 1741–1941*. Bethlehem, 1941.

Crews, Hall. *Old Salem: Now a Part of Winston-Salem, North Carolina*. New York, 1929.

Davis, Chester. *Hidden Seed and Harvest: A History of the Moravians*. Winston-Salem, 1959.

DeSchweinitz, Edmund. *The Financial History of the American Province of the Unitas Fratrum*. Bethle-hem, 1877.

——. *History of the Church Known as the Unitas Fratrum or the Unity of the Brethren*. Bethlehem, 1885.

——. *The Life and Times of David Zeisberger: The Western Pioneer and Apostle of the Indians*. Phila-delphia, 1870.

Dickson, Harold Edward. *A Hundred Pennsylvania Buildings*. State College, Pa., 1954.

Doddridge, Philip. *An Abridgement of Mr. David Brainerd's Journal Among the Indians.* London, 1748.

Doll, Eugene Edgar. *The Ephrata Cloisters: An Annotated Bibliography.* Philadelphia, 1944.

Downs, Joseph. *The House of the Miller at Millbach.* Philadelphia, 1929.

———. "A Pennsylvania-German House," *The Pennsylvania Museum Bulletin*, XXII, 108 (December, 1926), 265–75.

Eller, Ernest McNeil. *The Houses of Peace.* New York, 1937.

———. *Salem Star and Dawn.* Winston-Salem, 1962.

Erbe, Hellmuth. *Eine Kommunistische Herrnhuter Kolonie des 18. Jahrhunderts.* Stuttgart, 1929.

Faust, Albert Bernhardt, *Francis Daniel Pastorius and the 250th Anniversary of the Founding of Germantown.* Philadelphia, 1934.

———. *The German Element in the United States.* New York, 1909.

Fries, Adelaide L. *Distinctive Customs and Practices of the Moravian Church.* Bethlehem, 1949.

———. *Forsythe County.* Salem, N.C., 1898.

———. *Historical Sketch of Salem Female Academy.* Salem, N.C., 1902.

———. *The Moravian Church, Yesterday and Today.* Raleigh, N.C., 1926.

———. *The Moravians in Georgia.* Raleigh, N.C., 1905.

———. "Moravian Tile Stoves of Salem, North Carolina," *Proceedings of the Bucks County Historical Society*, IV (1917), 477–79.

———. *The Road to Salem.* Chapel Hill, N.C., 1944.

———. *The Town Builders.* Raleigh, N.C., 1915.

———. (ed.). *Records of the Moravians in North Carolina.* Raleigh, N.C., 1922–43.

Gnadenhuetten Monument Society. *A True History of the Massacre of Ninety Six Indians, at Gnadenhuetten, Ohio, March 8th, 1782.* New Philadelphia, Ohio, 1870.

Gray, Elma E. *Wilderness Christians.* Ithaca, N.Y., 1956.

Gross, A. Haller. "The Old Springhouses of Bucks County," *Proceedings of the Bucks County Historical Society*, IV (1917), 579–86.

Hacker, Hogan H. *Nazareth Hall.* Bethlehem, 1910.

Hall, Francis. *Travels in Canada and the United States in 1816 and 1817.* London, 1819.

Hamilton, John Taylor. *A History of the Church Known as the Moravian Church, or The Unitas Fratrum, or, The Unity of The Brethren.* Bethlehem, 1900.

Hamilton, Kenneth G. *Church Street in Old Bethlehem.* Bethlehem, 1942.

———. *John Ettwein and the Moravian Church during the Revolutionary Period.* Bethlehem, 1940.

Hamlin, Talbot Faulkner, *Benjamin Henry Latrobe.* New York, 1955.

Harbaugh, Henry. *The Life of Rev. Michael Schlatter; With a Full Account of his Travels and Labors among the Germans in Pennsylvania, New Jersey, Maryland and Virginia.* Philadelphia, 1857.

Hark, Ann. *The Seminary's Secret.* Philadelphia, 1936.

Heckewelder, John. "An Account of the History, Manners, and Customs of the Indian Nations who once Inhabited Pennsylvania and the Neighboring States," *American Philosophical Society Transactions*, Vol. I, No. 1 (1819), 1–347.

———. *A Letter to a Friend in which Some Account is Given of the Brethren's Society for the Furtherance of the Gospel Among the Heathen.* London, 1769.

———. *A Narrative of the Mission of the United Brethren Among the Delaware and Mohegan Indians from its Commencement in the Year 1740 to the Close of the Year 1808*, edited by William Elsey Connelley. Cleveland, 1907.

Heller, William Jacobs (ed.). *History of Northampton County and the Grand Valley of the Lehigh.* Boston, 1920.

Henry, James. *Sketches of Moravian Life and Character.* Philadelphia, 1859.

Hildreth, Samuel Prescott. *Contributions to the Early History of the North-West, Including the Moravian Missions in Ohio.* New York, 1864.

Holmes, John Beck. *Historical Sketches of the Missions of the United Brethren.* London, 1827.

Howland, Garth H. "An Architectural History of the Moravian Church, Bethlehem, Pennsylvania," *Transactions of the Moravian Historical Society*, XIV, Parts I and II (1947), 50–132.

———. "Reconstructional Problems Associated with the Moravian Buildings in Bethlehem," *Transactions of the Moravian Historical Society*, XIII, Parts III and IV (1944), 175–280.

Huebener, Francis Christian. *The Moravian Missions in Ohio.* Washington, D.C., 1898.

Huebener, Mary Augusta. *A Brief History of Lititz,* N.p., 1947.

Hulbert, Archer Butler. "The Moravian Records," *Ohio Archaeological and Historical Quarterly*, 18 (1909), 199–226.

Jordan, John Woolf. "Historical Sketch of the Widows' House at Bethlehem, Pennsylvania," *Transactions of the Moravian Historical Society, Nazareth*, IV (1895), 101–24.

———. "Moravian Immigration to Pennsylvania, 1734–1767," *Transactions of the Moravian Historical Society, Nazareth*, V, Part II (1896), 49–90.

Kachline, Susan Ada. *Old Nazareth: A Brief Sketch of Early Moravian Life.* Bethlehem, 1933.

Kalfus, Radim. *Die Brüderunität in Bildern.* Prag, 1957.

Kalm, Pehr. *Travels into North America.* London, 1772.

Keyser, Naaman Henry. *History of Old Germantown.* Philadelphia, 1907.

Kimball, Fiske. "Architecture in the History of the

Colonies and of the Republic," *American Historical Review*, XXVII (1921–22), 47–57.

Klees, Frederic. *The Pennsylvania Dutch*. New York, 1950.

Knauss, James Owen. *Social Conditions Among the Pennsylvania Germans in the Eighteenth Century*. Lancaster, Pa., 1922.

Kunckelii, Johannis. *Ars Vitraria Experimentalis*. Frankfurt und Leipzig, 1689.

Langton, Edward. *The History of the Moravian Church: the Story of the First International Protestant Church*. London, 1956.

Latrobe, Benjamin. *A Brief Account of the Mission Established Among the Esquimaux Indians on the Coast of Labrador by the Church of the Brethren, or Unitas Fratrum*. London, 1774.

Laux, James B. *Brother Albrecht's Secret Chamber: A Legend of the Ancient Moravian Sun Inn of Bethlehem*. Lititz, Pa., 1914.

Leibert, Augustus H. *A Chronicle of the First Century of Bethlehem, Pa., 1741–1841*. Bethlehem, 1921.

Leupold, Jacob. *Theatri Machinarum Hydraulicarum*. Leipzig, 1724.

Leutmann, M. Johann Georg. *Vulcanus Famulans*. Wittenberg, 1720.

Levering, Joseph Mortimer. *A History of Bethlehem, Pennsylvania, 1741–1892, With Some Account of Its Founders and Their Early Activity in America*. Bethlehem, 1903.

Loher, Franz von. *Geschichte und Zustande der Deutchen in Amerika*. Gottingen, 1855.

Loskiel, George Henry. *Extempore on a Wagon*, trans. J. Max Hark. Lancaster, Pa., 1887.

———. *Geschichte der Mission der Evangelischen Brüder unter den Indianeren in Nordamerika*. Leipzig, 1789.

MacMinn, Edwin. *On the Frontier with Colonel Antes*. Camden, N.J., 1900.

———. *A German Hero of the Colonial Times of Pennsylvania or, The Life and Times of Henry Antes*. Moorestown, N.J., 1886.

Martin, John Hill. *Historical Sketch of Bethlehem in Pennsylvania*. Philadelphia, 1873.

Mears, John William. *Heroes of Bohemia: Huss, Jerome and Zisca*. Philadelphia, 1879.

Mercer, Henry Chapman. *Ancient Carpenter's Tools*. Doylestown, Pa., 1929.

———. *The Bible in Iron*. Doylestown, Pa., 1914.

———. *The Decorated Stone Plates of Durham*. Doylestown(?), Pa., 1897(?).

———. "The Origin of Log Houses in the United States." *Proceedings of the Bucks County Historical Society*, V (1926), 568–83.

Merckleins, M. Albert Daniel. *Die Architectura Civilis*. Frankfurth und Leipzig, 1737.

Meyer, Henry Herman. *Child Nature and Nurture According to Nicolaus Ludwig von Zinzendorf*. New York, 1928.

Mittelberger, Gottlieb. *Gottlieb Mittelberger's Journey to Pennsylvania in the Year 1750 and Return to Germany in the Year 1754*. Philadelphia, 1898.

Moravian Historical Society. *Transactions of the Moravian Historical Society*, I——, 1858——.

Morrison, Hugh Sinclair. *Early American Architecture from the First Colonial Settlements to the National Period*. New York, 1952.

Mortimer, Charlotte B. *Marrying by Lot*. New York, 1868.

Myers, Elizabeth Fetter. *A Century of Moravian Sisters*. New York, 1918.

———. *History of the Bethlehem Pike*. Bethlehem, n.d.

———. "The Moravian Revolutionary Church at Bethlehem, Commonly Called 'The Old Chapel,'" *Pennsylvania-German Society Proceedings and Addresses*, Oct 5, 1923, Vol. 34 (1929), pp. 53–66.

———. *Sketch of Bethlehem*. Bethlehem, 1925.

———. *Story of the Gemein Haus*. Bethlehem, 1924.

Nazareth, Pennsylvania, Bi-Centennial Inc., *Two Centuries of Nazareth, 1740–1940*. Nazareth, 1940.

Neu Eroffnete Vorraths-Kammer. Frankfurt und Leipzig, 1760.

North Carolina Historical Records Survey. *Guide to the Manuscripts in the Moravian Church in America, Southern Province*. Raleigh, N.C., 1942.

Nutting, Wallace. *Pennsylvania Beautiful (Eastern)*. Framingham, Mass., 1924.

Oerter, Albert L. "Tile Stoves of the Moravians at Bethlehem, Pa.," *Proceedings of the Bucks County Historical Society*, IV (1917), pp. 479–81.

———. *The Whitefield House on the Ephrata Property at Nazareth, Pa., 1740–1914*. Bethlehem, 1914.

Ogden, John Cosens. *An Excursion into Bethlehem and Nazareth in Pennsylvania, in the year 1799*. Philadelphia, 1800.

Owen, Mary Barrow (ed.). *Old Salem, North Carolina*. Winston-Salem, 1941.

Pennsylvania Historical and Museum Commission. *Guide to the Published Archives of Pennsylvania*. Harrisburg, Pa., 1949.

Pennypacker, Samuel W. "Germans in Pennsylvania," *Philadelphia German Pionier-Verein*, Philadelphia, 1895.

Pochmann, Henry August. *German Culture in America*. Madison, Wis., 1957.

Proud, Robert. *The History of Pennsylvania*. Philadelphia, 1797–98.

Pückler-Muskau, Hermann Ludwig Heinrich. *Tutti-Frutti: Aus den Papieren des Verstorbenen*. Stuttgart, 1834.

Rau, Robert. "The First Apothecary in Bethlehem,"

Transactions of the Moravian Historical Society, XI, Part I (1931), 62–63.

——. "Historical Sketch of the Bethlehem Water Works," *Bethlehem Daily Times*, February 21, 1877.

Raymond, Eleanor. *Early Domestic Architecture of Pennsylvania*. New York, 1931.

Reichel, Edward H. *Historical Sketch of the Church and Missions of the United Brethren Commonly Called Moravians*. Bethlehem, 1848.

Reichel, Levin Theodore. *The Early History of the Church of the United Brethren, Commonly Called Moravians, in North America*. Nazareth, 1888.

——. *The Moravians in North Carolina*. Philadelphia, 1857.

Reichel, William Cornelius. *The Crown Inn, near Bethlehem, Pa., 1745*. Philadelphia, 1872.

——. *Friedensthal and its Stockaded Mill*. Nazareth, 1877.

——. *A History of the Rise, Progress and Present Condition of the Bethlehem Female Seminary*. Philadelphia, 1858.

——. *Historical Sketch of Nazareth Hall from 1755 to 1869*. Philadelphia, 1869.

——. *The Old Moravian Sun Inn, Bethlehem, Pennsylvania, 1758*. Philadelphia, 1893.

——. *A Red Rose from the Olden Time*. Philadelphia, 1872.

——. *Something About Trombones and The Old Mill at Bethlehem*. Bethlehem, 1884.

—— (ed.). *Memorials of the Moravian Church*. Philadelphia, 1870.

Reichmann, Felix, "Ephrata as Seen by Contemporaries," *Pennsylvania German Folklore Society*, 17 (1954), vii–xix, 1–206.

Reid, Grace Stuart. *The Barony of the Rose*. New York, 1904.

Rice, William Henry. *David Zeisberger and His Brown Brethren*. Bethlehem, 1897.

Rights, T. M., "Remarks on Tile Stoves," *Proceedings of the Bucks County Historical Society*, IV (1917), 481–82.

Risler, Jeremias. *Leben August Gottlieb Spangenbergs*. Leipzig, 1794.

Ritter, Abraham. *History of the Moravian Church in Philadelphia from its Foundation in 1742 to the Present Time*. Philadelphia, 1857.

Rochefoucauld Liancourt, François Alexandre Frederic. *Travels Through the United States of North America, the Country of the Iroquois and Upper Canada, in the years 1795, 1796 and 1797*. London, 1799.

Rodabaugh, James Howard. *Schoenbrunn and the Moravian Missions in Ohio*. Columbus, 1945.

Rondthaler, Edward. *The Memorabilia of Fifty Years, 1877 to 1927*. Raleigh, 1928.

Rupp, Israel Daniel. *A Collection of Upwards of Thirty Thousand Names of German, Swiss, Dutch, French, Portuguese and Other Immigrants in Pennsylvania; chronologically arranged from 1727 to 1776*. Harrisburg, 1856.

——. *History of Northampton, Lehigh, Monroe, Carbon and Schuylkill Counties*. Harrisburg, Pa., 1845.

Sachse, Julius Friedrich (trans.). *Falckner's Curieuse Nachricht von Pennsylvania*. Philadelphia, 1905.

——. *The German Pietists of Provincial Pennsylvania*. Philadelphia, 1895.

——. *The German Sectarians of Pennsylvania, 1708–1800*. Philadelphia, 1899.

——. "Quaint Old Germantown in Pennsylvania," *The Pennsylvania-German Society Proceedings and Addresses 1912*, XXIII (1915), 1–7.

Sawtelle, William Otis. *Thomas Pownall, Colonial Governor and Some of His Activities in the American Colonies*. Boston, 1931.

Schluter, Christoph Andreas. *Hütte-Werken*. Braunschweig, 1738.

Schnich, A. W. (comp.) *The Grist Mill: More about the Old Mill; W. C. Reichel's Tribute to the Old Mill; Petition for Stone Bridge at Luckenbach's Mill*. Bethlehem, 1925.

Schübler, Johann Jacob. *Synopsis Architecturae Civilis Eclecticae*. Nürnberg, 1732.

Schultze, Adolf. *Brief History of the Widows' Society of Bethlehem*. Bethlehem, n.d.

——. *Brüdermission in Wort und Bild*. Herrnhut, Germany, 1925.

Schultze, Augustus, "Guide to the Old Moravian Cemetery of Bethlehem, Pa., 1742–1910," *Pennsylvania-German Society Proceedings and Addresses, 1910*, XXI (1910), 1–218.

Schwarze, Edmund. *History of the Moravian Missions Among Southern Indian Tribes of the United States*. Bethlehem, 1923.

Schwarze, Margaret. *Old Moravian Chapel, 1751–1951*. Bethlehem, n.d.

Schwarze, William Nathaniel. *The Moravian Settlement of Bethlehem*. Princeton, 1940.

Schwarze, W. N. and Gapp, S. H. *A History of the Beginnings of Moravian Work in America*. Bethlehem, 1955.

Scopp, Johann Georg. *Scheuplazz des Mechanischen Mühlen Baues*. Frankfurt und Leipzig, n.d.

Sessler, Jacob John. *Communal Pietism Among Early American Moravians*. New York, 1933.

Snyder, Karl H. *An Architectural Monograph: Moravian Architecture of Bethlehem, Pennsylvania*. New York, 1927.

Spangenberg, August Gottlieb. *Idea Fidei Fratrum*. Leipzig, 1789.

————. *Leben des Herrn Nicolaus Ludwig, Grafen un Herrn von Zinzendorf und Potterdorf.* Barby, 1772–75.

Stocker, Harry Emilius. *Moravian Customs and Other Matters of Interest.* Bethlehem, 1918.

Sturms, Leonhard. *Grundliches Unterricht von Heng Oder Sprengenwerken.* Stockholm and Leipzig, 1726.

Van der Heiden, Jan, and Jan Van der Heiden de Jonge. *Slang-Brand-Spuiten en Haarewyze van Brand-Blussen.* Amsterdam, 1735.

Van Horn, Mrs. F. C. *The Moravian Contribution to the Town of Hope.* Hope, New Jersey, 1955.

Vardell, Charles Gildersleeve. *Organs in the Wilderness.* Winston-Salem, 1944.

Walters, Raymond. *Bethlehem Long Ago and To-day.* Bethlehem, 1923.

Waterman, Thomas Tileston. *The Dwellings of Colonial America.* Chapel Hill, N.C., 1950.

Watson, John F. "Notes of the Early History of Germantown," in *Register of Pennsylvania,* edited by Samuel Hazard, I, 1828, pp. 279–84, 289–93.

Weinlick, John Rudolf. *Count Zinzendorf.* Nashville, Tennessee, 1956.

Whitefield, George. *Expostulatory Letter Addressed to Nicholas Lewis, Count Zinzendorf and Lord Advocate of the Unitas Fratrum.* London, 1753.

Winkler, Angelina Virginia. *Souvenir of the Twin Cities of North Carolina, Winston-Salem, Forsyth County.* Salem, N.C., 1890.

Wood, Ralph Charles (ed.). *Pennsylvania Germans.* Princeton, 1942.

Zeisberger, David. *Diary of David Zeisberger: A Moravian Missionary Among the Indians of Ohio.* Cincinnati, 1885.

Zook, John G. *Historical and Pictorial Lititz.* Lititz, Pa., 1905.

INDEX